SOUTHERN BIOGRAPHY SERIES
Bertram Wyatt-Brown, *Series Editor*

Hamilton Gamble, ca. 1860

Courtesy Missouri Historical Society, St. Louis

Lincoln's Resolute Unionist

HAMILTON GAMBLE,
DRED SCOTT DISSENTER AND
MISSOURI'S CIVIL WAR GOVERNOR

Dennis K. Boman

LOUISIANA STATE UNIVERSITY PRESS   BATON ROUGE

Published by Louisiana State University Press
Copyright © 2006 by Louisiana State University Press
All rights reserved
Manufactured in the United States of America
FIRST PRINTING

DESIGNER: Melanie O'Quinn Smaha
TYPEFACE: Janson Text, Avalon
TYPESETTER: G & S Book Services, Inc.
PRINTER AND BINDER: Edwards Brothers, Inc.

Library of Congress Cataloging-in-Publication Data

Boman, Dennis K.
   Lincoln's resolute unionist : Hamilton Gamble, Dred Scott dissenter and
Missouri's Civil War governor / Dennis K. Boman.
      p. cm. — (Southern biography series)
   Includes bibliographical references (p.   ) and index.
   ISBN-13: 978-0-8071-3164-0 (cloth : alk. paper)
   ISBN-10: 0-8071-3164-4 (cloth : alk. paper)
      1. Gamble, Hamilton Rowan, 1798–1864.   2. Governors—Missouri—
Biography.   3. Unionists (United States Civil War)—Missouri—Biography.
4. Missouri—Politics and government—1861–1865.   5. Missouri—Politics
and government—To 1865.   6. Missouri—History—Civil War, 1861–1865.
7. United States—History—Civil War, 1861–1865.
I. Title.   II. Series.
   F466.G26B66 2006
   977.8'03092—dc22
   [B]

                                                          2005027769

For Jillon
Tecum vivere amen, tecum obean libens!

Contents

Preface

Our understanding of the Civil War era is gleaned from contemporary manuscripts, participant accounts, and their interpretation by historians. The sheer volume of materials pertaining to Missouri alone is remarkable in its extent. Articles and books continue to be written, often changing our perspective, expanding our knowledge, or at least modifying the narrative in some way. In particular, scholarly biography has been important to this process, for it provides a different window through which to view events, often thought to be well understood, but to which another participant's story provides crucial details and a new point of view. It is rare to discover a major actor like Hamilton R. Gamble, who has not been the subject of a published, book-length biography. For this reason, until now Gamble's role has been unknown to the wider public, and only partially understood even by specialists in Civil War history. As provisional governor of Missouri, Gamble shouldered the important tasks of establishing a militia, raising revenue, gaining the cooperation of unionists of often varied backgrounds and political principles, and harmonizing his efforts with federal military commanders and the Lincoln administration in the midst of a military struggle then being waged throughout the state.

Gamble was born in 1798 in Virginia, where he attended Hampden-Sydney College before moving to Missouri in 1818. Quickly distinguishing himself as a talented young lawyer, he was appointed district attorney in Howard and St. Louis counties and later secretary of state under

Governor Frederick Bates. After marrying and settling in St. Louis, for the next twenty years Gamble concentrated on his legal practice before circuit courts and the Missouri Supreme Court. As an elder of his church, he mentored young lawyers, offering spiritual and legal instruction, and supported students of the ministry financially. After refusing to run for various political offices, in 1844 he accepted the nomination of the Whig Party for state representative; he was elected and served one term.

In 1850, because of poor health, Gamble decided to end his partnership with Edward Bates, who later served as attorney general under President Abraham Lincoln, and to practice law only part-time. However, his dream of semiretirement ended when the bar of St. Louis sought his candidacy for judge of the Missouri Supreme Court in 1851. Because as state representative he had sought to make the judiciary of the state supreme court an elective office, Gamble believed that he could not in good conscience refuse to run. During his tenure as judge, the court adjudicated the *Dred Scott* case that later came before the U.S. Supreme Court. Dissenting from the decision of the majority, Gamble argued that the Missouri Supreme Court should uphold the past three decades' law and precedent in freedom suits and rule in favor of Scott. This decision was consistent with other opinions in which he strictly adhered to the jurisprudential principle that a judge's proper role was to interpret the law rather than legislate from the bench. In 1854 Gamble retired from the court because of his health. Before the advent of the Civil War, he occupied his time supervising the establishment of a farm for his oldest son and directing the education of his younger children. He also practiced as a lawyer but accepted only the most important and lucrative cases, some of which he argued before the U.S. Supreme Court.

During the secession crisis in early 1861, Gamble immediately rallied to the cause of the Union, presenting a nuanced and persuasive case against Missouri seceding. After his election as a delegate to the state convention, which was formed to decide whether Missouri would secede, Gamble chaired the Committee on Foreign Relations. In the majority report of the committee, which was primarily the work of his pen, Gamble argued that no justification for secession then existed and asserted that the federal courts were available to redress the South's grievances. This report was adopted by the convention. After the secessionist state government under Governor Claiborne F. Jackson fled the capitol, the state convention reconvened and established a provisional government, electing Gamble governor in late July 1861. He remained at this post until his death in early 1864.

As provisional governor during the conflict, Gamble played a central role in preserving Missouri in the Union. From the start, he sought to reconcile the various unionist factions while reassuring a substantial pro-Southern minority that their traditional rights, including the right to hold slave property, would be respected. As commander-in-chief of the state militia, Gamble faced many difficulties in building an effective military force and coordinating efforts with federal troops to protect against Confederate invasion and guerrilla attacks. Using his connections through Attorney General Bates, on several occasions Gamble traveled to Washington, D.C., and consulted closely with President Lincoln to gain funding for the militia and to work out various policy issues during the war. This cooperation became increasingly important when Gamble was later confronted with a determined radical unionist opposition to his administration.

Like Lincoln, Gamble adopted a flexible and pragmatic approach to governance. His policies dissatisfied every faction at some time, for as a statesman he sought to preserve the rights of all Missourians, even those noncombatants who sympathized with the South. Increasingly, the Radical Republicans believed Gamble was obstructing their political agenda. By the summer of 1862, the radicals accused him of being secretly disloyal and hampering the effort to put down the insurrection through his less than total war policies.

In his 1863 message to the legislature, Gamble presented a plan for the gradual emancipation of slaves in Missouri. In doing this he was responding to circumstances and to Lincoln's Emancipation Proclamation. Moreover, Gamble sought to gain the support of the less radical abolitionists, especially among a portion of the German population in St. Louis. Gamble's emancipation plan, however, was opposed by the Radical Republican legislators, who also failed to pass a plan of their own. For this reason, Gamble reconvened the state convention to pass an emancipation ordinance and to amend the state constitution where necessary. After a vigorous and often acrimonious debate, a plan very similar to Gamble's was passed calling for the gradual emancipation of Missouri's slaves. This achievement did not satisfy his critics and efforts to undermine his authority continued unabated to the end of his administration. Despite the unfailing criticism and opposition, Gamble retained a substantial corps of supporters who recognized his desire to act justly and fairly as governor, understanding that he did not have the luxury to speak or act without considering the effect such pronouncements and policies would have on the war effort. More important, Gamble's organization of militia forces enabled out-of-state Union troops to augment Grant's forces in the West, despite the continued threat of attack from Confederate armies and guerrilla forces operating in Missouri and Arkansas. Without these additional forces, Grant would have found it more difficult to take Vicksburg and hold it against the Confederate forces marching to its rescue. Without the contributions of Gamble and other loyal war governors, the war in the West could not have been won.

I would like to thank the archivists and staff of the Missouri Historical Society in St. Louis for their professionalism in providing access to the papers of Hamilton R. Gamble and to their many other valuable manuscript collections. The archivists and staffs of the Missouri State Archives in Jefferson City and the State Historical Society of Missouri in Columbia also deserve recognition for their help in directing me to sources illuminating the context of Gamble's life and Civil War Missouri. And finally, although I cannot thank each of my friends individually, I want to express my appreciation to them collectively for their encouragement during the research and writing of this book.

Lincoln's Resolute Unionist

Chapter One

Formative Years

On November 29, 1798, in Winchester, Virginia, a seventh child was born to Joseph and Anne Gamble, who named him Hamilton Rowan. Joseph and Anne were natives of Ireland and had immigrated to the United States in 1784. Hamilton's paternal grandfather, also named Joseph, had immigrated to British North America in 1752, but after two years had returned to Ireland. Joseph's eldest son Archibald (and Hamilton's uncle) returned to America, gained a college education, and later taught Greek and Latin at the University of Pennsylvania. During the Revolutionary War, Hamilton's uncle served as an engineer for the American Army at the siege of Charleston, South Carolina.[1]

Growing up in early nineteenth-century Virginia, Hamilton could point with pride to his state's leadership in the struggle for independence and to the prominent role of many of its statesmen in forming a new country under the Articles of Confederation and the Constitution of the United States. Before the Revolutionary War, both Patrick Henry and Thomas Jefferson made important contributions in drawing the colonies closer to independence. Henry's fiery rhetoric in his opposition to the Parsons' tax, in which Parliament had imposed taxes for the support of

---

1. Archibald Gamble, "Family Record by Archibald Gamble," 15 January 1858 and 15 January 1863, Hamilton R. Gamble papers, Missouri Historical Society, St. Louis, Missouri; hereinafter cited as Gamble papers. *In Memoriam: Hamilton Rowan Gamble, Governor of Missouri* (St. Louis: George Knapp, 1864), 85. John F. Philips, "Hamilton Rowan Gamble and the Provisional Government of Missouri," *Missouri Historical Review* 5 (October 1910): 1.

Anglican ministers without the consent of Virginians, was founded on principles expounded in English Whig opposition literature, Enlightenment thought, and classical writings. Jefferson similarly imbibed these rich sources of republican ideology, which he expounded ably in his treatise "A Summary View of the Rights of British America" (1774) and the Declaration of Independence (1776). In these writings Jefferson argued that political authority derived from the people and could not be ignored by Parliament and the king. The contributions of George Washington and James Madison in establishing a new constitutional system founded on the same republican ideals deepened further the legacy of leadership and statesmanship in which every Virginian could take pride. These men and much of their generation believed that a republican form of government, that is, a political system in which the people are in charge through the election of representatives, cannot work properly unless the people themselves are virtuous. To promote virtue, young people must be educated to cherish a simple manner of living, preferably working industriously on their own land as farmers. Many Virginians associated life in the cities with squalor, avarice, and corruption. They believed, on the other hand, that an agricultural economy would best cultivate a population independent from factions seeking to foster their own interests, often to the detriment of the interests of the community and country. Moreover, this political philosophy, today referred to as agrarian republicanism, championed limited government as a check against executive ambition, opposed the maintenance of standing armies as a threat to the people's freedom, and waged a vigorous campaign against the federal government fostering an English-style economy through the establishment of a national bank, protective tariffs, and the use of federal monies to build roads to promote commerce and industry.[2]

While little evidence exists revealing his early political beliefs, Hamilton could not have been unaware of the legacy of these great men, who

2. For the influence of English Whig opposition literature see Bernard Bailyn, *The Ideological Origins of the American Revolution* (Cambridge, Mass.: Harvard University Press, 1992). For an excellent analysis of agrarian republicanism see Drew R. McCoy, *The Elusive Republic: Political Economy in Jeffersonian America* (Chapel Hill: University of North Carolina Press, 1980). For the influence of republican ideology in Virginia see Dan Monroe, *The Republican Vision of John Tyler* (College Station: Texas A & M University Press, 2003), 8–23.

would have inspired him and other young Virginians to aspire to serve their country and achieve great things as well. If he was an exponent of agrarian republicanism, Hamilton later adopted a different philosophy developed by members of the American Whig Party, who championed a vigorous use of the powers of the federal government to foster domestic and international commerce through the imposition of tariffs to protect American industry; the use of federal funds to build roads, canals, and railroads; and the creation of a national bank. However, the principle of government by the people and their representatives was the foundation of Hamilton's political philosophy and guided him when, during the crisis of 1861 as a member of the state convention in Missouri, he led the fight against secession. In particular, after the departure of Missouri's governor and legislators, Hamilton asserted forcefully that the convention as representatives of the people had the power to form a new state government. Unless the people or their representatives had limited the convention's powers it had the same authority as if the people were gathered together "in one vast plain."[3]

While little is known about Hamilton's boyhood, as the youngest child he probably received a good deal of attention and nurturing from his parents and siblings. However, his upbringing was also strict, for his father "was a ruling Elder in the Presbyterian Church" and raised his children according to the "straitest sect" of the denomination. This is probably a reference to Hamilton's religious education in the "Old School" branch of the Presbyterian Church. The Old School believed in man's total depravity and his inability to save himself. Therefore, God alone determined who was predestined to faith and an afterlife with Him in heaven. Soon Hamilton grew tall, strong, and athletic, and proved to be uncommonly intelligent. In 1812, at the age of thirteen Hamilton was sent to Hampden-Sydney College, a Presbyterian school in Prince Edward County, Virginia. Founded on the eve of the American Revolution, the college was small and underfunded at the time of Hamilton's arrival. This

3. Merrill D. Peterson, ed., *The Political Writings of Thomas Jefferson* (Monticello: Thomas Jefferson Memorial Foundation, 1993), 23–29. Merrill D. Peterson, *Thomas Jefferson and the New Nation, A Biography* (New York: Oxford University Press, 1970), 69–77. St. Louis *Missouri Republican*, 2 August 1861. *Proceedings of the Missouri State Convention Held at the City of Jefferson, July 1861* (St. Louis: George Knapp, 1861), 73–74, 86–87, 95, 109.

circumstance would continue for some time after, for although the Anglican Church had lost its state support and was then in decline in Virginia,
many of its former members failed to join evangelical churches, finding
their teachings on sin and the revivalism of the Second Great Awakening
unfamiliar. Probably most disturbing of all to most Southerners, however,
was the teaching of many Presbyterian, Baptist, and Methodist ministers
who denounced slavery and gentry recreations such as dancing, gambling,
horse racing, and cockfighting. For these reasons, most of the increases
in evangelical membership came among Scot-Irish immigrants like Hamilton's family, a minority segment of the population that would not gain
acceptance among established Southerners for some time.[4]

Moses Hoge, a noted Presbyterian minister, was then president of
Hampden-Sydney College. Under his administration, religious training
was emphasized, especially for ministerial students whom Hoge had personally recruited. All students were required to attend chapel twice daily,
although this apparently did not prevent some students from playing
pranks and getting into trouble. Because of these problems, students in
early 1813 were required to read and sign a statement declaring that they
understood college rules and would abide by them. No doubt, discipline
was very important at a Presbyterian institution founded where a Southern planter ethic of honor and Enlightenment rationalism dominated.
According to the accounts of students and others attending Hampden-
Sydney at the time, Hoge labored diligently to convert unbelieving students to the faith and to lead others to a more intimate spiritual life. His
ministry, modeled on a tradition of German Reformed Pietism, emphasized one's personal relationship to God premised on repentance and the
development of spirituality through the study of scripture, fellowship
with other Christians, and prayerful meditation on God and His creation.
This tradition was very much in harmony with the evangelical and reviv-
alist "New Light" preaching of Jonathan Edwards, Cotton Mather, and
George Whitefield. These men had revolutionized the spiritual world of

4. *In Memoriam*, 70 and 85–86. John Luster Brinkley, *On this Hill: A Narrative History of
Hampden-Sydney College, 1774–1994* (Hampden-Sydney, Va.: Camdus, 1994), 14–15. Herbert
Clarence Bradshaw, *History of Hampden-Sydney College: From the Beginnings to the Year 1856*,
vol. 1 (privately printed, 1976), 122. Christine Leigh Heyrman, *Southern Cross: The Beginnings of
the Bible Belt* (New York: Alfred A. Knopf, 1997), 3–27. Donald G. Mathews, *Religion in the Old
South* (Chicago: University of Chicago Press, 1977), 163–65.

New England and the middle colonies, and their teaching was then beginning to have some impact on the South, although, as has already been noted above, to a much lesser degree than in the North.[5]

In addition to spiritual training, the curriculum of Hampden-Sydney College provided instruction in translating Latin and Greek prose and poetry, and in the other core subjects of mathematics, geography, geometry, trigonometry, surveying, navigation, logic, and moral and natural law. At the end of each session, students endured public examinations by the president, trustees, and teachers. Students failing these exams were not promoted to the next class. Before graduation, each student was also required to compose an original essay and present it before the public and trustees.[6]

After leaving college, Hamilton studied law. While at Hampden-Sydney College, he may have decided to become a lawyer after watching trial proceedings at Prince Edward Courthouse. Occasionally, President Hoge permitted students to go and observe John Randolph of Roanoke and other lawyers argue cases in court. Randolph had developed a friendship with Hoge, who became his spiritual adviser and through whose guidance Randolph eventually converted. In 1817, Hamilton was recommended to Virginia's superior court, which granted him his law license on May 20. Sometime after this, he departed from Virginia for Tennessee, where he practiced law for a few months before removing to St. Louis. His decision to leave Virginia was probably based on more than one consideration. Perhaps Hamilton recognized that establishing a lucrative legal practice without strong ties to the planter elite, who still dominated the professions and politics in Virginia, would be difficult. Another factor in his decision may have been the desire of many young men to strike off on their own into the unknown. In the West, especially in the frontier regions, many opportunities for young lawyers abounded. Hamilton's eventual decision to settle in Missouri was most probably at the behest of his brother Archibald, who was many years his senior and as clerk of the St. Louis circuit court could offer Hamilton employment. By the time of

5. Bradshaw, *History of Hampden-Sidney College*, 122, 128, 130, and 133–34. Arthur Dicken Thomas Jr., "Moses Hoge: Reformed Pietism and Spiritual Guidance," *Journal of Presbyterian History* 7, no. 2 (Summer 1993): 95–98. Mathews, *Religion*, 15–23.

6. Bradshaw, *History of Hampden-Sidney College*, 135–36.

his arrival, Hamilton, who had grown into full manhood, may have been difficult for Archibald to recognize at first.[7]

On September 20, 1819, after serving as deputy clerk to his brother, Gamble was examined by Silas Bent, a justice of the territorial supreme court, and was granted a license to practice law in Missouri. Perhaps wishing to gain more independence from his older brother and hearing of the greater opportunities farther west, Gamble soon moved to the central part of the state, to the town of Franklin located on the northern bank of the Missouri River opposite Boonville. When he arrived, Franklin had been founded only three years before, but already had nearly 1,000 residents and was the seat of Howard County, then "extending from the Osage River on the east and south to the territorial line on the west, containing a population of about 7,000." Only a handful of the town's buildings were brick or framed; the rest, approximately 120, were built of logs supplied from timber growing along the Missouri River. Business and industry quickly followed immigrants to the region. Soon the town of Franklin was bustling with the activities of two mills, two smith shops, and brickmakers, shoemakers, potters, wool-carders, saddlers, and hat makers. These products were sold to the local residents in one of the town's thirteen mercantile stores or were sent down the Missouri River to markets elsewhere. After 1822, with the establishment of the northern terminus of the Santa Fe Trail in Franklin, the market to Mexico was opened to anyone willing to brave the arduous and dangerous journey. For entertainment men frequented Franklin's four taverns and two billiard rooms, or they gathered on the main square, where the offices of doctors and lawyers were located, as well as the headquarters of the Franklin *Missouri Intelligencer*, then the country's westernmost newspaper. Until the channel of the Missouri River changed course and flooded the town, Franklin continued to grow for several more years, offering Gamble and other young lawyers a fine opportunity to begin the practice of law.[8]

7. Ibid., 129; *In Memoriam*, 86; William V. N. Bay, *Reminiscences of the Bench and Bar of Missouri* (St. Louis: F. H. Thomas, 1878), 288. Recommendation of J. A. Keith of Frederick County, Virginia, for Gamble to the judges of the superior courts to receive law license, May 1817, and Gamble's Virginia law license, 20 May 1817, Gamble papers. Thomas, "Moses Hoge," 101–2.

8. Bay, *Bench and Bar*, 58 and 288. Gamble's Missouri law license, 20 September 1819, Gamble papers. Franklin *Missouri Intelligencer*, 15 November 1819 and 1 April 1820. Jonas Viles, "Old

In November 1819, soon after moving to Franklin, Gamble began the practice of law in the circuit courts of the extensive First Judicial District, which at the time included most of central and northwestern Missouri. He also argued cases before the Missouri Supreme Court. In September 1820, after gaining appointments as circuit attorney of the First Judicial District and the St. Louis Circuit, Gamble formed a partnership with Cyrus Edwards. These appointments were probably made through the influence of Gamble's brother Archibald and David Todd, judge of the First Judicial District. Judge Todd and the lawyers often traveled together on horseback from county to county, covering thousands of miles each year. Able to carry only the barest necessities and a law book or two, the men shared the hardships and tedium of their journeys and filled the monotonous hours in conversation, debate, and practical jokes. Peyton R. Hayden, a member of this legal fraternity, later complained to Gamble that after his departure from Franklin, the lawyers no longer enjoyed "the pleasures & joy which we used to ha[ve] traveling around this laborious Circuit. Indeed, there is not that warm hearted fellowship with us now, as was when you & I, Dabney Carr, Edwards, etc., traveled here together." Another lawyer, who knew him only in his later years, verified that Gamble possessed a "rich vein of humor which, now and then, in conversation enlivened as a glad sunbeam his serious face."[9]

Of course, traveling in a frontier region was often inconvenient and was sometimes dangerous. Because of the primitive condition of roads and facilities along the way, the traveling lawyer could expect to find himself in a difficult situation from time to time. Such a circumstance befell Gamble while traveling with St. Louis lawyer John F. Darby from the town of Union, the seat of Franklin County, to Mount Sterling, the location of the Gasconade circuit court. In their journey, the two men took a shortcut, but because "this new road consisted merely of blazes and notches

Franklin: A Frontier Town of the Twenties," *Mississippi Valley Historical Review* 9 (March 1923): 269–82.

9. Bay, *Bench and Bar*, 58–61 and 288. Franklin *Missouri Intelligencer*, 2 September 1820. St. Louis *Missouri Argus*, 19 June 1835. William Francis English, "The Pioneer Lawyer and Jurist in Missouri" (Ph.D. diss., University of Missouri-Columbia, 1943), 49. Wilbert Henry Rosin, "Hamilton Rowan Gamble: Missouri's Civil War Governor" (Ph.D. diss., University of Missouri, 1960), 15. Peyton R. Hayden to Gamble, 23 November 1826, Gamble papers. Philips, "Gamble," 1.

on the trees, made with an axe, to indicate the location of the road," the two men soon found themselves lost with night fast approaching. Darby proposed that by heading north they might find the Newport road, which also led to Mount Sterling.

> We started in a direct line due north, as indicated by the star, and went down one of the steepest hills possible for a horse to travel. When we reached the bottom of the ravine, there was such a thick, matted undergrowth that it was impossible for a man to ride through it. The darkness was so dense down in the bottom as to become almost visible, and the undergrowth was a perfect tangle. Mr. Gamble got unhorsed in his efforts to force the animal into the brush, but he held on to the reins and retained possession of the animal. . . . [Gamble then] denounced Gasconade County, with some pretty heavy oaths, as an "outlandish, miserable, backwoods place."

Deciding to spend the night in the woods, after some difficulty the two men built a campfire and awaited morning. The next day they continued their journey, making 25 miles to Mount Sterling without seeing a single farmhouse or building along the way.[10]

On the frontier the need for judicial proceedings often preceded the construction of a courthouse. For this reason sometimes court was held in a tavern or house, or as happened during the first session of the Boone circuit court, suits were tried "under the branches of a spreading sugar tree in the town of Smithton." As circuit attorney in early 1821, Gamble attended the inaugural sessions of both the Boone and Lillard (afterward renamed Lafayette) circuit courts.[11]

Most of Gamble's early practice involved debt suits. According to Missouri law, if the debtor lost the suit and could not pay, property was sold at public auction to settle the account. Sometimes legal action was brought

---

10. John F. Darby, *Personal Recollections of Many Prominent People Whom I have known, and of Events—especially of those relating to the History of St. Louis—During the First Half of the Present Century* (St. Louis: George Knapp, 1880), 176–80.

11. North Todd Gentry, *The Bench and Bar of Boone County Missouri, Including the History of Judges, Lawyers and Courts, and an Account of Noted Cases, Slavery Litigation, Lawyers in War Times, Public Addresses, Political Notes, etc.* (Columbia, Mo.: Author, 1916), 282. William Young, *History of Lafayette County, Missouri*, vol. 1 (Indianapolis: B. F. Bowen, 1910), 250. Bay, *Bench and Bar*, 61.

to recover items sold to the debtor. This property could be store goods, land, or slaves. Some of these actions were instituted by the administrators of estates, who were charged with collecting the debts and paying the creditors of the deceased. Other suits were breach of contract cases, divorce actions, attachments, and civil suits brought for assault and battery. In his capacity as circuit attorney, Gamble also prosecuted persons charged with committing violent assaults, murders, fraud, theft, and other crimes against the state.[12]

During his residence in Franklin, Gamble involved himself in the social and civic affairs of the town and state. Gamble participated in a town meeting to improve Franklin's streets, prevent disease and crime, and establish a city government. At the meeting, he was appointed to a committee to draft articles of incorporation and was part of a group that later presented these to the legislature. He also helped to found a Masonic lodge in Franklin, and in 1822 organized and commanded a volunteer militia company, the Franklin Guards. Gamble trained the guards, who demonstrated their proficiency in military maneuvers and marching at public events. At a celebration of Missouri's admission into the Union, Gamble toasted statehood, but in so doing made it clear that he, like most Missourians who had emigrated from Southern states, resented the attempt by Northern congressmen to restrict slavery as a condition for the state's admittance.[13]

Gamble's reaction was typical of many immigrants to Missouri, who carried with them not only their belongings, but their customs and attitudes as well. Like their counterparts in the South, Franklin's residents raced horses, gambled, and competed in a variety of athletic contests. Occasionally, these activities erupted into disputes and even violence, especially when someone's integrity or bravery was questioned. Among Franklin's elite, primarily composed of its professional class and those with significant property holdings, sometimes disputes were settled according to the code of honor by fighting a duel. While these affairs were rare, duels were most frequently fought by lawyers and politicians, and

12. Howard Circuit Court Records, 1819–23. Gamble's legal notebook, Gamble papers. See also Anton-Hermann Chroust, "The Legal Profession in Early Missouri," *Missouri Law Review* 29 (1964): 129–37.

13. Franklin *Missouri Intelligencer*, 16 April 1821; 13 August, 24 September, 10 and 15 October 1822; 13 February, 17 and 24 June, and 1 and 8 July 1823.

often resulted from disputes that had begun in court or on the political stump. Although he never fought one himself, Gamble served as a second to one of the principals in two different duels. Fortunately, neither of these ended in bloodshed. In the first, Gamble carried a challenge from U.S. Senator David Barton to Governor Alexander McNair. Although the disputed issue was ostensibly over legislation then pending before the General Assembly, Barton and McNair soon attacked one another personally, their animosity stemming ironically from McNair's failure to prosecute the killer of Barton's brother Joshua in a duel. McNair's refusal to accept the challenge ended the affair.[14]

Many of the particulars of the second duel have been lost. However, it is known that the two parties journeyed separately to Louisiana, Missouri, where the duel was to be fought on the Mississippi River. Gamble and Abiel Leonard were the seconds and the disputants are thought to have been Charles French and Peyton R. Hayden, both of whom were lawyers. Fortunately, after imbibing drinks at a local bar, both men settled their differences and the group traveled home together as friends. From these incidents it is difficult to know how much of the code of honor Gamble accepted. One possibility is that he wished to support a friend and felt duty-bound to act as a second. Such behavior, of course, did not require that he accept the code and the practice of dueling without reservation. More likely, he, like many of his contemporaries, believed that under special circumstances a duel was the proper manner to settle a dispute between gentlemen. These special circumstances were probably drawn narrowly for himself, for he never challenged anyone to a duel.[15]

Eventually, Gamble's professional and social success got the better of him, for as early as 1821 some of his friends had become concerned about his drinking habits. By 1823 this problem was serious enough to prompt him to resign as circuit attorney of Howard County and remove to St. Louis. Perhaps his brother Archibald, believing that some of his younger

14. Dick Steward, *Duels and the Roots of Violence in Missouri* (Columbia: University of Missouri Press, 2000), 108–10.

15. Ibid., 112–13; and John F. Philips, "Hamilton Rowan Gamble and the Provisional Government of Missouri," *Missouri Historical Review* 5, no. 1 (October 1910): 2. The seminal work on dueling and the code of honor in the antebellum South is Bertram Wyatt-Brown, *Southern Honor: Ethics and Behavior in the Old South* (Oxford: Oxford University Press, 1982).

brother's associations in Franklin tended to promote the problem, encouraged him to move back to St. Louis. Apparently by late 1824, Gamble had overcome his drinking problem, for Governor Frederick Bates felt confident enough to appoint him as secretary of state. The particulars of his battle with the bottle are unknown, but later in life he occasionally imbibed alcohol without slipping back into his former dissipation.[16]

As prescribed by the legislature, the secretary of state maintained the governor's papers, preserved the state accounts and books, and served as an amanuensis to the governor and the legislature. Gamble was also required to make a quarterly report to the state auditor of all remissions of fines and forfeitures granted by the governor, and to make up an abstract and index of all commissioned civil and military officers.[17]

At the time of Gamble's appointment, the legislature met in St. Charles. Without an executive mansion, Governor Bates remained at his home in the country whenever the legislature was adjourned, but once a week he traveled the short distance from his home to St. Charles to administer the duties of his office as circumstances required. During the governor's absences, Gamble served as chief of staff and representative of the executive. These duties involved investigating citizens' claims for property lost during an Indian conflict, making recommendations on possible judicial appointments, and arranging for a special election to fill vacant House seats.[18]

Governor Bates died unexpectedly before the expiration of his term in

16. Franklin *Missouri Intelligencer*, 18 November 1823 and 27 November 1824. Bay, *Bench and Bar*, 288–89. Edward Bates's diary, 29 January 1851, Bates family papers, Missouri Historical Society, St. Louis, Missouri; hereinafter cited as Bates papers. William C. Rodgers to Abiel Leonard, 20 June 1821, Abiel Leonard papers, Western Historical Manuscript Collection, Columbia, Missouri; hereinafter cited as Leonard papers. From contemporary sources, the extent of Gamble's drinking problem is unclear. Rosin, "Gamble," 18.

17. *Laws of a Public and General Nature of the District of Louisiana of the Territory of Missouri and of the State of Missouri up to the Year 1824*, vol. 1 (Jefferson City: W. Lusk and Son, 1842), 712–13. *Laws of a Public and General Nature of the State of Missouri, Passed Between the Years 1824 and 1836, Nor published in the Digest of 1825 Nor in the Digest of 1835*, vol. 2 (Jefferson City: W. Lusk and Son, 1842), 93–94.

18. Darby, *Personal Recollections*, 55. William Latham to Gamble, 15 January 1825; T. Mosely Jr. to Gamble, 2 October 1825; and Lilburn W. Boggs to Gamble, 16 June 1826, Gamble papers.

August 1825. Because Lieutenant Governor Benjamin H. Reeves had resigned earlier to accept a federal commission to survey the Santa Fe Trail,
a special election was held to supply the vacancy. Upon his election, John
Miller, a resident of Franklin, retained Gamble as his secretary of state.
Miller knew Gamble well and probably wished to have an experienced
lieutenant on whom he could depend for advice and information. Because
Gamble was a capable administrator, Miller could also rely upon him to
handle the daily functions of office whenever the legislature was not in session. In January 1826, Gamble delivered Governor-Elect Miller's address
before a joint session of the General Assembly. The following summer,
the legislature, desiring to establish the state capitol in a more convenient
location for a majority of its members, passed a bill to remove the seat of
government to Jefferson City. This measure probably prompted Gamble
to resign his office and to return to the full-time practice of law. Governor
Miller appointed Spencer Pettis as Gamble's replacement.[19]

In July 1826, Gamble again removed to St. Louis, then a growing and
prosperous city. The population of St. Louis would increase from 3,000
to almost 6,000 by 1830. This growth sparked a good deal of construction that continued throughout Gamble's life. This activity created a great
amount of hustle and bustle and contributed to poor air quality from the
fumes of brickmaking kilns. This pollution, coupled with the smoke from
residential and business fires, presented a nuisance and occasionally a
health hazard to the town's residents.[20]

Sometime after his resignation, Gamble met Caroline J. Coulter, who
was probably then visiting her brother David in St. Louis. Little is known
about their courtship, but it may have continued by correspondence after
Caroline returned to her home in Columbia, South Carolina. In November 1827, Gamble traveled by horseback to South Carolina, where he and
Caroline were married. According to all accounts, the match was a happy
one and, after they had returned to St. Louis, the couple quickly settled
down together to their new domestic responsibilities. In time, probably

19. Thomas J. Boggs to Gamble, 3 November 1825; John Miller to Gamble, 11 November 1825; receipt from Spencer Pettis for state property in his possession, 29 July 1826, Gamble
papers. St. Louis *Missouri Republican*, 26 January and 31 August 1826.

20. James Neal Primm, *Lion of the Valley: St. Louis, Missouri*, 3d ed. (Boulder, Colo.: Pruett,
1998), 132.

through his wife's and brother's influence, Gamble rediscovered his faith and became an active member of the local Presbyterian church.[21]

Just how Gamble's religious rebirth occurred is unclear, but the transformation was apparently genuine, for he remained a faithful and active participant in church affairs for the rest of his life. His devotion was evident from his deportment and from his influence on others to lead a pious life. This influence was particularly strong among young lawyers, who, by the 1830s, admired Gamble as a successful lawyer, a mature man, and someone from whom they could gain solid legal and religious advice. This generosity with his time and advice was very much in the tradition of his former mentor, Moses Hoge, at Hampden-Sydney College.[22] Often inviting young men home after Sunday church services, Gamble took particular interest in the welfare of young lawyers, one of whom years later wrote that

> there was no subject in the range of the law that he [Gamble] was not capable of reducing to its last analysis, nor any application of legal principles to facts which he was not able to make more clearly and masterfully than any other man I knew. His moral power was equal to his intellectual. Whatever came before him as a duty, he did to the uttermost, leaving all consequences to God. His nature was not emotional, neither was it cold, but calm, collected, self poised, and controlled by strong religious principle. . . . Many a time, with great kindness, he helped me out of his abundant store of law knowledge; but more often, after I made a profession of religion in 1840, and united with the church he was a Ruling Elder, he opened to me his store of spiritual knowledge and experience to my great benefit. I do not think I ever knew a man of deeper religious experience than his.[23]

Gamble also took an interest in the welfare of young ministerial students, corresponding with them and providing advice and money for their edu-

21. St. Louis *Missouri Republican*, 27 December 1827. Bay, *Bench and Bar*, 289–90. *In Memoriam*, 36 and 86.

22. Covenant between J. Spalding and John Kerr to pay $50 whenever they used tobacco, 15 September 1834; and Gamble's pledge to give at least one-tenth of his income to God, October 1835, Gamble papers. Thomas, "Moses Hoge," 98.

23. Charles D. Drake, "Autobiography," 476–78 and 531–33, Western Historical Manuscripts Collection, Columbia, Missouri. See also Philips, "Gamble," 4.

cation. Once again he was following the example of Hoge by supporting ministerial students financially. Such a willingness to participate in religious affairs was very valuable and rare, and led to even greater responsibilities for Gamble as an elder of the local Presbyterian church, and as a legal adviser to the regional Presbyterian association. In one instance, he consented to represent Marion College in an important trial to determine the ownership of large donations. His role was "*to assist the resident counsel,*" but quickly took over the management of the case, "not by any assumption of his own, but by respectful deference on the part of his colleagues." His co-counsels' confidence in him was not misplaced, for Gamble offered a very important instruction to the jury, which undermined the opposition's case and led to victory for Marion College.[24]

Moreover, Gamble participated in organizations that sought to improve the community and reform people's lives. No doubt remembering the harm alcohol had done him, he joined a local temperance society established to warn the public about its dangers. As a member, he donated money to provide lecturers and supported efforts to limit the accessibility of alcohol in St. Louis and on steamboats.[25]

Gamble was also a member of the St. Louis branch of the American Colonization Society. The organization's goal was to emancipate slaves and colonize them in Africa. In 1816, when the society was first established, it was largely uncontroversial, for most Americans in the North and South considered the gradual eradication of slavery to be a worthwhile goal. More than anything else this organization served as a safety valve for moderate antislavery idealism in the North and South. James Madison became president of the organization until his death in 1836, when another slaveholder, Henry Clay, was elected to replace him. By this time, however, most of the Revolutionary generation's elder statesmen in the South had passed from the scene. Over time, in reaction to Northern

24. George C. Sibley to Gamble, 5 June 1837; Rev. A. Bullard to Gamble, 16 July 1837; Rev. William C. Wimer to Gamble, 12 July 1837; receipt for pew, 6 July 1837; J. W. Allen to Gamble, 17 April 1838 and 15 February 1839; William S. Potts to Gamble, 21 May and 20 July 1838, 16 February 1839, and 20 December 1842; and William P. Cochran to Gamble, 18 March 1839, Gamble papers. Thomas, "Moses Hoge," 98. See also *In Memoriam*, 51, and the St. Louis *Missouri Republican*, 31 October 1834 and 21 July 1835. The case was *Dr. Ely v. Marion College*.

25. St. Louis *Missouri Argus*, 30 September 1837, and Drake, "Autobiography," 477.

criticism, many of the new Southern generation began to defend slavery as a positive good, beneficial to slave and slaveholder alike.[26]

Gamble's attitudes and relationship to slaves and the institution of slavery were complex, for he, like many Southerners, acted in seemingly contradictory ways. Although a member of the colonization movement, he was also a slaveholder and a lawyer who represented both slaves and slaveholders in emancipation suits. As circuit attorney in St. Louis County, he prosecuted blacks who had violated the restrictive codes governing their behavior in St. Louis County. As a public official, Gamble was duty-bound to enforce state and county law. As a slaveholder, he probably shared white concerns that too much freedom for free blacks and slaves would lead to trouble. Occasional newspaper stories about slave rebellions, free blacks helping slaves run away, and crimes committed by free blacks and slaves probably exacerbated the normal fears of whites in slaveholding communities. Other articles revealed the callous and harsh treatment of blacks accused of criminal activity. Often lynchings were reported in a matter-of-fact manner, although occasionally they were condemned as illegal measures to which whites should never resort.[27]

In reaction to some of the excesses that these stories exposed, many reform-minded members of society, of whom Gamble was a part, sought to change the circumstances to mitigate the severity of slavery. This desire explains Gamble's law enforcement efforts. Reflecting the values and prejudices of the age, his first concern was to protect whites, but he also wanted to maintain better control of slaves and free blacks to prevent tragedies from occurring. One way to achieve this was to restrict the freedom of blacks, both slave and free, and to arrange for the humane and voluntary removal of free blacks whose presence and influence would cause discontent and ambition for freedom among their brethren in bonds. No doubt Gamble also understood that some members of the colonization movement had joined to undercut the efforts of radical abolitionists, such

26. St. Louis *Missouri Republican*, 17 May 1831 and 3 February 1835. See also Daniel Walker Howe, *The Political Culture of the American Whigs* (Chicago: University of Chicago Press, 1979), 133–37; and William Lee Miller, *Arguing About Slavery: The Great Battle in the United States Congress* (New York: Alfred A. Knopf, 1996), 72–75.

27. For example, see the St. Louis *Missouri Republican*, 21 April 1829; 22 August 1834; and 27 February, 8 and 22 March 1844.

as Elijah Lovejoy, who for a short time resided in St. Louis. Moreover, it is important to remember that Gamble and most supporters of the colonization movement never argued for black equality; in fact, the entire black colonization effort was founded on the premise that free blacks could never become full-fledged citizens and therefore should be removed from white society.[28]

Gamble's efforts to improve and reform himself and society were an extension of his religious awakening and efforts to live according to the evangelical principles he had learned in his youth. Although preferring to work through ecumenical channels whenever possible, he recognized that comprehensive change could best be effected through the political process. His political activities, however, were largely limited to supporting the reforms he most strongly believed in, and for many years after joining the local Presbyterian church he was unwilling to run for political office.

28. See note 26 above.

Chapter Two

State Representative

$\mathcal{F}$rom the very beginning of his residence in Missouri, Hamilton R. Gamble developed important alliances with prominent members of its legal and political world. One of these contacts was Edward Bates, who in 1824 had persuaded his brother Frederick, who was then governor, to appoint Gamble secretary of state. This association was strengthened by marriage ties when Gamble married the sister of Bates's wife. Their friendship would endure for over forty years and was apparently characterized by mutual respect. Both men shared a conservative outlook, occasionally worked on cases together, and collaborated in politics as members of the Whig Party for the rest of their lives. However, disliking the rough and tumble of Missouri politics, and preferring to devote himself to his duties as elder of his church, Gamble demonstrated a strong reluctance to run for political office himself.[1]

In 1828, Gamble supported the candidacy of John Quincy Adams for reelection as president and attended a state convention to organize support in Missouri. At the convention, Gamble was appointed to a committee that prepared an address to the people of the state. He also supported

1. Marvin R. Cain, "Edward Bates and Hamilton R. Gamble: A Wartime Partnership," *Missouri Historical Review* 56 (January 1962): 146–55. W. V. N. Bay, *Reminiscences of the Bench and Bar of Missouri* (St. Louis: F. H. Thomas, 1878), 289–90. Edward Bates to Frederick Bates, 24 August 1824, Bates papers. Edward Bates to Gamble, 24 January, 1 and 30 April 1828; and 9 February 1829, Gamble papers.

the candidacy of his brother-in-law Bates for the U.S. House of Representatives. After Bates's election, the two corresponded about political and legal matters. In his letters from Washington, D.C., Bates primarily discussed bills he had written and proposed. This legislation included the establishment of a new territory on Missouri's northern border, wherein Native American rights would be extinguished and the region secured for settlers; the sale of lead mines and salt works in Missouri; a bill to secure Missouri's land records; the settlement of Spanish claims to Louisiana Purchase lands; and military protection of the Sante Fe Trail, upon which Missouri's entrepreneurs carried an important trade with Mexico. These bills addressed issues important to many Missourians and especially to the interests of the political minority of which Bates and Gamble were a part. The bills pertaining to land sales were of special importance to Gamble, for much of his legal work concerned conflicting claims of title to land. In the ensuing years, Gamble gained a reputation for his expertise in these types of cases, of which there were many in Missouri's courts. The main difficulty in securing a title in Missouri was that Congress had failed to define clearly the law as it pertained to valid claims based on Spanish and French land grants and New Madrid claims. These difficulties were greatly exacerbated because accurate land records were not available to prevent the posting of conflicting claims.[2]

The political minority of the time was primarily a conservative movement in opposition to the Jacksonian Democrats, who dominated politics in Missouri from 1828 into the 1850s, controlling both the governor's mansion and the General Assembly. Because the governor appointed all the circuit court and supreme court judges, even the judiciary was controlled by Democrats, excepting only those judges who were holdovers from the pre-1828 period. The Jacksonians achieved this success by effectively using egalitarian rhetoric to promote their policy initiatives, which were designed to help farmers and laborers of moderate means. These

2. Edward Bates to Gamble, 24 January, 1 and 30 April 1828; and 9 February 1829, Gamble papers. William Francis English, "The Pioneer Lawyer and Jurist in Missouri" (Ph.D. diss., University of Missouri, 1943), 54–90. William Foley, *A History of Missouri*, vol. 1 (Columbia: University of Missouri Press, 1971), 171–73. Walter A. Schroeder, "Spread of Settlement in Howard County, Missouri, 1810–1859," *Missouri Historical Review* 64 (October 1968): 10–11. Fayette *Missouri Intelligencer*, 7 March 1828.

initiatives included making public land more affordable and available to the common man, reducing taxes, making government more answerable and responsive to the public by advocating the rotating of elected and appointed officials in and out of office, and ending the lifetime tenure of federal and state judges. The Jacksonians' most important measure, however, was the proposal to sell small lots of public land at a low price per acre. By making land available at a lower price, they hoped to provide opportunity in the West for persons of modest means to own land. To the Jacksonians, this policy was congenial in two respects, for it promoted an independent yeomanry and provided their party with a valuable patronage to dispense. That this policy was popular in Missouri was evident from the fact that even David Barton, the state's conservative U.S. senator, voted with Senator Thomas Hart Benton for the measure.[3]

The minority party, under the leadership of Henry Clay and others, offered the American System as an alternative legislative program to the Democrats' proposals. By diversifying the economy and fostering industry, it was argued, the United States would be less dependent on foreign producers and could provide more wealth and jobs for its citizens. This goal could be achieved by placing protective tariffs on other countries' products that competed with American goods and by federal funding of road- and canal-building projects throughout the interior of the United States. In this way, American manufacturers could compete with their foreign competitors and reach many more people with their goods. Another important component of the American System was the Bank of the United

---

3. A good deal has been written about Andrew Jackson and the Jacksonian Democrats. For information on the Jacksonians in Missouri see Perry McCandless, "Benton v. Barton: The Formation of the Second-Party System in Missouri," *Missouri Historical Review* 79 (July 1985): 425–38, and "The Political Philosophy and Political Personality of Thomas H. Benton," *Missouri Historical Review* 50 (January 1956): 145–58. Raymond D. Thomas, "A Study in Missouri Politics, 1840–1870," *Missouri Historical Review* 21 (January 1927): 166–84. Some of the more important works on the Jacksonian movement are Arthur M. Schlesinger Jr., *The Age of Jackson* (New York: Book Find Club, 1945). Marvin Meyers, *The Jacksonian Persuasion: Politics and Belief* (New York: Vintage, 1957). Lee Benson, *The Concept of Jacksonian Democracy: New York as a Test Case* (Princeton: Princeton University Press, 1961). Richard P. McCormick, *The Second American Party System: Party Formation in the Jacksonian Era* (Chapel Hill: University of North Carolina Press, 1966). Harry L. Watson, *Liberty and Power: The Politics of Jacksonian America* (New York: Hill and Wang, 1990).

States, an institution that provided capital to businessmen and exercised some control over the speculative propensities of many state banks. The proponents of this plan, sometimes referred to as the Opposition or the Anti-Jacksonians, were an on-again, off-again coalition of conservatives alarmed by the Jacksonians' efforts to democratize American society. While reluctant to organize, the Anti-Jacksonians' alarm eventually caused them to create the Whig Party in Missouri and throughout the country.[4]

As an Anti-Jacksonian and Whig, Gamble supported Clay's American System and was a strong advocate of the colonization and temperance movements. This agenda appealed to Gamble and his associates (many of whom were men of property and eminence), who sought to improve American society by making use of the power and wealth of the federal government. While Gamble himself was reluctant to seek public office, he willingly worked on committees promoting the Anti-Jacksonians' goals and supported their candidates.[5]

In 1831, Gamble and other Anti-Jacksonian leaders in Missouri sought to find an electable candidate for the U.S. House of Representatives. After they were unable to urge Abiel Leonard, a prominent central Missouri lawyer, to run for the office, a public meeting of "the Friends of the American System" nominated former Senator David Barton for Congress. Gamble and Bates, with others, drafted a letter to Barton asking him to be their nominee, to which he agreed. However, probably to no one's surprise, Barton lost to the Jacksonian candidate Spencer Pettis.[6]

During the 1830s and 1840s St. Louis continued to grow. In 1835, over 8,000 people resided there. Until then, the city had grown steadily,

4. For fuller accounts about the Whig Party and its formation in Missouri see Daniel Walker Howe, *The Political Culture of the American Whigs* (Chicago: University of Chicago Press, 1979). John Vollmer Mering, *The Whig Party in Missouri*, University of Missouri Studies, vol. 91 (Columbia: University of Missouri Press, 1967).

5. St. Louis *Missouri Argus*, 19 June 1835 and 11 June 1840. Edward Bates to Gamble, 1 April 1828, Gamble papers.

6. George C. Sibley to Abiel Leonard, 25 March 1831; and Edward Bates, 4 April 1831, Leonard papers. St. Louis *Missouri Republican*, 5 July 1831. John F. Darby, *Personal Recollections of Many Prominent People whom I have known, and of Events—especially of those relating to the History of St. Louis—during the First Half of the Present Century* (St. Louis: George Knapp, 1880), 39–40.

but moderately. This pace of growth, however, quickened so that by 1840 the town had a population of over 16,000 and over 35,000 by 1845. Such a phenomenal increase had advantages and disadvantages. Immigrants brought capital and labor when the rest of the country was suffering from an economic downturn. Most of the new arrivals were Americans, but a significant number came from Germany seeking a new start in a free and democratic country. Skilled laborers in the construction fields were especially welcome, and although many settled in St. Louis they were unable to build enough homes and other buildings to meet the demand. Between 1833 and 1845, thirty-one new additions to the city were established. City government was inadequate to meet the need for water and sewage disposal, the pavement of streets and sidewalks, and city police and fire services. Because the state legislature exercised a good deal of control over city government, the council was handicapped in its attempts to meet these and other needs.[7]

In 1836 town leaders and boosters promoted the construction of a railroad from St. Louis to Fayette, a town located in Howard County, a prosperous and populous region of central Missouri. Mayor John F. Darby asked the Board of Aldermen to organize support for the railroad project. At a public meeting, Gamble spoke with "great force and power" in favor of building the railroad. After it was agreed to hold a convention to mobilize support, Gamble nominated delegates to represent St. Louis County. The convention was held in St. Louis on April 20. Delegates from eleven counties attended and agreed to support the construction of two railroads, one leading to Fayette and the other to the Iron Mountain region. In the 1836–37 legislative session, these projects and sixteen more railroads were approved. In addition, eleven turnpike companies were chartered. Because of the pressing need for better roads, these bills were passed by legislators; even Democrats recognized the importance of expediting the transport of goods and people to all parts of the state. These roads, it was hoped, would open up new markets to merchants and industry and enable farmers to transport their produce to wider markets. However, in the end,

7. James Neal Primm, *Lion of the Valley: St. Louis, Missouri, 1764–1980*, 3d ed. (St. Louis: Missouri Historical Society Press, 1998), 132–33, 142–48, 151–57.

because of a nationwide depression the legislature was unable to appropriate the necessary funds.[8]

ATTACKS ON THE JUDICIARY

An issue of great importance to both the Jacksonians and Anti-Jacksonians concerned the character of judicial offices. Missouri's constitution provided for the lifetime appointment of circuit and supreme court justices by the governor. When Missouri's Jacksonian Democrats were swept into office in 1828, they immediately attempted to amend the constitution to make judicial positions elective and to limit the terms to six years. In part, this effort, which would be renewed repeatedly for many years thereafter, was undertaken to make judges, like most other public officials, answerable to the people.[9]

Anti-Jacksonians and other conservatives did not share the Jacksonians' confidence in the people's ability to elect competent men as judges. By making judicial offices elective, the Anti-Jacksonians feared that the independence of the judiciary would be undermined and that Jacksonian candidates would be elected who, instead of administering the law, would cater to the whims of the people on the stump and in the courtroom.[10]

Although they composed a considerable majority in the state legislature, the Jacksonians were unable to amend the constitution for some time because a two-thirds majority was required. While unable to change the character of the judiciary, they exercised a more radical option available by bringing articles of impeachment against some of the judges. The first impeachment occurred during the 1828–29 legislative term against

8. Darby, *Recollections*, 202–10. Primm, *Lion of the Valley*, 200–201. After the meeting, the Democrats accused Gamble of nominating only Anti-Jacksonians to represent St. Louis County at the convention. See the St. Louis *Missouri Argus*, 11 and 18 March 1836.

9. Charles F. Hobson, *The Great Chief Justice: John Marshall and the Rule of Law* (Lawrence: University of Kansas Press, 1996), 111–49. Charles Warren, *The Supreme Court in United States History*, rev. ed., vol. 1, *1789–1835* (Boston: Little, Brown, 1926), 169–230 and 652–728.

10. William E. Foley, "The Political Philosophy of David Barton," *Missouri Historical Review* 58 (April 1964): 281. Mering, *Whig Party in Missouri*, 19–20 and 30–31. Dennis K. Boman, *Abiel Leonard, Yankee Slaveholder, Eminent Jurist, and Passionate Unionist*, Studies in American History, vol. 38 (Lewiston: Edwin Mellen, 2002), 66–67. See also *Federalist* No. 78, Alexander Hamilton's classic argument against elective judicial offices.

David Todd, an Anti-Jacksonian judge in the First Judicial Circuit. Todd was charged with judicial misconduct in three trials over which he had presided. Spearheaded by Speaker of the House John Thornton and other Jacksonian representatives, this effort was apparently motivated by politics and personal animosity; however, in the end, Todd was acquitted of all charges against him.[11]

Jacksonian legislators again attempted to rid themselves of a conservative judge during the 1832–33 legislative session, bringing charges against William C. Carr, judge of the Third Judicial Circuit. Charles H. Allen, chairman of the judiciary committee, presented to the House a petition signed by citizens of St. Louis County charging that Carr was an unfit judge. Behind the petition were Luke E. Lawless, Arthur L. Magennis, and George Shannon, all of whom were Jacksonian partisans. Most prominent of these was Lawless, who formerly had conducted a long campaign to impeach and convict U.S. Circuit Court Judge John M. Peck. Despite Peck's acquittal before the U.S. Senate, Lawless apparently had not lost his animosity to judicial authority and his taste for impeachment proceedings.[12]

Judge Carr chose Gamble and Henry S. Geyer to represent him before the legislature. Undoubtedly, Carr considered them to be the most talented lawyers practicing before his court. Gamble and Geyer, however, faced great difficulties in their defense of Judge Carr, for the Jacksonian Democrats, who were in the majority, controlled every aspect of the trial and were able to overrule any of Gamble's and Geyer's objections to the proceedings. Their greatest difficulty was that the evidence presented against Carr before the House Judiciary Committee was kept secret from them. In addition to this, when the trial was almost over Gamble and Geyer were not allowed to offer into evidence depositions from persons too infirm or otherwise unable to attend the trial. Josiah Spalding, a well-

11. Dennis K. Boman, "Impeachment Proceedings as a Partisan Tool: The Trial of Judge David Todd," *Missouri Historical Review* 94 (January 2000): 146–59.

12. *Journal of the House of Representatives of the State of Missouri at the First Session of the Seventh General Assembly, Begun and Held at the City of Jefferson, On the Nineteenth Day of November, in the Year of our Lord, one thousand eight hundred and thirty-two* (St. Louis: John Steele, Free Press Office, 1833), 93–94. Jo. Gamble to Gamble, December 1833, Gamble papers. Eleanore Bushnell, "The Impeachment and Trial of James H. Peck," *Missouri Historical Review* 74 (January 1980): 137–65. The facts in the Peck impeachment and trial strongly indicate that the judge was a victim of congressional animosity toward the judiciary.

respected St. Louis lawyer and an important witness for Gamble and Geyer's case, could not testify, for he had been prevented from leaving home until the trial was almost over because of his wife's serious illness.[13]

The House presented to the Senate one charge and fourteen specifications as grounds for Carr's impeachment. The charge asserted that "Carr is wholly unqualified" for his office. This was a strange assertion for the prosecution to make in its only charge, for it did not constitute an impeachable offense. The specifications, which normally provide factual evidence to prove a charge, were really accusations, some of which, if proven, were impeachable offenses, while others were not. Apparently, this irregularity was intentional, for it enabled the prosecution to present numerous charges without specific evidence. Throughout the trial, Gamble and Geyer emphasized how unfairly Judge Carr was being treated. Another irregularity in the proceedings was that both houses sat as jurors, instead of only the Senate as in Todd's trial. Certainly, this was not unknown to the House managers, for Phillip Cole had served as prosecutor in the Todd case as well.[14]

In Carr's formal answer, Gamble and Geyer stated that many of the trial's specifications came from disgruntled lawyers seeking to blame him after they had lost cases. These eight specifications were repetitious and accused Carr of prejudice against and favor toward some attorneys, of lacking a proper judicial temperament, of ignorance of the law, and of favoring the rich over the poor. Apparently, witnesses for the prosecution provided only opinions and no specific instances of Carr's judicial misdeeds, for none of these were ever publicly debated.[15]

13. St. Louis *Missouri Republican*, 19 February 1833. Josiah Spalding to Gamble, 19 and 21 January 1833, Gamble papers.

14. Boman, *Abiel Leonard*, 44. St. Louis *Missouri Republican*, 5 February 1833. St. Louis *Free Press*, 7 February 1833. *Journal of the Senate of the State of Missouri at the First Session of the Seventh General Assembly, Begun and the Held at the City of Jefferson, on the Monday the Nineteenth Day of November, in the Year of our Lord, One Thousand eight hundred and thirty-two* (Jefferson City: Calvin Gunn, Jeffersonian Office, 1833), 137.

15. The major sources for information on the trial are *Journal of the House, Seventh General Assembly*, 93–94, 141, 150–51, and 231. *Journal of the Senate, Seventh General Assembly*, 126–27, 130–31, 132–35, 136–37, 196, 199–201, 203–6, 212–14, 218, 223–24, 227–31, and 234. St. Louis *Missouri Republican*, 29 January, 5, 12, and 19 February 1833. St. Louis *Free Press*, 7 and 21 February 1833. The specifications here referred to are two, three, six, seven, eight, ten, thirteen, and fourteen.

Four other specifications stated that Carr lacked legal ability, was "negligent" in the administration of his duties, and had lost the public's confidence. To the first of these charges, Gamble and Geyer gave a history of Carr's career as a lawyer in Missouri until his appointment by Governor John Miller in 1826, demonstrating that he had practiced law for fifteen years before retiring in 1819. They also noted that he had never sought the judicial post and had accepted it only reluctantly. Concerning the petitions presented to the House complaining of Carr's behavior as a judge, Gamble and Geyer replied that a small number of people had signed the documents only after a few disgruntled lawyers had incited them to do so.[16]

The trial took only a few days, beginning January 28 and ending February 6. Before the joint session of the General Assembly, one of the managers gave his concluding argument and was followed by Gamble and Geyer. After them, three of the four remaining prosecutors gave concluding statements. When the final manager had concluded, it was moved to end the trial, in this way preventing Gamble and Geyer from offering a rebuttal to the concluding remarks of the last three prosecutors. After this the House and Senate separated to consider and vote on the charge and remaining specifications—three, five, eight, and eleven had been dismissed. To convict, two-thirds of both houses would need to vote against Carr. In the House, he was convicted on four specifications: the second and seventh, which were almost identical, for allegedly showing favoritism to some lawyers and for oppressing others; the ninth, because public sentiment was against him; and the thirteenth, because he lacked a judicial temperament. The Senate convicted Carr on the fourth specification, alleging that he was "inattentive and negligent in discharging his duties as a Judge." However, because both houses did not agree to convict on the same charge or specification, Carr was acquitted of them all.[17]

While no record exists of Carr's reaction to his acquittal, it was no doubt a bittersweet victory at best, and probably led to his decision to resign his office in 1834. He and his supporters were not happy when Governor Daniel Dunklin appointed Lawless to replace him. Lawless resigned his judgeship in 1836, but later changed his mind and sought

16. St. Louis *Missouri Republican*, 5 February 1833.

17. *Journal of the Senate, Seventh General Assembly*, 212–14, 227–31, and 234. St. Louis *Missouri Republican*, 12 and 19 February 1833.

reappointment. In response to this development, Gamble and fourteen other lawyers in St. Louis County held a meeting of the bar on December 8 to object to Lawless's reappointment. From the record of the proceedings it is clear that Gamble and Geyer were very much at the forefront of the effort to embarrass Lawless and to demonstrate the majority of the legal profession's displeasure with him.[18]

Gamble and four others were appointed to draft a letter to the governor "expressing the objections of the Bar, to the reappointment" of Lawless as judge. In this document, consisting of eight allegations, the drafters echoed some of the complaints brought against Judge Carr, arguing that Lawless did not possess the judicial temperament necessary to the proper administration of his duties. According to them, Lawless was "too passionate and impatient . . . to admit a calm and full examination of causes" and that he was "imperious overbearing and disrespectful in his manner to the members of the bar." Moreover, Lawless's bias in causes often influenced jurors; he was "wanting in punctuality in attending" to his duties, and was "indifferent to the faithful recording" of court proceedings. A vote was taken on each allegation, all of which were adopted by a strong majority, Gamble and Geyer voting in favor of all the allegations. Nevertheless, Governor Dunklin reappointed Lawless and his nomination was reconfirmed by the Senate.[19]

During the late 1830s, Gamble also served on committees promoting the Whig Party in Missouri, occasionally spoke in public, and opposed Thomas Hart Benton's candidacy for the U.S. Senate. In 1840 he declined the Whig nomination for state representative and did little to promote the candidacy of Whig presidential candidate William Henry Harrison. However, despite his reluctance to run for political office, his fellow Whigs in St. Louis County still regarded him as an electable candidate for the state legislature and finally persuaded him to run in the summer of 1844 after Luther Kennett, the original candidate, dropped out of the race.[20]

18. St. Louis *Farmers' and Mechanics' Advocate*, 20 March 1834. Record of a St. Louis County bar meeting, 8 December 1836, Gamble papers.

19. Bar meeting, 8 December 1836. Notes on interview of Beverly Allen, senator from St. Louis County [1837], Gamble papers.

20. St. Louis *Missouri Argus*, 2 and 9 December 1837; 23 February and 21 June 1838; and 11 June and 10 October 1840. St. Louis *Missouri Republican*, 20 June 1844. It is likely that

In July, Gamble, with seven other St. Louis County Whig candidates for the General Assembly, published a policy statement opposing a sales tax, currency bills, and a landlord and tenant law. Moreover, they favored a mechanics lien law, amending Missouri's constitution to establish a more equitable system of representation in the General Assembly, creating new congressional districts, providing for greater compensation to jurors and witnesses in Missouri's courts, improving the roads, reducing state debt, and maintaining citizens' equal rights and privileges. All eight Whig candidates were elected, seven (including Gamble) as state representatives and one as state senator. Of the twenty candidates for state representative in St. Louis County, Gamble received the most votes (3,527), demonstrating the confidence of contemporaries in his judgment and integrity. St. Louis County's election followed a statewide trend in which the Whig Party gained twenty seats in the General Assembly, although they remained the minority party with fifty-three seats to the Democrats' eighty.[21]

STATE REPRESENTATIVE

Perhaps Gamble would not have run for state representative, despite Kennett's withdrawal from the race, if the legislature was not due to revise state law as it was mandated to do every ten years by the constitution. Because of his reputation as a knowledgeable and accomplished lawyer, Gamble was appointed to the judiciary committee and the joint committee on the revision of state laws. After electing officers, the House met in joint session with the Senate and elected Thomas H. Benton and David R. Atchison to the U.S. Senate. The legislature then turned to the issue of amending the state constitution to limit judges' terms in office. For several years, the Democrats had sought this reform, in part, to replace circuit and supreme court judges (appointed for life), many of whom were members of the Anti-Jacksonian opposition. After the 1834–35 session of the General Assembly, much of the fervor for this reform was lost when an

---

Gamble declined running for the legislature to attend the Presbyterian Synod of Missouri as an elder-delegate.

21. St. Louis *Missouri Republican*, 24 July 1844. Jefferson City, *Jefferson Inquirer*, 14 November 1844. St. Louis *Mill Boy*, 10 August 1844. Mering, *Whig Party in Missouri*, 121.

amendment passed ending the terms of the judges then in office. New judges were appointed by a Democratic governor, who naturally chose men from his own party.[22]

The traditional Whig position was that judges should serve lifetime tenures during good behavior, because limiting their terms to six years for circuit court judges and to ten years for supreme court judges would undermine the independence of the judiciary and make them subject to the executive branch for reappointment. Gamble agreed with this and first sought to delay the vote on this and other amendments by having them sent to a select committee to ascertain "whether the requirements of the constitution ha[d] been complied with in regard to the publication of these amendments." This constitutional provision required the General Assembly, before it could consider an amendment, to have it published several times in all state newspapers at least one year before the general election. This ensured that the matter would be debated by candidates for the legislature. William V. N. Bay and Benjamin F. Stringfellow, Democrats from Franklin and Chariton counties respectively, opposed Gamble's resolution on the grounds that it was unnecessary to have a select committee investigate the matter and that the constitutional provision was only "directory, and not imperative." Stringfellow also accused Gamble of playing politics, to which he replied

> that he had submitted the motion in good faith. That the committee was subject to the power of the House, and could be compelled to return the amendments to the House at any time. He desired to know if any member of the House was prepared to lay his hand upon his heart, and vote for these amendments, if they had not been published as required by the constitution. . . . Could they engraft a provision on the constitution in the face and in total disregard of the plain provisions of the constitution? In regard to electioneering on this subject, he knew nothing about it; but he would say this, that he had been bred a lawyer, and had entertained the idea that the

22. *Journal of the House of Representatives of the State of Missouri of the First Session of the Thirteenth General Assembly, Begun and Held at the City of Jefferson, On Monday, the Eighteenth Day of November, in the Year of our Lord One Thousand Eight Hundred and Forty-Four* (Jefferson City: James Lusk, printer to the state, 1845), 47 and 53. For information about the 1834–35 legislative session and the issue of making judgeships elective see Boman, *Abiel Leonard*, 66–67.

tenure of the judiciary during good behavior was one of the safeguards of
the constitution and of the liberties of the people; but of late, since he had
seen men appointed, not from their knowledge of law, or the abstruse and
intricate questions which must come before them, nor from their virtue or
their talents, and solely because he preferred this or that man for President
of the United States, he had begun to doubt.[23]

Two weeks later, Gamble presented resolutions arguing that the amendments limiting judges' tenures "would have subjected the Judiciary to the
Executive department, and thereby virtually impaired the independence
of the Judiciary." For this amendment to be acceptable, he argued, the
judiciary's independence must be vouchsafed and this could be accomplished only by providing for the election of judges. While Gamble's resolutions pinpointed an important flaw in the proposed amendments, he and
his Whig counterparts also recognized an important benefit to making
the judiciary elective, for this reform might enable Whigs occasionally to
gain judgeships that they would never fill so long as Whigs failed to elect a
governor. For this reason, Gamble and his party championed making the
judiciary elective, a measure that Democrats had long advocated on the
principle that judges should be answerable to the people. However, with
Whig support behind this reform, some Democrats in the legislature began to reconsider the issue and to oppose it, recognizing that they would
lose control of this important source of political patronage. Apparently,
for these reasons, the amendments eventually failed.[24]

Another important issue to Gamble's constituents concerned the repeal
of a law that confiscated the land of those who had failed to pay their state
taxes. Gamble moved for the law's repeal, but was opposed by Representative Stringfellow, who argued that many of the petitioners against the law
were land speculators (nonresidents buying land as an investment), and

23. Jefferson City *Jefferson Inquirer*, 14 and 21 November, and 19 and 26 December 1844.
St. Louis *Missouri Republican*, 6 December 1844.

24. Jefferson City *Jefferson Inquirer*, 26 December 1844; 4 January and 8 February 1845; and
29 December 1846. After rejection of these amendments, the provisions were included in the
new constitution proposed to the people by the state constitutional convention held in 1846.
After the new constitution was rejected, the amendments were again submitted to the General
Assembly in 1846, but were not adopted until the 1850–51 session. See St. Louis *Missouri Republican*, 1 July 1850 and 12 April 1851.

those unaffected by the law. He stated that his constituents in Chariton County had already suffered under the statute and it was unfair to exempt others from it now. Moreover, some means of compelling nonresidents to pay their taxes was needed.[25]

Gamble replied that Stringfellow was mistaken to assert that the petitioners were speculators who stood to lose their land for failing to pay their taxes. Gamble argued that even if Stringfellow was correct the law should be repealed, for it "was wrong and unjust, and on that [basis] alone he asked members to vote for its repeal, and not as a boon to St. Louis." After more debate the House voted to repeal: seventy-eight in favor and fifteen against.[26]

As a representative from St. Louis County, Gamble promoted an act to improve the harbor at St. Louis, which was passed and authorized the mayor and city council to borrow up to $100,000 and levy a tax to remove obstructions and make other improvements. He also proposed the amendment of an incorporation act of a St. Louis school, pushed through the House a special tax for St. Louis County to provide better compensation to jurors, and presented a petition asking the House to pass an act to make "trespassing on lands . . . an indictable offense."[27]

One of the more time-consuming duties Gamble performed as state representative involved his work on a committee to investigate the operations of the state tobacco warehouse in St. Louis. The committee was charged with making arrangements for selling out the operation, for it was doing very little business and operating at a loss. Apparently, the warehouse had been established to provide tobacco farmers with an alternative to the Planters' Tobacco Warehouse, which was also located in St. Louis. Some concern was expressed in the majority report that without competition the Planters' Tobacco Warehouse would pay low prices for tobacco and charge exorbitant fees for inspection and storage. They recommended that the state continue to maintain its warehouse, regulate

25. *House Journal of the Thirteenth General Assembly,* 49 and 55. St. Louis *Missouri Republican,* 2 December 1844.

26. Ibid.

27. *House Journal of Thirteenth General Assembly,* 188, 475, and 488. St. Louis *Missouri Republican,* 26 March and 3 April 1845.

the inspection process, and fix the prices paid for tobacco and for the cost of storage.[28]

The minority report, with which Gamble was probably in agreement, sought to determine "the condition, prospects, cost, &c., of the Tobacco Warehouse" and whether to keep the warehouse or sell it. After considering operation costs, the expense of paying the 10 percent loan on the building, and the amount of fees collected during the first fourteen months of its operation, the minority concluded that the state warehouse should be sold to avoid incurring large losses. If the state wanted to maintain the warehouse, it would be cheaper to lease it out. They also expressed concern that the owners of the Planters' Tobacco Warehouse not be treated unfairly, and that nothing be done to destroy their business after they had ventured the capital to establish it.[29]

In the end, the House and Senate decided to maintain the state warehouse and regulate the inspection and storage of tobacco. The bill also provided for the establishment of county warehouses and the appointment of inspectors by county courts. These measures were adopted to break up what many considered to be a monopoly of the Planters' Tobacco Warehouse on the inspection, buying, and storing of tobacco in Missouri.[30]

After returning from St. Louis, Gamble missed a good part of the session (February 3–March 16, 1845), partly due to cases he had pending before the Missouri Supreme Court, but mostly because of a serious illness. Although the disease took the lives of several legislators, Gamble recovered and returned to his legislative duties. Apparently, his illness did nothing to diminish his willingness to participate in partisan controversy, for almost immediately after returning to his seat he took the lead in debating some of the session's most divisive issues.[31]

Perhaps the most important of these matters concerned whether the United States should annex Texas, which was then an independent repub-

28. *House Journal of the Thirteenth General Assembly*, 142–43, 504, and 242–54 of appendix. St. Louis *Missouri Republican*, 3 April 1845.

29. Ibid.

30. Ibid.

31. *House Journal of the Thirteenth General Assembly*, 267 and 462. St. Louis *Missouri Republican*, 10 February 1845.

lic and had requested admission into the Union. Most Whigs were against annexation, fearing that expansion would agitate the slavery issue, endanger the Union, and provoke war with Mexico. Democrats, on the other hand, were split into two factions, one supporting U.S. Senator Thomas H. Benton's stand against annexation, and the other desiring the admission of Texas into the Union as a slave state. Sharing the Whigs' fear that the slavery issue could tear the country apart, Benton vigorously opposed annexation and provoked the hostility of the leaders of the proannexation faction of his party. One of the advocates for annexation was Claiborne F. Jackson, who, along with other Democrats, declared himself opposed to Benton's reelection during the campaign of 1844. This split in his party caused Benton to consider soliciting support from Whig legislators, but eventually he was able to work out a deal with proannexation Democrats whereby they supported his reelection in return for concessions to proannexationists. These concessions included supporting Claiborne F. Jackson for the House speakership, backing a resolution instructing Missouri's congressmen to support annexation "at the earliest practicable moment" (replacing the proannexation faction's call for immediate annexation), and antiannexation support for congressional redistricting.[32]

In an effort to prevent the adoption of resolutions instructing Missouri's congressmen to vote for annexation, Gamble offered amendments recommending that Texas be split into a state no larger than the largest state. The rest of the region would become a territory, part of which would be set aside as a sector where slavery was prohibited. Moreover, he warned that annexing Texas would provoke a war with Mexico and saw the annexation scheme as an intrigue by some in the South to secede from the Union. In conclusion, he praised Benton's stand against annexation. In presenting these resolutions, Gamble was probably motivated by genuine concern that the slavery issue could tear the Union apart and that annexing Texas could lead to war with Mexico, and by a desire to exploit the split within Democratic ranks. These and other Whig amendments to the resolutions failed.[33]

Another wedge issue that Gamble and others used to split Democratic

32. *House Journal of the Thirteenth General Assembly*, 121–22, and Mering, *Whig Party in Missouri*, 121–23.

33. *House Journal of the Thirteenth General Assembly*, 108–10, 121–22, 136–41.

unity concerned pay for sundry state officials. Here the Whigs took a page from the Democrats' political strategy book by seeking to reduce the cost of government, a favorite campaign theme of Democrats. Twenty-five Democrats and every Whig in the House supported the bill, which fixed the governor's salary at $1,000, a supreme court judge's pay at $800, and the compensation of circuit court judges at $600. These wages were exceedingly low and caused a great deal of concern among those opposed to it, for the measure had enough support to pass. After obtaining an adjournment, Representative William Bay, a Democrat opposed to the measure, asked Gamble as he left the House "how he could conscientiously vote to give a governor $1,000 and a supreme judge $800. 'Why,' said he (laughing till his sides shook), 'there is not a judgeship in the state filled by a Whig, and if you Democrats want to reduce the pay of your own officers, how can you expect that we Whigs, who are stripped of all official patronage, shall oppose you?' And again he laughed heartily at our apparent distress." The next day, however, those in opposition to the bill attached an amendment greatly reducing the salaries of the president of the state university and its other officers. This attack on a favorite Whig institution produced the desired result, defeating the measure.[34]

Stung by Whig tactics exploiting their disunity, Democrats met in caucus and restored some measure of unity within their ranks. When the issue of compensation for state officers was considered again, salaries were set at rates that often provided a lucrative patronage for the Democratic faithful. Some of these officers, such as the court clerk and county sheriff, were paid additional fees for copying subpoenas and serving them, activities that were really part of their duties. Gamble and others were unsuccessful in seeking to limit how much these state officers could receive by directing the surplus to the treasury.[35]

In a similar attempt to limit the total compensation of a state officer, Gamble presented an amendment to a bill establishing the office of state printer. Formerly, during each legislative session printers submitted bids for the state printing contract. In caucus, the Democrats decided to use the printing patronage to maximize its political benefit by creating the of-

34. Bay, *Bench and Bar*, 292–93.
35. St. Louis *Missouri Republican*, 24 March 1845.

fice of state printer. The state printer, in return, was expected to publish a partisan newspaper advocating Democratic measures. While Gamble and others offered amendments to this bill without any expectation of their passing, they hoped to expose the added expense of establishing this new office. Gamble argued that it was wrong for a printer to profit from the sales of publications for which he had already received just compensation, and thought the profit from sales should go to the state. Moreover, he asserted that the bill was designed to provide a state-supported organ for the Democratic Party. Another Whig from St. Louis County, Willis L. Williams, protested that the printing would cost significantly more than under the bid system and "saw no reason why there should be a State Printer elected to do the printing, any more than there should be a State Builder, to build and repair all the State buildings, or a State Wood-chopper, to furnish all the wood which the State officers burned." Other amendments were presented but were all defeated. However, the Whigs achieved some success in demonstrating the partisan nature of the measure, when Democratic Representative J. C. Griffin attempted to stop any further amendments from being offered. When Griffin was "asked to withdraw his motion to let in the amendment," he remarked "that it was useless for the opponents of the bill to offer amendments, as they would be all voted down." Griffin was then asked how he could know that all amendments would be defeated. "Was there any agreement or understanding by which amendments, however right or proper, were to be voted down?" Griffin did not reply and Speaker of the House Jackson stated that he hoped the bill's opponents would be allowed to offer their amendments and that the bill's friends would defeat them. Perhaps the most galling of the amendments was presented by John D. Coalter, Gamble's brother-in-law, who sought to restrict eligibility for the office to "an experienced, practical mechanic, who had served his time at the business, and by whose hard labor the work was to be done." This was to prevent the "fat office" from being filled by "a lawyer or a trading politician." In conclusion, he stated that "he wished to see how many of those who professed to be so much in favor of supporting laborers and mechanics, would vote for confining this, one of the most lucrative offices in the State, to practical mechanics."[36]

36. Ibid.

Despite his participation in these very partisan fights, even most Democrats held Gamble in high esteem. According to Representative Bay, "he was on good terms with all, . . . had a good word to say to every one," and was known to enjoy a good laugh. This reputation was very different from that of an austere and cold nature that his political opponents later sought to fix on the public mind. During that winter, he attended exhibitions of mesmerisms, wherein the practitioner used magnets and other devices to induce a hypnotic state on volunteers. Even though he was not an adherent and did not believe the practitioner's claims, Gamble found these displays entertaining and amusing. No doubt, Gamble's popularity with his political opponents was partly due to the magnanimous manner in which he treated Speaker Jackson, arguably the most partisan House member of either party.[37]

Late in the legislative session, Jackson resigned his office after the House had voted to appoint seven members to a conference committee to negotiate the differences between the House and Senate versions of a bill to reapportion representation in the General Assembly. Because sparsely populated regions were organized into counties and were entitled to at least one representative, very small numbers of people from these new counties had as many representatives as did more densely populated counties. Furthermore, St. Louis and Howard counties, then Missouri's two most-populous counties, were underrepresented when compared to those of average size. Lieutenant Governor James Young appointed members to the Senate conference committee who were all strong proponents of the Senate bill. Representatives from the small counties in the House and many Democrats from other counties sought to prevent passage of the Senate bill because of the political advantage the system provided them. Knowing that Speaker Jackson (who represented Howard County) was in sympathy with the Senate bill, Representative Joseph H. Reynolds moved on the House floor to appoint members who would fight for the House bill. This was very unusual, for the Speaker normally appointed members to conference committees. In consequence, Jackson resigned as Speaker.[38]

After the initial shock of the Speaker's resignation, Representative

37. Bay, *Bench and Bar*, 291–93.
38. St. Louis *Missouri Republican*, 26 March 1845.

Richard F. Richmond called for the election of a new Speaker. Recognizing that Jackson had acted impetuously, and knowing that a Whig could not be elected, Gamble immediately nominated Jackson for reelection. This motion carried unanimously and Gamble with two other House members were appointed to a committee to inform the Speaker of his election. Jackson soon accepted the House's overture, explaining that he had resigned because he had thought Reynold's resolution had "manifested a want of confidence in me. . . . the members have shown, however, that they did not intend to censure me by their unanimous selection of me as Speaker."[39]

Gamble's service in Missouri's House of Representatives was distinguished by pragmatic action, creative presentation of ideas in debate, and careful representation of his constituents' interests, many of the same qualities that made him a fine lawyer. Although a confirmed Whig, he understood that an effective legislator did not always stand on principle, but must sometimes devise mutually beneficial compromises with the opposition to obtain a part, if not the whole, of one's goals. When he considered it expedient, Gamble was a capable partisan fighter who, from many years of practice in the courtroom, knew how to ferret out his opponents' weaknesses and exploit them. As a member of the minority party, however, he and his Whig colleagues were often reduced to presenting amendments to the Democrats' bills, either to strengthen an otherwise weak bill or to embarrass the majority party. By all accounts and by his decision not to seek reelection, it is evident that at the end of his term Gamble was uninterested in pursuing a political career. His temperament was much better suited for the legal profession, and besides, his devotion to his family and church required most of the spare time available to him.

39. Ibid. The issue of reapportionment was addressed in the state constitutional convention in which the delegates reapportioned county representation more democratically. However, the new constitution was narrowly rejected by the people.

Chapter Three

Judge Hamilton R. Gamble

fter his service in the state legislature, Hamilton R. Gamble restricted his political activities to attending meetings and occasionally drafting policy statements on behalf of the Whig Party. Given his strength in the contest for state representative, it is not surprising that Whig newspapers sometimes mentioned him as a possible candidate for different state and national offices. Despite his popularity, Gamble was content to return to his lucrative legal practice, which often involved important issues of law and property. Valuing his good reputation, he preferred to limit his activities in the community to the promotion of education and to providing leadership as an elder in his church. However, after members of the St. Louis bar urged him to run for the position of judge of the Missouri Supreme Court, Gamble reluctantly agreed to allow his name to be placed on the ballot. In doing so, he stipulated that he would only run as an independent, believing that candidates for judicial office should be elected on the basis of their legal qualifications rather than their political affiliations. Newspaper editorialists throughout the state praised Gamble's position, forcing the other candidates and their supporters to adopt the same policy. In subsequent elections, this focus on the legal education and abilities of candidates for judicial office made it difficult for anyone to run as a Whig or Democrat partisan.[1]

1. Liberty *Tribune*, 19 May 1848. Columbia *Missouri Statesman*, 7 April 1848. St. Louis *Missouri Republican*, 4 April 1850 and 18 April 1851. Request of St. Louis bar to present Gamble's name as a candidate for judge of the Missouri Supreme Court, 22 March 1851, Gamble

By the time of his election to the state legislature, Gamble was part of a small, elite group of lawyers in St. Louis entrusted with the region's most important cases. Over the years Gamble sometimes teamed with other lawyers, but his most enduring and significant professional relationship was with his brother-in-law Edward Bates, with whom he established the firm of Bates and Gamble. Such business arrangements with relatives were often established in the nineteenth century. The partners specialized in property and commercial law before the various St. Louis County courts, the Missouri Supreme Court, and the U.S. circuit courts, and the U.S. Supreme Court. Most of their clients sought Gamble's and Bates's representation in property suits, and a significant number of their clients were merchants, steamboat owners, and insurance companies. The promotion of commercial interests of this sort was both lucrative and congenial to Gamble's political-economic principles as a member of the Whig Party and of the successful professional class in St. Louis. However, from this one should not conclude that through his work as a lawyer Gamble primarily sought to promote the interests of capitalism and industrialization in Missouri, for he also represented the underdogs of society in cases against the powerful. Moreover, one must remember that often litigants, rather than lawyers, decided who would represent them. As Gamble's reputation as a lawyer grew so did the fees he could command for his representation, thereby limiting the number of potential clients who could afford his services. Those persons with limited means, then as today, often hired young lawyers—both Whigs and Democrats—who were willing to take cases for small fees. Furthermore, when Gamble's judicial decisions are scrutinized, no evidence of bias in favor of Missouri's social or economic elite is manifest.[2]

As in other parts of the West, many of the most important cases before Missouri's courts were disputes over legal title to land. As part of

papers. *In Memoriam: Hamilton Rowan Gamble, Governor of Missouri* (St. Louis: George Knapp, 1864), 10–12.

2. Accounts for the firm of Bates and Gamble, Gamble papers. Gail Williams O'Brien, *The Legal Fraternity and the Making of a New South Community, 1848–1882* (Athens: University of Georgia Press, 1986), 79–92. For the argument that lawyers and judges promoted capitalism and industrialization through the cases they argued and the decisions handed down see Morton J. Horwitz's book, *The Transformation of American Law, 1780–1860* (Chapel Hill: University of North Carolina Press, 1977).

the treaty to purchase the territory of Louisiana from France, the United States agreed to honor land titles granted to individuals by the French and Spanish governments. The governors and other authorities under whom the territory had been administered often had granted title to lands without defining the acreage and borders. Most persons, however, were living on land without a title. At the time, because no one dreamed that Louisiana was soon to become part of the United States, a title seemed unnecessary to the inhabitants of the very sparsely populated frontier regions. In fairness to those persons with land on which they had lived and improved, Congress passed legislation allowing them also to establish title. This was important for, encouraged by liberal land policies to establish homesteads in unoccupied land, large numbers of Americans soon began immigrating to Louisiana. These circumstances led to competing claims to some of the best land in the region.[3]

Suits to establish title to land were not easily resolved, especially after Congress passed a series of laws that were often unclear and contradictory. By the time Missouri had become a state, the courts were confronted with complicated issues of U.S., Spanish, and French law, and even more complicated questions of fact that could only be resolved after scrutinizing many documents, wills, and witness testimonies. The legal questions of these suits were many and varied. For instance, who of the Spanish and French crown's representatives had authority to convey title to land? What were the obligations of the United States under the Louisiana treaty agreement? What were women's property rights under French, Spanish, and American law? What right did one have to restrict the use of property bequeathed to heirs? Especially difficult was the interpretation of congressional acts. Some of Gamble's land cases were eventually argued before the U.S. Supreme Court and provided important precedents on which later law would be based.[4] In the other important staple of their legal practice,

---

3. William Francis English, "The Pioneer Lawyer and Jurist in Missouri" (Ph.D. diss., University of Missouri, 1941), 54–90. William Foley, *A History of Missouri*, vol. 1, *1673 to 1820*, ed. William Parrish (Columbia: University of Missouri Press, 1971), 171–73. Paul Wallace Gates, "Private Land Claims in the South," *Journal of Southern History* 22 (May 1956): 185.

4. 4 Mo. Rep. 380, *Lindell v. McNair*; 5 Mo. Rep. 380, *McNair v. Hunt*; 6 Mo. Rep. 510, *Bird v. Montgomery*; 7 Mo. Rep. 16, *MacKay v. Dillon* and *Chouteau v. Eckert*; 8 Mo. Rep. 446, *Hammond v. St. Louis Public Schools*; 9 Mo. Rep. 446, *Clamorgan et al. v. Lane*; and 49 U.S. Rep. 317–66 and 569–86, *Bissell v. Penrose*, *Mills v. Stoddard et al.*, and *Mills et al. v. St. Clair County et al.*;

Gamble and Bates tried suits touching commercial law. In these suits, the partners often litigated issues of contract law, debt collection, partnership agreements, bills of exchange, transfers of stock, insurance policies, and the transport of goods.[5]

Having decided to go into semiretirement at the age of fifty-two, Gamble ended his partnership with Bates to have more time to direct his children's educations and to restore his health, which had been unsound for some time. Moreover, this decision enabled him to concentrate his professional efforts on important cases. During his career several of his cases had been heard before the U.S. Supreme Court, but Gamble did not personally practice before the country's highest tribunal until 1850. Because the journey to Washington was very arduous and time-consuming, the custom of western lawyers was to employ congressmen from their state or prominent lawyers in the East to represent their clients' interests.[6]

By 1850, however, water and land travel had improved substantially, enabling Gamble to journey to Washington, D.C., and argue two important cases. *Bissell v. Penrose* and *Mills v. Stoddard et al.* were similar in many respects, involving valuable land and many of the same legal issues that turned on the interpretation of French and Spanish law, twenty-three acts of Congress, and the proper application of legal precedent. According to a St. Louis newspaper account, the land in dispute between Lewis Bissell and Mary Penrose was worth half a million dollars. Gamble's client Bissell, having lived there for twenty-six years, had improved the land and increased its value. Both Bissell's and Adam Mills's titles descended from New Madrid certificates issued by Congress to replace land ruined by a se-

---

51 U.S. Rep. 348–76, *Landes v. Brant;* and 56 U.S. Rep. 358–66, *Forsyth v. Reynolds.* See below for Gamble's practice before the U.S. Supreme Court.

5. 4 Mo. Rep. 338 and 601, *Graham and others v. O'Fallon, executor of Mullanphy;* 6 Mo. Rep. 317, *Drake v. Rogers and Shrewsbury;* 7 Mo. Rep. 228, *Potter v. Dillon;* 8 Mo. Rep. 704, *Walker v. Bank of Missouri;* 9 Mo. Rep. 149 and 411, *St. Louis Perpetual Insurance Company v. Goodfellow* and *Citizens Insurance Company of Missouri v. Glasgow, Shaw, and Larkin;* and 10 Mo. Rep. 6, *Walsh v. Homer.*

6. Edward Bates diary, 10 March 1851, Bates papers. Certificate granting right to practice before the U.S. Supreme Court, 13 February 1849, Gamble papers. Gamble employed Missouri's U.S. Senator Thomas H. Benton in *Farrar and Brown v. the United States,* 30 U.S. Rep. 373–89. Attorney General of the United States Benjamin F. Butler in *Chouteau v. Marguerite, a woman of colour,* 30 U.S. Rep. 507–10.

ries of earthquakes in 1812 near the town of New Madrid in southeastern Missouri. The Penrose and Stoddard claims traced their titles to Spanish land grants. The Court ruled that the Penrose and Stoddard claims were valid, although Justice McLean wrote in dissent that the Court had applied the wrong precedents in the case and had overlooked the lower court's mistakes in its evidentiary rulings.[7]

The Court's decisions in these cases were criticized and debated in the St. Louis newspapers, in large part because the decisions dispossessed Bissell and Mills from land they had purchased many years before. The St. Louis *Missouri Republican* argued that they were the victims of ill-advised and haphazard legislation by Congress. Having no other remedy available, the *Republican* urged them to appeal to Congress for compensation of their losses. A Washington correspondent with close ties to Judge McLean wrote to Gamble that "the Court is really ignorant, prejudiced, and, which is perhaps best described as 'notional.' A *notion* strikes them, or some one of them, and it is allowed to prevail: there is but little *professional* pride now existing upon the bench; hence the most crude fancies of any one of them are often permitted to assume the form of a 'decision' of the Court, unread and uncared for by the balance." What is unclear is whether Gamble agreed with this criticism of the Court. However, it is evident that the complicated issues of fact and law in these cases made their determination very difficult, for everything turned on judgments about the interpretation of a great amount of evidence and congressional legislation.[8] The frustration of many lawyers and landowners was well summarized by Bates, Gamble's former law partner, who confided to his diary that "the unsettled & precarious state of our land titles is a very serious evil. Hardly any man feels safe; and no lawyer can rely confidently upon his own judgment. However clear his own judgment, he cannot feel at all certain that any particular principle will be established, or if established, that it will, for any reasonable time, be adhered to."[9]

7. 49 U.S. Rep. 317–66. St. Louis *Missouri Republican*, 24 and 28 January 1850. James Lal Penick Jr., *The New Madrid Earthquakes*, rev. ed. (Columbia: University of Missouri Press, 1981), viii and 15–51.

8. St. Louis *Missouri Republican*, 3 and 18 February 1850. 49 U.S. Rep. 341–45. Abel Rathbone Corbin to Gamble, 6 February 1850, Gamble papers.

9. Bates diary, 24 January 1850, Bates papers.

In his final case before the Court during the January 1850 term, Gamble represented Adam Mills and others in a suit against St. Clair County, Illinois, and James Harrison. At issue was whether the Illinois legislature had the right to rescind the terms of a contract originally made with Samuel Wiggins to operate a ferry on the Mississippi River between Illinois and St. Louis. Later, the Illinois legislature gave Harrison the right to operate a ferry on a portion of Wiggins's land that St. Clair County had condemned. Gamble argued that this action was a violation of Wiggins's contract and that the compensation paid for the condemned land was almost fraudulently low. Daniel Webster submitted a printed brief supporting Gamble's side in the case. In his decision, Justice Catron agreed that Gamble's client had been the victim of "an invasion and illegal seizure of private property on pretence of exercising the right of eminent domain," but declined to remedy this violation because he believed that the Court had no jurisdiction in the case.[10]

Having lost his first three cases before the U.S. Supreme Court, Gamble must have been disappointed. Perhaps he gained some satisfaction in having, under difficult circumstances, represented his clients' interests well.

CANDIDATE FOR JUDGE

In the spring of 1851, 150 members of the St. Louis bar—only nine refused—signed a letter requesting Gamble to run as a candidate for judge of the Missouri Supreme Court. While conceding that Gamble would lose money by accepting the position, the bar believed that the public interest justified such a sacrifice. Years later Gamble verified this loss, stating in a letter to a friend that he had sometimes made more money in legal fees from one case in private practice than he had received in annual salary as a judge.[11]

In his reply to the St. Louis bar's request, Gamble warned that he would not campaign for the judgeship, but, if elected, would accept it as "a duty to the public. . . . [and was] willing to make any reasonable sacrifice which the people may call me to make, in discharging the duties of a public

10. *Mills et al. v. St. Clair County et al.*, 49 U.S. Rep. 569–86.

11. St. Louis *Missouri Republican*, 18 April 1851. Gamble to Charles S. Rannels, 17 February 1857, Gamble papers.

station." Gamble's refusal to campaign reflected both his dislike of campaigning for public office and his strongly held belief that those elected to the judiciary should be chosen on the basis of their legal knowledge and jurisprudence rather than their political affiliation. While a conscientious concern to fulfill his public responsibilities was undoubtedly the main reason he agreed to serve, perhaps Gamble was reluctant to disappoint so many of his friends and colleagues by refusing the office. Moreover, now in his early fifties, he may have wished to make a more lasting contribution to his profession.[12]

Because Missouri's constitution had been amended only recently, and supreme court justices had formerly been appointed by the governor, the August 1851 election was the first in which the voters would decide who sat in the state's highest judicial office. The election returns from many counties came in slowly, but by mid-August Gamble had received over 23,000 votes, exceeding his closest competitor's backing by over 7,000 votes. This was an overwhelming display of support for a Whig candidate in a predominately Democratic state. In recognition of Gamble's popularity with the people and the bench and bar, his newly elected colleagues selected him to serve as the court's chief justice.[13]

Gamble and his fellow judges, John F. Ryland and William Scott, took their seats on the Missouri Supreme Court during the October 1851 term. Although the justices disagreed in politics, it is apparent that they were careful not to allow their differences to affect their relations with one another. This was important, for over the next three years the justices spent very long days together hearing and deciding cases. They decided 728 cases in all, averaging more than four decisions per week. Ryland, who was affiliated with the Benton wing of the Democratic Party, was courtly and dignified in his manners, epitomizing the Southern gentleman. Classically educated and an Old School Presbyterian, he shared with Gamble many values and interests. Moreover, both men knew each other well,

12. Ibid. That Gamble's view concerning the nonpartisan nature of judicial elections prevailed is demonstrated best by his own landslide election in a state where Democrats significantly outnumbered Whigs. For another interpretation of this first election of justices to the Missouri Supreme Court see Kenneth C. Kaufman, *Dred Scott's Advocate: A Biography of Roswell M. Field* (Columbia: University of Missouri Press, 1996), 175.

13. *Missouri Republican*, 19 August 1851.

having begun the practice of law together on the Missouri frontier some thirty years before.[14]

Scott, an anti-Benton Democrat and zealous proslavery advocate, had served previously on the supreme court (1841–49). According to a Democrat and lawyer who had tried cases before him for many years, Scott occasionally interpreted the law so that he could rule in a manner that, in his opinion, "best tended to subserve the ends of justice." While this tendency was inconsistently indulged, it was sure to bring him into disagreement with Gamble, who adhered strictly to precedent in almost every case he heard, even when in his opinion the decision was contrary to true justice in a case. However, it should be noted that almost all of the Gamble court's decisions were unanimous and fewer still elicited dissenting opinions.[15]

CONSERVATIVE JURIST

On the Missouri Supreme Court, Gamble and his associates reviewed lower court decisions, mediated disputes between rival office seekers, and determined the constitutionality of legislation and the actions of officeholders. In the review of lower court decisions, the court ensured the proper administration of the law and regulated the behavior of lower court judges, prosecutors, and lawyers. Moreover, the Gamble court conformed its decisions to the common law (the corpus of English and American precedent) and Missouri's statute law.

In performing his duties as chief justice of the Missouri Supreme Court, Gamble relied heavily on his experience as a lawyer and his knowledge of the law and its practice in Missouri. From his written opinions, it is clear that his goal was to administer the law in strict accord with the

14. W. V. N. Bay, *Reminiscences of the Bench and Bar of Missouri* (St. Louis: F. H. Thomas, 1878), 271–76. Wilbert Henry Rosin, "Hamilton Rowan Gamble: Missouri's Civil War Governor" (Ph.D. diss., University of Missouri, 1960), 96–97.

15. Bay, *Bench and Bar*, 324–30; 7 Mo. Rep. 2 and 9 Mo. Rep. 2. Contrast Gamble's decision in *Kissell v. St. Louis Public Schools*, 16 Mo. Rep. 553–96 to Scott's in *Eberle v. St. Louis Public Schools*, 11 Mo. Rep. 257; State at the relation of *Tredway v. Lusk*, 18 Mo. Rep. 333–57; and *Chauvin v. Wagner*, 18 Mo. Rep. 531–57. If my count is correct, only twelve dissents were presented by any of the justices during the three years of Gamble's tenure on the court.

U.S. Constitution and the Missouri constitution, and in conformity to legal precedent and statute. In this he was very successful, demonstrating a principled approach to judicial decision making. For the state's first Whig supreme court justice it must have been difficult to resist the temptation of occasionally issuing a partisan ruling, for the legislature and the courts had been under Democratic control since 1828. However, it is apparent from his opinions that he did not indulge his own political preferences and sense of justice. Only rarely did he overturn a decision, believing it better to let an improper ruling stand once it had become a settled matter of law.[16]

> It is only when we are satisfied that an error has been committed in the decisions of our predecessors, which may be corrected before it has become a rule of property, that we feel willing to interfere with previous adjudications. In our state, where the tenure of the judicial office is but for a short period, it is of the utmost importance that great delicacy should be observed in overruling or shaking the authority of previous decisions. If in the change to which the court must be subject, the spirit of innovation and disregard of precedents shall find place, the administration of the law will become too uncertain, and too dangerous to the rights of the people to be endured. While we entertain this opinion, we feel that in a case like the present, we will unsettle no title, and do no injury by overruling [the former decision of this court].[17]

While certainty of the law was important, Gamble also recognized the necessity of taking into account the evolving nature of the law in his decisions. This evolution in American jurisprudence had come about primarily through the necessity of adjusting the law to changing circumstances and new legislation. As noted above, the most troublesome to the court were property and land suits that required an investigation not only of

16. *Hamilton and Treat v. St. Louis County Court*, 15 Mo. Rep. 3–28; and *Kissell v. St. Louis Public Schools*, 16 Mo. Rep. 553–96.

17. *Huff v. Knapp*, 17 Mo. Rep. 420. In this Gamble agreed with the prevailing attitude of most jurists of his time. See Carl F. Stychin, "The Commentaries of Chancellor James Kent and the Development of an American Common Law," *American Journal of Legal History* 37 (October 1993): 448.

American common law, but also an understanding of French and Spanish law. These cases became Gamble's specialty on the court.[18]

While courts in other states may have been more directly involved in promoting change, the Gamble court largely reacted to change as circumstances dictated. Moreover, it did not actively legislate from the bench to promote economic prosperity or to serve ulterior political motives. The court was not innovative, but instead was conservative and pragmatic in its jurisprudence and learned in its application of precedent, preferring to react to change rather than to cause it. In these respects, the court reflected perfectly the personality and predilections of Gamble.[19]

Of all the cases that Gamble ruled on as chief justice of the Missouri Supreme Court, the most important type involved the interpretation of Missouri's constitution and of state and federal legislation. These cases were important because the court's decisions often determined the ownership of very valuable property, the proper occupant of a political office, and the limits of judicial and legislative authority. Moreover, the cases had far-reaching implications in establishing precedent for later rulings on such important matters. Because the interpretation of the constitution and legislation was sometimes more an art than a science, Gamble believed that he must exercise great care and strictly apply the law without

18. *Schulenburg and Company v. Charles Gibson*, 15 Mo. Rep. 281–88; *Holmes v. Hill*, 19 Mo. Rep. 159–70; *Harrison v. Page*, 16 Mo. Rep. 182–210; *Kissell v. St. Louis Public Schools*, 16 Mo. Rep. 553–96; *Gamache et al. v. Piquignot et al.*, 17 Mo. Rep. 310–25; *Charleville v. Chouteau*, 18 Mo. Rep. 492–509; and *Moreau v. Detchemendy*, 18 Mo. Rep. 522–31. For an account of similar difficulties encountered in Tennessee see Timothy S. Huebner, *The Southern Judicial Tradition: State Judges and Sectional Distinctiveness, 1790–1890* (Athens: University of Georgia Press, 1999), 50–55.

19. Much scholarship has been devoted to understanding nineteenth-century jurisprudence, and especially in accounting for the great amount of change to the law then occurring. In Horwitz's book, *The Transformation of American Law, 1780–1860*, it is argued that many judges legislated from the bench to promote economic development. For a different point of view see Peter Karsten, *Heart versus Head: Judge-Made Law in Nineteenth-Century America* (Chapel Hill: University of North Carolina Press, 1997). For an account of the jurisprudence of Missouri's nineteenth-century judges see Thomas C. Clark, "The Impact of Nineteenth Century Missouri Courts upon Emerging Industry: Chambers of Commerce or Chambers of Justice?" *Missouri Law Review* 63 (1998): 51–114. Gamble's jurisprudence accords best with Karsten's and Clark's analysis, which rejects the idea that judges, as part of a socioeconomic elite, promoted a market economy in their decisions.

regard to consequences. To do otherwise, he feared, would undermine the public's faith in the court and the administration of law, even if the ruling favored a legal verdict over true justice in the case.[20]

An important case demonstrating Gamble's commitment to the judicial principle of strict application of the law was *Hamilton and Treat v. the St. Louis County Court.* Two judges of St. Louis County brought suit to gain payment of expense accounts they had presented to the court. The dispute arose out of legislation passed in 1851 doubling the amount the judges could claim for expenses and requiring St. Louis County to pay them. Over the previous decade, the population of St. Louis had grown rapidly. With this growth came a proportionate increase of cases in the county courts and of expenditures required of its judges.[21]

The lawyers representing the county court, Edward Bates and Thomas Gantt, raised several objections to the legislation. The most important of these was that the legislature had acted illegally, for the state constitution did not expressly give the General Assembly the right to tax a county in such a manner. They also asserted that the additional economic burden was unjust, for it unfairly required the county to pay its own cost of administering justice when all other counties' expenses were paid out of state taxes. Therefore, the residents of St. Louis County would pay for the administration of justice in their own county and aid in the payment of the rest. Without its own government, this burden was exacerbated by the legislature's failure to allow the county to raise an additional tax to meet the expenditure. Moreover, Bates and Gantt argued that the language of the statute could be interpreted to allow the St. Louis county court some discretion in deciding which of the judges' expenditures it would pay.[22]

In his decision, Gamble addressed the different objections presented in argument and explained his conclusions fully, some of which were *obiter dicta*, that is, extralegal and usually nonbinding expressions of opinion. These *dicta* provided guidance to the county court in conforming to his decision. While he agreed that "the act is awkwardly phrased," Gamble also believed that "the intention of the legislature is sufficiently plain, and

20. *Chauvin v. Wagner,* 18 Mo. Rep. 531–57; and *Thomas v. Meier,* 18 Mo. Rep. 573–79.
21. *Hamilton and Treat v. St. Louis County Court,* 15 Mo. Rep. 3–28.
22. Ibid.

that that intention does not vest the county court with the discretion they claim."[23]

While he agreed that the law unfairly burdened St. Louis County, Gamble believed that there was no constitutional reason to repudiate the statute. He noted that he could name numerous types of injustices operating under the current system for which there were no remedies, such as the governor appointing an "unworthy man" to fill an important office, or unwise or unjust legislation.[24] "It may therefore be stated, as a principle, in construing the constitution, that the mere fact, that a law is unjust in its operation, or even in the principles upon which it was adopted, does not authorize any expansion of the prohibitions in the constitution, beyond their natural and original meaning, in order to remedy the evil in the particular case."[25]

Finding nothing repugnant to the state constitution in the statute, Gamble believed he had no choice, in spite of its unfairness, but to enforce it. In conclusion, he stated that "we are not at liberty to give our judgment of expediency, or even of justice, a controlling power over acts of the General Assembly. Our duty, then, alone remains for us to perform, and that is to enforce the law."[26]

Gamble's principled stand on the limits of judicial authority and power, however, did not satisfy everyone. Then, as now, lawyers often bemoaned the idiocy of the judiciary. His former law partner and losing attorney in the case, Edward Bates, criticized the ruling in his diary, stating that it allowed the legislature to pass any legislation not prohibited by the state constitution, calling it "a monstrous blunder."[27]

In *Mason v. Woerner*, another case involving the St. Louis County courts, the Missouri Supreme Court was asked to decide whether or not the circuit court and court of common pleas could continue to hear land suits after the legislature had passed a statute establishing a new land court. The legislation gave the new court jurisdiction over all land cases in St. Louis County, but the statute did not indicate, as was normal in

23. Ibid.
24. Ibid.
25. Ibid., 23–24.
26. Ibid., 28.
27. Bates diary, 6 December 1851, Bates papers.

such legislation, when jurisdiction over land suits would transfer to the new court.[28]

As a consequence of this omission, lawyers, whose clients would benefit from a delay, brought suit to prevent the hearing of their land cases in the old courts. Gamble in considering the case agreed that the natural understanding of the statute's language would lead one to conclude that the legislature intended immediately to end the old courts' jurisdiction over land cases. However, he noted factors that tended to oppose this interpretation. First, the state constitution provided that the people should have free access to the courts without delay, and the statute, if taken literally, would violate that provision. Moreover, a literal interpretation of the statute would create a great deal of mischief in preventing cases from being heard. To give the statute this interpretation seemed absurd to Gamble, when the purpose in passing the law was to expedite the hearing of land cases in a county where the courts were overwhelmed by pending litigation. Taking these factors into account, he concluded that the legislature had used imprecise language in the statute.[29]

Perhaps the most controversial cases that Gamble was called to rule on were disputes over political office. In *Missouri at the relation of Richardson v. Ewing*, the court was requested to settle a dispute between Ephraim B. Ewing and John M. Richardson, both of whom claimed the office of secretary of state. In 1851 the legislature had amended the constitution, making the post elective. After his election, Richardson demanded the state seal and other property of the office, but Ewing refused to comply, insisting that his term had not expired and that no one could supersede him until then.[30]

The issue in the case concerned the language of the amendment, which, once again, was not explicit in stating whether it was intended that the appointee Ewing must give way before the end of his term to Richardson. Under these circumstances, Gamble believed that he must exercise his best judgment, and that his decision should be guided by the language of the amendment in light of the legislature's intent. Following this course,

28. *Mason v. Woerner*, 18 Mo. Rep. 566–73.
29. Ibid., 572.
30. *Missouri at the relation of John M. Richardson v. Ephraim B. Ewing*, 17 Mo. Rep. 515–20.

Gamble ruled that the legislature had intended for the incumbent Ewing to remain in office until a successor was elected. Upon his election, the successor was to begin his tenure as secretary of state. Gamble believed this decision to be best, for it "prevents any interregnum, preserves the government from the confusion that would otherwise be introduced into its affairs, and gives effect to the intention of the people and the general assembly."[31]

In *State at the relation of Tredway v. Lusk*, the court was asked to determine who was entitled to fill the office of state printer. Established by the General Assembly in 1845 when Gamble was serving in the state House of Representatives, the office of state printer provided a lucrative patronage and helped support a partisan Democratic newspaper. Gamble and his Whig colleagues, recognizing the partisan purpose of the measure, had sought to prevent its passage, but the majority had pushed the measure through over their objections.[32]

The ordinance provided for an election in the General Assembly and for the state printer to hold office "for two years, *and until his successor shall be duly elected and qualified.*" The controversy had arisen when after two years, the incumbent James Lusk had refused to give way to Tredway, who had been appointed by the governor after the General Assembly had failed to elect a successor. The state contended that after two years Lusk's term ended and the office became vacant. Therefore, it was the governor's right to appoint a new printer. Counsel for the state also argued that Lusk could not continue to serve, for he would then be serving without bond, it having expired after two years.[33]

Lusk's counsel, Abiel Leonard, a prominent Whig lawyer, argued that the statute's language was precise and clearly provided for the state printer to serve a minimum of two years, but that he could continue on indefinitely so long as no successor was elected to replace him. Leonard further

---

31. Ibid., 520. This decision stands in contrast to that of Thomas Ruffin, justice of the North Carolina Supreme Court, in *Hoke v. Henderson.* Ruffin ruled that Henderson, who had been appointed to office, could not be superseded by an election, for the office was his property until the end of the term. See Huebner, *Southern Judicial Tradition,* 135–38.

32. See chapter 2 for Gamble's service in the legislature. St. Louis *Missouri Republican,* 24 March 1845; and *State at the relation of Tredway v. Lusk,* 18 Mo. Rep. 333–57.

33. *State at the relation of Tredway v. Lusk,* 18 Mo. Rep.

argued that Lusk had bonded for his term of office, not for two years, and even if it turned out that his bond was only good for that period, this merely proved "that our legislature has blundered, in providing that the incumbent might, in certain contingencies, continue in office for a longer period than his securities are bound." Obviously, Leonard relished making the Democrats feel some discomfiture over the unintended consequences of a partisan bill they had muscled through the legislature against the protests of Whigs a few years before.[34]

In his decision, Gamble ruled that the only question to decide was whether or not the office of state printer became vacant when the General Assembly failed to elect a replacement. Unconvinced by the argument of the state's counsel, Gamble ruled that the office did not become automatically vacant upon the expiration of two years. The statute's language provided no time limit to the term of office; indeed, two years was the minimum, rather than the maximum, time that the state printer could serve, barring death or resignation.[35]

Judge Scott, in a transparently partisan effort, wrote a lengthy dissent in an often convoluted defense of the Democratic administration's position. In it, he asserted that the constitution provided for the governor to make appointments to vacant offices, and that the legislature had acted unconstitutionally if it had intended to make the term of office continue until a successor was elected. This provision in the statute would be unconstitutional, he argued, for it "cannot restrain the constitutional power vested in the governor." The only difficulty with Scott's reasoning was that the office had never become vacant, for Lusk remained in office and, according to the statute, could remain there until the General Assembly elected a successor. Other elective offices followed the same procedure and Scott never explained why the office of state printer was different.[36]

Because the legislature would not pass an unconstitutional statute, Scott reasoned that legislators had not intended for the state printer to remain in office, despite the fact that no language in the statute supported his assertion. This intention, he lamely admitted, was not expressed in the statute, and blamed this omission on "the imperfection of language."

34. Ibid.
35. Ibid.
36. Ibid., 342–57.

Moreover, in the interpretation of statutes, Scott argued that if the intent of the lawmakers could be ascertained, it should be operative even when it is contrary to the language of the statute. Moreover, he thought that if this rule was not followed in this case, the state would be harmed, for Lusk would continue to serve without a bond guaranteeing his faithful service. However, recognizing the dangerous ground of his position, Scott added that "it will not be contended, that the legislature cannot give words a signification variant from their literal import."[37]

Another case relating to Gamble's service in the legislature was a divorce case, *Bryson v. Bryson*. While a member of the legislature serving on the judiciary committee, Gamble had worked with others to reform the administration of justice. One of the bills reported out of the committee declared legislative divorces unconstitutional. However, this bill did not pass and the legislature continued to grant divorces through petitions presented by members of the General Assembly on behalf of constituents.[38]

In the case of *Bryson v. Bryson*, the legislature had granted a divorce to the husband, but the wife had contested it in court. The case was then appealed to the supreme court. The main issue was the constitutionality of a legislative divorce. Despite previous supreme court decisions declaring legislative divorces unconstitutional, the General Assembly continued to grant them.[39]

In his opinion, Gamble noted that although legislative divorces had been declared unconstitutional, "the question is again presented, no doubt, with the hope that, in a change in the judges, there may be a change in the views of the court." He believed the issue to be important, for it involved the question of the proper separation of powers between the legislature and the judiciary. "It is perfectly obvious, that if sentences may be pronounced by the legislature, between two individuals, by which their rights and relations may be conclusively determined, all the powers designed to be exercised by courts of justice may be drawn to the general assembly,

37. Ibid., 346.
38. *Journal of the House of Representatives of the State of Missouri of the First Session of the Thirteenth General Assembly, Begun and Held at the City of Jefferson, On Monday, the Eighteenth Day of November, in the Year of our Lord One Thousand Eight Hundred and Forty-Four* (Jefferson City: James Lusk, printer to the state, 1845), 111 and 212–14 of appendix.
39. *Bryson v. Bryson*, 17 Mo. Rep. 590–95.

and the whole judicial power of the state may be absorbed by that body."[40] Moreover, Gamble argued that legislative divorces presented a fundamental problem to those obtaining them in that the legislature did not have the power to dissolve the financial obligations the husband and wife owed to one another. Because of this, the husband still retained control over his wife's property and was responsible for any debts incurred by her.[41]

Another case with important political ramifications was *Missouri at the relation of Douglas v. Scott.* The dispute centered on legislation establishing Vernon County. Its territory was taken from Bates County. Douglas, the sheriff of Bates County, had brought suit against Scott for operating as sheriff in the new county. Douglas's attorney claimed that the legislation creating Vernon County was unconstitutional, for it dropped the population of Bates County below the constitutional minimum necessary for a county to be recognized as a legal entity, and the county thereby would lose its representation in the General Assembly.[42]

In his opinion, Gamble noted that all counties were interested in this question, for otherwise a county might gain "full representation" in the legislature even though it had only "a fraction of representative population." For many years, much controversy had surrounded this question of representation in the General Assembly. In 1844, an unsuccessful effort had been made to amend the constitutional provision limiting the number of representatives in the General Assembly to 100. Moreover, this provision directed that all counties should have at least one representative each. The result of these directives was that smaller counties had more representatives per person than did larger counties. Small counties, comprising only one-third of the population, held a majority of representatives in the General Assembly. St. Louis County, by far the largest in the state, felt the inequity of the system most, only having seven representatives in 1844, when it should have had twenty-one, if representation had been based strictly on population. With only 7 percent representation in the legislature, St. Louis County paid one-third of the state's taxes.[43]

40. Ibid., 591.
41. Ibid., 592.
42. *Missouri at the relation of Douglas v. Scott,* 17 Mo. Rep. 521–29.
43. Ibid., 526. St. Louis *Mill Boy,* 10 February and 9 March 1844.

While it is unknown whether these factors influenced Gamble's decision, the illegality of the legislation was evident, for the ordinance dropped the population of Bates County below the constitutional limit. Therefore, he ruled in Douglas's favor. Later, however, the law went into effect once the population of Bates County had increased to allow its division without dropping below the constitutional minimum population.[44]

During Gamble's term, several cases were presented before the court stemming from controversies concerning the interpretation of the new legal code passed by the legislature in 1849. In reforming Missouri's legal code, the General Assembly simplified the practice of law to ensure that legal technicalities would not obstruct the administration of justice. In this effort the legislature was largely unsuccessful, for by removing most of the pleadings—the written statements used to determine the legal point in dispute—"the court and jury [were left] to grovel in the dark with respect to the matter they were to try." Later, the legislature amended this simplified code of civil procedure until it adopted a "New Code of Civil Procedure" in 1943.[45]

In one of the legal code cases, *Fine v. Rogers*, because the legislature had apparently omitted to enumerate many of the circumstances for which appeals should be granted, Gamble found it necessary to supply the deficiency in the code. In ruling thus, he was forced to legislate from the bench to ensure that all litigants had full access to the judicial process. In justifying this action he explained that it was in keeping with the spirit of

44. *Missouri at the relation of Douglas v. Scott,* 17 Mo. Rep. 521–29.

45. Daniel J. Boorstin, *The Mysterious Science of the Law: An Essay on Blackstone's* Commentaries *Showing How Blackstone, Employing Eighteenth-Century Ideas of Science, Religion, History, Aesthetics, and Philosophy, Made of the Law at once a Conservative and a Mysterious Science* (Chicago: University of Chicago Press, 1941; reprint, 1996), 242. Bay, *Bench and Bar,* 261–62. Bates diary, 18 February 1849, Bates papers. The code sought to regulate cases concerned with the conveyance of property, proper pleading in court, the powers and jurisdictions of different courts, rules of evidence, taking depositions, statutes of limitation, and writs of *mandamus.* See *Brant v. Robertson,* 16 Mo. Rep. 129–49; *See and Brother v. Cox,* 16 Mo. Rep. 166–68; *Hunt v. Hernandez,* 16 Mo. Rep. 170–72; *Winston v. Wales,* 17 Mo. Rep. 370–73; *Miller v. McKenna,* 18 Mo. Rep. 253–54; *Smith and Kinzer v. Dean,* 19 Mo. Rep. 63–65; and *Smith v. St. Francois County Court,* 19 Mo. Rep. 433. Lawrence M. Friedman, *A History of American Law* (New York: Simon and Schuster, 1973), 340–43.

the statutes in which the legislature sought to simplify the practice of law and to provide greater access to the courts.[46]

In another case in which the new legal code was at issue, *Butcher v. Death and Teasdale*, the Gamble court was forced to decide very basic questions about the proper conduct of trials. In his decision, Gamble ruled that the defendant must deny every allegation or otherwise it must be considered true. He also held that the judge in instructing the jury must indicate which facts were to be tried and which had been denied. Moreover, under the new law code, one could amend pleadings "even at the trial, in order to conform the petition to the proof, and avoid a non suit on account of a variance." In ruling this way, Gamble demonstrated his commitment to upholding the new legal codes in which the legislature intended to simplify the practice of the law. One of the most important ramifications of the reformed code was that persons represented by less experienced lawyers would not lose their cases because of some technical error. Certainly, if he had wished to retain the advantage for himself and other experienced lawyers under the common law pleading system, Gamble could have undermined the simplified code, especially where the legislation was silent about courtroom procedures. These same advantages more often than not accrued to the benefit of clients wealthy enough to afford higher-priced representation. For this reason, simplification of the legal code increased the probability that the facts of a case, rather than the technicalities of the law, would determine the outcome of a suit and thereby transformed the judicial system into a more egalitarian institution.[47]

46. *Fine v. Rogers*, 15 Mo. Rep., 315–22. Certainly, Missouri's attempt to simplify its law code bore out Chancellor James Kent's prediction that the common law's technicalities and complexities were not easily reducible into clear principles. He also predicted that ambiguous and unclear language would present difficulties to those practicing and interpreting the law. Kent believed it was better to change the law incrementally. See Carl F. Stychin, "The Commentaries of Chancellor James Kent and the Development of the American Common Law," *American Journal of Legal History* 37 (October 1993): 461–62.

47. *Butcher v. Death and Teasdale*, 15 Mo. Rep. 271–75. Evidently while still on the court, Gamble suggested revisions of the legal code to James O. Broadhead, who, as a member of Missouri's General Assembly, was then attempting to amend it. See Samuel T. Glover to James O. Broadhead, 3 January 1853, James O. Broadhead papers, Missouri Historical Society, St. Louis, Missouri.

Business and Property Law

The Gamble court's treatment of contract law was very much in accord with common law tradition, strictly interpreting and enforcing the terms of the contract so long as all the parties understood to what they were agreeing without the presence of fraud or deceit. While legal protections for the consumer and the regulation of business were not as well developed then as today, Missouri law was typical of its time. In his decisions, Gamble followed this precedent, which made it the legal responsibility of individuals, not the courts, to protect themselves from making bad business deals. Moreover, the law expected parties to an agreement to be prudent in their planning and to make provision for different contingencies that might render the deal bad or make it impossible for them to meet their obligations.[48]

In *Denny v. Kile et al.*, Denny, the owner of a drying house, had contracted with the defendants to cultivate and deliver broom corn. The suit alleged that the broom corn had not been delivered according to the terms of the contract, for which Denny sought damages. In the agreement, Denny had promised to provide equipment for the defendants. However, Gamble ruled that this equipment was inadequate for the task, and that Denny, who was very familiar with the business, had deliberately provided faulty machinery to make it impossible for the defendants to satisfy their part of the agreement. This constituted a breach of contract and released the defendants from their bargain with Denny.[49]

In another business contract case, *Collier v. Swinney*, Collier contracted with Eaton, the steamboat captain on the *Wapello*, to transport tobacco from Glasgow, Missouri, to St. Louis. In the agreement, Eaton had promised to deliver the tobacco even if the Missouri River was too low for the *Wapello*. After his tobacco was not delivered as promised, Collier sued Swinney, the owner of the *Wapello*, for failure to meet the terms of the contract.[50]

In his decision, Gamble ruled that the lower court had erred by in-

48. Peter Karsten, *Heart versus Head*, 47–61; and *Harrison v. Town and Dixon*, 17 Mo. Rep. 237–46.
    49. *Denny v. Kile et al.*, 16 Mo. Rep. 450–55.
    50. *Collier v. Swinney*, 16 Mo. Rep. 484–90.

structing the jury to disregard Eaton's agreement to carry the "tobacco on another boat," if the *Wapello* was unable to transport it. Moreover, the lower court had erred when it had instructed the jury that low water was "an act of God which excused the defendant from the performance of his contract, and the jury must find for the defendant." Under normal circumstances, an act of God or of a public enemy excused a common carrier from his otherwise absolute duty to transport goods or persons. However, Eaton had promised to deliver the tobacco, even if the Missouri River was low. For this reason, Gamble ruled in favor of Collier, a judgment one would not expect from a judge who sought to promote and protect the interests of business.[51]

Nevertheless, strict adherence to the terms of contracts could cut both ways. This is best demonstrated in *Vai v. Weld*. Vai had leased from Weld a building in which to operate his store. After the roof began to leak, Vai testified that Weld had refused to repair it. Moreover, he claimed that the stench from a nearby privy prevented him from conducting business there. Gamble ruled that the owner of the property was not responsible for repairs unless this was stated expressly in the contract. The renter of the property had no remedy for the bad smell against the owner unless Vai could prove that Weld had caused the problem. However, this ruling, Gamble noted, did not prevent the renter from bringing suit once he presented proof that Weld or someone else was responsible.[52]

Under most circumstances during this period, financial arrangements were accomplished by written agreement in which it was expected that the parties involved would strictly adhere to the terms of the contract. However, recognizing that some individuals were vulnerable to coercion, the Missouri legislature passed statutes to protect them from unscrupulous individuals inclined to take advantage of others. An example of such provisions were those protecting women from being coerced by their husbands into selling property in which they both had an interest. Often a woman brought property into a relationship, but even if she had not, upon her husband's death she was entitled by law to one-third of his property. Similarly, a woman's property was protected from her husband's creditors,

51. Ibid.
52. *Vai v. Weld*, 17 Mo. Rep. 232–33.

and even a prenuptial agreement or the husband's last will and testament could not rescind a woman's dower right. These laws protected property that was needed to support a widow and her children.[53]

In 1825 the General Assembly passed a statute enabling a couple to sell a woman's property, but provided safeguards against a husband coercing his wife to go along with the arrangement. The law stipulated that a woman relinquishing her dower must go to court alone and swear that she was doing so voluntarily. The court was to determine that the woman understood "the contents of the deed" and that she agreed to convey the property voluntarily.[54]

In *Chauvin v. Wagner*, the issue before the court regarded Mrs. Chauvin's relinquishment of her dower by certificate. Her heirs had brought suit against Wagner, claiming that the certificate had not been properly accomplished and thereby claimed ownership of the land. In his decision, Gamble agreed with Chauvin's heirs, for "the certificate does not, in any manner, refer to Mrs. Chauvin's willingness, at the time of the acknowledgement, to give effect to the deed." The defendant's counsel argued that because Mrs. Chauvin lived in St. Louis where the property was located and knew that Wagner was using and developing the property, it was reasonable to assume that she had agreed to the sale of her dower, for otherwise she would have brought suit to regain it upon the death of her husband. Gamble ruled that unless the defendant could prove that Mrs. Chauvin was aware of Wagner's activities on the land, this objection could have no effect. In rendering this judgment, Gamble was displeased with the result, for he apparently believed that Mrs. Chauvin's heirs had taken advantage of a technicality to take Wagner's property from him. "I have thus, as briefly as possible, considered the questions in the case, and the conclusion at which I have arrived is one unfavorable to the title of the defendants, as presented on the record. It is a conclusion attained by yielding to what I regard as the demands of strict law, against my sense of the justice of the case. But the court has no power to dispense with any requirements which the law makes."[55]

53. For a discussion of these dower rights see Dennis K. Boman, *Abiel Leonard, Yankee Slaveholder, Eminent Jurist, and Passionate Unionist*, Studies in American History, vol. 38 (Lewiston: Edwin Mellen, 2002), 192–94.

54. *Chauvin v. Wagner* and *Thomas v. Meier*, 18 Mo. Rep. 531–57 and 573–79.

55. Ibid., 531–55.

In his dissent, Scott argued that in Missouri it was difficult to find men who could skillfully execute legal documents without making some error. For this reason he felt it important to make some allowance for this, otherwise he feared that many titles would be challenged in court and that this would lead to much injustice. Undoubtedly, Gamble agreed with Scott's assessment of the effect of his judgment, but also recognized that if he had ruled in Wagner's favor the decision might set a precedent undermining the protection provided to other women under the 1825 statute.[56]

Of all the cases that the court decided, the most complex and difficult were land suits. Because of the expense of having a survey made and providing documentation to officials, few of the inhabitants of Louisiana had obtained a completed title. According to Gamble, during his career as a lawyer and judge, he had seen no more than two or three completed Spanish land titles. Congress had recognized this difficulty and passed statutes directing the land boards to approve the claims of those who could prove they had lived on and cultivated the land before December 20, 1803. As the process unfolded, however, it became clear that many of the original inhabitants were unable to provide evidence of occupation or title to satisfy the land title boards appointed to sift through the claims. The difficulties in determining legal ownership was expressed by a commissioner on one of the land boards who complained that his duties were complicated by

> the refusal by the Spanish officials to deliver the plats and books relating to foreign grants; the refusal of the late deputy surveyor south of Tennessee to deliver to his successor his field-notes, plats, etc.; the meagerness and inaccuracy of the description of titles and boundaries given to the old boards of commissioners by claimants; bad translations of the old titles, which were sometimes very bad French, Spanish, or English, or a mixture of the three; and last but not least, the refusal or neglect of parties to point to true locations, or to give any assistance to the deputies while employed in the field, together with misdirections by others, with a view to obtain a

---

56. Ibid., 555–57. In *Moreau v. Detchemendy* Gamble ruled that a couple married under Spanish law was not affected by the 1825 statute and that a woman could not own property so long as she was married. Therefore, the husband had a vested right to dispose of all property held "in community" by the couple as if the Spanish legal system was still in authority, 18 Mo. Rep. 522–31.

tract of land free of interference with other claims, or through ignorance of their rights.

After many of the original inhabitants' claims were denied, Congress, in an effort to treat fairly the original inhabitants of the territory, extended the deadlines for claims and relaxed the standard of proof somewhat. Because of this action, many of the claims approved under these directives were of a more questionable nature, and undoubtedly some were fraudulent.[57]

In *Gamache et al. v. Piquignot et al.*, counsel for the heirs of John Baptiste De Gamache Sr. sought to recover an outlot of the town of Carondelet. Originally, the heirs had sought to perfect their title in accord with an 1824 congressional statute, but the surveyor-general then in office rejected their claim. Apparently, their evidence, a land survey, was considered untrustworthy. However, in 1839 the heirs presented the testimony of an old inhabitant who asserted that he had worked on the Gamache farm in 1797 or 1798, and that Gamache had cultivated the land for some years after. Based on this testimony another surveyor-general approved Gamache's title twelve years after the deadline for approval of claims had expired.[58]

After gaining approval of their title by the surveyor-general, Gamache's heirs brought suit to recover the land from the town of Carondelet, which had been awarded the land after Gamache's claim had been rejected in 1827. Gamble stated that if Gamache's claim had not been disputed by the U.S. government, the court would have had no objection to it. However, because the claim was denied by the federal government, the court "will examine his acts, and give them effect only so far as they conform to the law." Because Gamache's title was entered long after the congressional deadline had passed, Gamble believed the court was bound to deny it as a valid claim. This decision was affirmed by a U.S. Supreme Court opinion in which Justice John Catron quoted several paragraphs of Gamble's decision and concluded by expressing his confidence in the past and future decisions of state supreme courts in suits involving complicated state law.[59]

57. Eugene Morrow Violette, "Spanish Land Claims in Missouri," *Washington University Studies* 8 (1921): 167–200. Quotation taken from Gates, "Land Claims," 187. Undated document in Gamble's handwriting explaining land law and precedent, Gamble papers.

58. *Gamache et al. v. Piquignot et al.*, 17 Mo. Rep. 310–25 and 57 U.S. Rep. 451–69.

59. Ibid.

In another land case, *Kissell v. St. Louis Public Schools*, Kissell appealed a ruling of the St. Louis circuit court to evict him from property claimed by the St. Louis County school commission. Kissell's case was based on a preemption claim that was confirmed by the land register in 1836. However, the school commission based its right of ownership to the same land on acts of Congress passed in 1812, 1824, and 1831.[60]

In his decision, Gamble weighed the conflicting claims and concluded that the interpretation of the congressional statutes by Kissell's counsel was flawed. According to them, the 1831 statute superseded those of 1812 and 1824 and left the disputed land subject to preemption. Gamble disagreed with this interpretation, noting that the 1824 and 1831 acts were supplementary to the 1812 statute. In it unclaimed land in towns was set apart for the use of education. The 1824 act directed anyone with a land claim to present it for verification within a specified time. After the expiration of the time limit, the surveyor-general was to determine what land was available for educational purposes. With this accomplished, Congress in 1831 relinquished the title of the United States to those with verified land claims and to towns, including St. Louis, claiming land for the use of schools.[61]

Because the St. Louis school commission had gained prior title, the burden of proof fell on Kissell to show some defect that would render it void. Gamble believed that Kissell's counsel, whose case was founded on the meaning of certain terminology and legal technicalities, had not accomplished this. In handing down his opinion, Gamble noted the inconsistency of the court's decisions on some of these issues. "On some of these points there has been hesitation in giving an opinion that differs so far from those expressed by other Judges of this court on former occasions, and it is hoped that, as this case depends entirely upon the construction of laws of the United States, it will be taken to the tribunal in which such questions may be finally settled."[62] And indeed, Gamble's decision was appealed by Kissell's counsel to the U.S. Supreme Court. In his opinion, Justice Catron again affirmed both Gamble's reasoning and decision in the case.[63]

60. *Kissell v. St. Louis Public Schools*, 16 Mo. Rep. 553–96 and 59 U.S. Rep. 19–28.
61. 16 Mo. Rep. 580–96.
62. Ibid., 590.
63. 59 U.S. Rep. 19–28.

In *State v. Ham,* suit was brought against Ham in circuit court for trespass and destruction of property. The state claimed that Ham, who had leased land from Thomas Fleming, was actually residing on land reserved for public education. Ham appealed his conviction and fine to the Missouri Supreme Court.[64]

For his part, Fleming traced his title back to an 1801 Spanish concession called Mine la Motte. After Louisiana was sold to the United States, President Thomas Jefferson appointed a land title board to investigate land claims. In 1811 this board rejected the Mine la Motte concession, but Congress in 1828, in response to a petition, confirmed the land grant, although it relinquished the title of the United States only. Moreover, Congress stipulated that a third party might still have a legal right to the property "either by purchase or donation." Apparently, Congress was unaware that the federal government had already donated the land to Missouri to fund education. It was on this basis that the state had brought suit against Ham (and later Fleming).[65]

In his opinion, Gamble believed the congressional statutes did not prohibit future efforts to confirm rejected claims. Although the same right, he noted, was not accorded to those claiming land within the sixteenth sections of townships designated for the benefit of education. Therefore, because the federal government had designated the land in dispute as a sixteenth section in 1820, the state of Missouri had a "superior" title to that derived from the Spanish concession. Once again, Gamble's decision was later affirmed by the U.S. Supreme Court.[66]

CRIMINAL LAW

In the private practice of law, Gamble seldom represented defendants in criminal suits, finding commercial and land law more lucrative. However, while still a young lawyer, he had extensive experience in criminal law as circuit attorney in the First Judicial Circuit and in St. Louis County. While most of the court's opinions in criminal cases were written by Judge

64. *Ham v. the State of Missouri,* 19 Mo. Rep. 592–607 and 59 U.S. Rep. 126–34.
65. Ibid.
66. 19 Mo. Rep. 606 and 59 U.S. Rep. 126–34.

Ryland, who specialized in that type of law, occasionally Gamble wrote opinions for such cases as well.[67]

Again, in these cases it is clear that Gamble carefully followed the law and ruled accordingly, even when this meant overturning a conviction on a technicality. For example, in *State v. Curran*, Gamble ruled that because the state had accused Curran of assaulting Silas Melville instead of Silas Melvin, the correct name of the victim, the lower court judge should have acquitted Curran on a variance. Moreover, he clarified the rules by directing that simple misspellings or the use of nicknames would not be grounds for acquittal. Similarly, in *State v. Dillihunty*, Gamble overturned a murder conviction and remanded the case for a new trial because the prosecution had misidentified the victim.[68]

In another criminal case, *State v. Lopez*, Gamble overturned Lopez's conviction for embezzlement, citing the omission of the words "against the peace and dignity of the state" in the indictment. In his opinion, Gamble also ruled that the circuit attorney had no right to make an agreement with the defendant not to prosecute six indictments in return for pleading guilty to four others. Therefore, the defendant could still stand trial for any of the other indictments.[69]

In two *habeas corpus* cases, Gamble ruled against the defendants. In *Ex Parte Ruthven*, Gamble refused petition to free Ruthven after the lower court had dismissed the jury. Ruthven's counsel had argued that the judge could not dismiss the jury without the defendant's permission. Gamble noted in his opinion that no precedent was available to guide him, but that the statute on writs of *habeas corpus* was clear in its prohibiting the release of any person under indictment. Moreover, if there were facts and law that should void the indictment, this must be determined in trial.[70]

In the second *habeas corpus* case, *Ex Parte McKee*, Gamble was asked to free the editor of a newspaper who had been jailed for contempt. McKee had been subpoened to testify before a notary public and had refused to

---

67. Bay, *Bench and Bar*, 276.

68. *State v. Curran* and *State v. Dillihunty*, 18 Mo. Rep. 320–21 and 331–32. Gamble's willingness to overturn convictions based on technicalities sets him apart from many judges of his era. See Boman, *Abiel Leonard*, 195–96. Huebner, *The Southern Judicial Tradition*, 5.

69. *State v. Lopez*, 19 Mo. Rep. 254–55.

70. *Ex Parte Ruthven*, 17 Mo. Rep. 541–44.

divulge the identity of the anonymous writer of an article in the paper he edited. His counsel argued that McKee considered the identity of the author confidential, that the question was immaterial to the suit, and that the deposition had a political object. Moreover, he asserted that the notary public did not have the authority to imprison McKee. Gamble, however, ruled against McKee, arguing that to do otherwise would impair the ability of litigants to collect relevant information necessary to their causes. Therefore, the witness did not have the right to refuse to testify if the court determined otherwise.[71]

In his decisions, Gamble, as the first Whig justice of the Missouri Supreme Court, demonstrated how a principled judge could rule according to the law and rise above political partisanship and economic self-interest. To him maintaining the integrity and consistency of the law was more important than the momentary political or economic advantages that might be gained through judicial activism. To do otherwise would end in the politicization of the judiciary and an imbalance in the constitutional system he so admired. Moreover, following precedent and adhering carefully to positive law in conformity with the state and national constitutions appealed to Gamble's conservative philosophy. He believed it dangerous to upset principles and institutions that had been developed through trial and error over decades and even centuries. However, his principles of jurisprudence and judicial statesmanship were tested in the consideration of a case that later became the most controversial of its time.

71. Ibid., 601.

Chapter Four

Law, Politics, and the *Dred Scott* Case

amilton R. Gamble's attitudes toward slavery were complex and influenced by different factors. Born and raised into manhood in Virginia, he disliked Northern criticism of "the peculiar institution," although he never adopted the extreme proslavery views of some. As he matured and came to recognize the political and social problems of slavery, Gamble supported the American Colonization Society as an organization with a reasonable plan for the emancipation of slaves. A pragmatic man who disliked radical solutions, Gamble probably hoped that voluntary emancipation and colonization might solve the problem gradually and with a minimum of social disruption. As a lawyer, he represented both slaves and slaveholders in freedom suits, providing his clients with the best representation possible. This sometimes required him to press hard on the limits of plausible legal argument, an unwelcome task that all lawyers undertake from necessity when arguing weak cases. As chief justice of the Missouri Supreme Court, Gamble carefully applied law and precedent in the *Dred Scott* case and other suits involving slavery. At stake, he understood, was the delicate condition of Northern and Southern cooperation on the slavery issue in the courts and elsewhere. Similarly, Northern and Southern congressmen had settled disagreements over slavery through compromise or avoidance of the issue. These political and legal precedents, established on the principle of comity and enlightened self-interest, coincided well with Gamble's political and jurisprudential principles. The majority opinion in *Scott v. Emerson*, however, marked the beginning of a steady erosion of this arrangement of convenience between the North and South.[1]

When Gamble moved to Missouri after the War of 1812, the territory had adopted the common law and much of Virginia's and Kentucky's slave law as its own. For this reason, because he had first studied law in Virginia, Gamble's adaptation to Missouri's legal system was simple. As in other slave states, according to Missouri law slaves were both property and persons with limited legal rights. Because slaves were property, Missourians bought and sold them, provided them as gifts to others, and bequeathed them in their wills. In case of their harm, escape, or death at the hands of others, slaveowners could sue for damages in court. Moreover, creditors could force the sale of slaves to satisfy the debts of a slaveowner.[2]

As persons with rights, slaves were protected from cruel treatment and murder, and when accused of a felony were guaranteed trial by jury. In most respects, however, slaves had little control over their lives or those of their spouses and children. Of course, their circumstances depended much on the character of their master and the community in which they lived.[3]

While it was uncommon for slaves to gain their freedom, the period from the American Revolution to the mid-1830s was the time in the

1. See chapter 1 for Gamble's early education and attitudes toward slavery. This chapter is revised from my article "The Dred Scott Case Reconsidered: The Legal and Political Context in Missouri," *American Journal of Legal History* 44, no. 4 (October 2000): 405–28. The best account of the *Dred Scott* case remains Don E. Fehrenbacher's *The Dred Scott Case: Its Significance in American Law and Politics* (Oxford: Oxford University Press, 1979). For an excellent account of Congress's handling of the issue of slavery see Harry V. Jaffa, *Crisis of the House Divided: An Interpretation of the Issues in the Lincoln-Douglas Debates*, with a new preface (Chicago: University of Chicago Press, 1959; reprint, 1982).

2. *Laws of a Public and General Nature, of the District of Louisiana, of the Territory of Louisiana, of the Territory of Missouri, and of the State of Missouri, up to the Year 1824*, vol. 1 (Jefferson City: State of Missouri, 1842), 27–33. Harrison Anthony Trexler, *Slavery in Missouri, 1804–1865*, Johns Hopkins University Studies in Historical and Political Science, series 32, no. 2 (Baltimore: Johns Hopkins Press, 1914), 59–62, 68–69, and 77. For a variety of suits involving slaves as property see 1 Mo. Rep. 178–79; 4 Mo. Rep. 361–63; and 7 Mo. Rep. 221–24. For cases Gamble decided as a judge see 15 Mo. Rep. 191–93, 240–44, 400–403, 494–99; 16 Mo. Rep. 98–101; 18 Mo. Rep. 249–52, 411–15; and 19 Mo. Rep. 453–54.

3. Don E. Fehrenbacher, *Slavery, Law, and Politics: The Dred Scott Case in Historical Perspective* (Oxford: Oxford University Press, 1981), 16. Trexler, *Slavery in Missouri*, 68–69 and 77.

nation's history most opportune for emancipation. The Enlightenment ideology of natural rights and liberty, which had stoked the fires of patriot fervor and rhetoric, had also motivated most state legislatures to loosen restrictions on the manumission of slaves. With an increase in manumissions came disappointment to many who had expected soon to inherit or receive slaves as gifts. Some of these disappointed relatives contested the wills in court or simply retained control of the slaves illegally. Moreover, slaves' manumissions were sometimes disputed because of the debts of their owners whose property was subject to sale before the estate could be divided. To resolve these issues and to ensure that slaves were treated fairly, laws guaranteed legal counsel to slaves and established a regular procedure in such cases. In Missouri an 1824 statute directed judges to appoint an attorney at state expense to represent any slave presenting evidence supporting a case for freedom. The judge was then to prohibit the slave's master from punishing or preventing the slave from meeting with counsel.[4]

During this period, slaves gained another opportunity for freedom when much of the North and West was closed to slavery. First, the Northern states passed legislation to emancipate slaves gradually and to prohibit the immigration of slaves into the region. In addition to this, the U.S. Congress passed the Northwest Ordinance—first approved by the Confederation Congress in 1787—prohibiting slavery from its holdings north of the Ohio River. In effect, a large portion of the old Northwest was closed to slave property. To this point, the legal systems of the North and South had been very similar and little difficulty had occurred through the conflict of laws. However, from that point questions would arise about how far each region would be willing to accommodate the interests of the other.[5]

Until slavery became a controversial issue, most legislators and judges in the North and the South were willing to treat the laws of the other with respect and dignity. A slaveholder could travel with a slave through a free

4. Fehrenbacher, *Dred Scott Case*, 8–9. Paul Finkelman, *An Imperfect Union: Slavery, Federalism, and Comity* (Chapel Hill: University of North Carolina Press, 1981), 181–82. Timothy S. Huebner, *The Southern Judicial Tradition: State Judges and Sectional Distinctiveness, 1790–1890* (Athens: University of Georgia Press, 1999), 23–25. 2 Mo. Rep. 157.

5. Fehrenbacher, *Dred Scott Case*, 26–40. Finkelman, *Imperfect Union*, 13–16.

state or visit friends and relatives without fear of the authorities interfering. In the South the courts demonstrated their respect for Northern prohibitions of slavery by freeing slaves who had resided in the North with their masters but had then returned to a slave state.[6]

For many years, these arrangements between the North and South promoted harmonious relations. As lifetime appointees, the judges of the first Missouri Supreme Court vigorously enforced Missouri's freedom statute, ruling against masters who had brought or allowed their slaves to reside in free territory. One of the judges in particular, George Tompkins, held strong views against slavery and ruled in favor of freedom in many suits. Although a native Virginian, in writing about the Northwest Ordinance he commented that "when the states assumed the right of self government, they found their citizens claiming a right of property in a miserable portion of the human race. Sound national policy required that the evil should be restricted as much as possible." This "evil," he stated, had already been restricted in Europe and other regions of the world through the benevolent influence of Christianity. Moreover, he argued "that freedom is the birthright of every human being" and that "whenever one person claimed to hold another in slavery the *onus probandi* [Latin for "burden of proof"] lies on the claimant."[7]

Despite the support of many legislators and judges for the right of slaves to sue for their freedom, one must not forget that such a right was inoperative unless slaves were aware of it and willing to assert it. Despite the measures of the 1824 statute intended to protect slaves suing for their freedom, it is clear that a slave could not undertake such action lightly because of the potential for retaliation after the trial's conclusion, especially, but not exclusively, if the slave lost. The greatest deterrent of all was the threat that slaves and loved ones could be sold "down South." Moreover, whatever legal protections were available to slaves ended with the trial's conclusion. Another deterrent to slaves suing for their freedom was the difficult situation that most free blacks experienced in Missouri. Free blacks had poor prospects for supporting themselves and their families and often less protection from whites than slaves, who, at least, could usu-

6. Finkelman, *Imperfect Union*, 50–51 and 70.

7. William V. N. Bay, *Reminiscences of the Bench and Bar of Missouri* (St. Louis: F. H. Thomas, 1878), 30–36. 1 Mo. Rep. 475; 3 Mo. Rep. 548–49 and 553; and 4 Mo. Rep. 596.

ally rely on their masters to protect them, if for no other reason than owners' desire to preserve their substantial investment. Suspicious that free blacks might foment an insurrection among their enslaved counterparts, whites were not reluctant to deal decisively and violently with them. For these reasons, slaves often sued for their freedom only after the impetus of some crisis such as the intention of their owner to sell them or a family member, or the realization that the promise of emancipation would not be honored.[8]

During the November 1824 term the Missouri Supreme Court ruled in its first freedom suit, *Winny v. Whitesides*. According to testimony in the St. Louis circuit court trial, around the turn of the century Winny had resided in Illinois with her owner for three or four years and then had moved with her to Missouri. In his opinion Tompkins held that Winny was free because her owner, Phebe Whitesides, had introduced slavery into a region where Congress had prohibited it. Tompkins rejected the argument of Whiteside's counsel that Congress did not have the power to prohibit slavery from the territories, noting that "it is too late now to raise a doubt on that subject. It is a rule of the national, as well as of the common law, that the acts of a government *de facto* are binding on all future governments." Moreover, Tompkins ruled that Winny's former status as a slave did not reattach itself to her when she returned to Missouri. This followed precedent established by other Southern courts in similar cases.[9]

Tompkin's 1824 decision in *Winny v. Whitesides* would remain the most important freedom suit heard in Missouri until *Scott v. Emerson* overturned it in 1852. *Winny* provided the main precedent on which all other suits of its kind rested: Congress's prohibition of slavery in the territories is constitutional; the residence of a slave in a free state or territory makes

---

8. Cases indicating these dangers include *Maria Whiten v. Garland Rucker*, November 1829 term, case number 14; *Cary, a man of color v. Benjamin Wilder*, March 1831 term, case number 53; *Thenia v. Green Crowder*, March 1832 term, case number 9; *Harriet, an infant v. Samuel T. McKinney and James Walker*, July 1833 term, case number 17; *Abraham Dutton, a free boy of color v. John Paca*, July 1834 term, case number 115; and *Delph, a mulatress v. Stephen Dorris*, March 1836 term, case number 4, St. Louis County Circuit Court. See also a discussion of cases related to slaves owned by Jonathan Ramsey in Dennis K. Boman, *Abiel Leonard, Yankee Slaveholder, Eminent Jurist, and Passionate Unionist*, Studies in American History, vol. 38 (Lewiston: Edwin Mellen, 2002), 133–35.

9. 1 Mo. Rep. 472–76.

him or her free; and a return to slave soil does not reattach slave status on the freedman or freedwoman. Subsequent freedom suits clarified the law, defining the limits of freedom and slavery for both the slaveowner and slave. The state legislature, apparently considering the matter a judicial one, was content to allow the courts to determine on what basis a slave should be granted his or her freedom under the 1824 statute.[10]

As a young lawyer, soon after the 1824 freedom suit statute was passed by Missouri's legislature, Gamble began representing both slaves and owners in a number of cases over the next decade and a half. He probably considered most of these cases as routine legal matters, although for the parties involved—especially the slaves—the stakes were very high. In most of these cases slaves sued for their freedom, claiming that they had resided in free territory or that their master had bequeathed their freedom to them. In one unusual case Gamble represented an individual who apparently had purchased a slave to manumit him but had stopped installment payments after learning that the black man was already free. Sometimes Gamble benefited from the errors or the incompetence of other lawyers. In one of these cases, a lawyer misplaced the names of persons who could give depositions in Galena, Illinois, supporting the claims of a slave who had resided there. The judge ruled that the case must be tried without this testimony, leading to the slave's loss of his case. In another suit Gamble won a case representing an owner after the opposing lawyer had made a technical error in the presentation of evidence. Most of these cases were settled at the circuit court level, although a few of his cases were appealed to the Missouri Supreme Court.[11]

In his first freedom suit before the Missouri Supreme Court, *Marguerite v. Chouteau*, Gamble represented the slave Marguerite. His client was

10. For the particulars of these cases see 1 Mo. Rep. 725–26; 2 Mo. Rep. 20–23, 36–39, 70–93, 144–45, 155–58, 214–17; 3 Mo. Rep. 194–97, 270–77, 306–8, 400–402, 540–77, 588–94; and 4 Mo. Rep. 350–54, 592–99.

11. *Maria Whiten v. Garland Rucker*, November 1829, case number 14; *Cary, a man of color v. Benjamin Wilder*, March 1831, case number 53; *Dunky, a woman of color v. Andrew Hay*, July 1831 and 1832, case number 12; *Thenia v. Green Crowder*, March 1832, case number 9; *Coleman Duncan for the use of James S. Thomas v. Jonathan Duncan*, March 1832, case number 29; *Susan, a girl of color v. Lemon Parker*, November 1832, case number 7; *Nelson Kerr, a free man of color v. Mathew Kerr*, July 1834, case number 104; and *Andrew Dutton, a free boy of color v. John Paca*, July 1834, case number 114, St. Louis County Circuit Court.

of Native American and black descent and in 1806 had unsuccessfully sued Pierre Chouteau for her freedom in the territorial superior court of Upper Louisiana. However, having never given up her hope of freedom, in 1825 Marguerite requested permission from the St. Louis circuit court to sue her master. When this request was denied she appealed to the Missouri Supreme Court, which ordered the lower court to give her a trial or provide a reason for the denial. Judge Tompkins considered the lower court's reason unacceptable and ordered the issue to go to trial.[12]

Following the dictates of the 1824 statute, the lower court appointed Gamble and Isaac McGirk, the brother of Missouri Supreme Court justice Mathias McGirk, to represent Marguerite. Chouteau hired Luke E. Lawless, later judge of the St. Louis circuit court, and Henry S. Geyer, who would serve in the U.S. Senate and represent John Sanford before the U.S. Supreme Court in *Scott v. Sandford*. In the 1827 trial Gamble and McGirk argued that Marguerite's Indian ancestry entitled her to freedom. This argument was founded on the legal principle of "*partus sequitur ventrem*—the child inherits the condition of the mother." Because her maternal grandmother was reputed to be Native American, Gamble and McGirk argued that Marguerite was not a slave, for under Spanish rule all Native Americans were declared free. When the judge instructed the jury that Marguerite's maternal grandmother was an Indian *slave*, Gamble and McGirk objected, preparing the way for an appeal to the Missouri Supreme Court.[13]

When the case came before the state's highest court in May 1828, Judge Mathias McGirk's absence left only two justices, Tompkins and Robert Wash, to hear arguments and decide Marguerite's fate. The court rendered a split decision, Tompkins ruling that Indian ancestry was *prima facie* evidence of freedom and Wash holding that Marguerite's slave status had descended from her grandmother. Because the court split, the lower court's ruling was upheld and Marguerite remained Chouteau's slave.[14]

However, Marguerite's determination to gain her freedom must have

12. William E. Foley, "Slave Freedom Suits Before Dred Scott: The Case of Marie Scypion's Descendants," *Missouri Historical Review* (1985): 9–14.

13. Ibid., 15–18. Kenneth M. Stampp, *The Peculiar Institution: Slavery in the Ante-Bellum South* (New York: Vintage, 1956), 193.

14. 2 Mo. Rep. 71–93.

impressed both Gamble and McGirk, for six years later they petitioned the Missouri Supreme Court to rehear the case. Tompkins and McGirk granted a new trial during the October 1834 term of the court. While no new issues were introduced in trial, it is apparent from the tenor of Tompkin's opinion that his opposition to slavery was as strong as ever. This time the result was different, for McGirk joined Tompkins in ruling that the lower court had misdirected the jury and ordered a new trial. The retrial was held in the Jefferson County circuit court and resulted in the jury finding in Marguerite's favor. Revealing equal determination to prevail in the suit, Chouteau then appealed the case to the U.S. Supreme Court, where it was heard during the January 1838 term. Gamble and McGirk retained Benjamin F. Butler, former attorney general of the United States, to argue the case. The Court, in conformity with past decisions, ruled that it did not have jurisdiction in the suit and let the decision stand. This determination was final and ended Indian slavery in Missouri.[15]

In another freedom suit, *Julia v. McKinney*, Gamble represented Samuel McKinney, who had bought Julia from Mrs. Carrington in Illinois. Before her sale, Julia had stayed for a month in Illinois with her former owner and had been hired out for a day or two before being sent just across the border to Louisiana, Missouri. In a short time, Julia became ill and was sent back to Mrs. Carrington, who cared for her until she recovered. Julia was then sent to St. Louis, where she was sold to McKinney.[16]

In the lower court case, which he won, Gamble argued that Mrs. Carrington, in bringing Julia to Illinois, had not intended to make her a resident or to introduce slavery there. He also contended that a literal interpretation of the Illinois constitutional provision prohibiting slavery would prevent slaveowners from even traveling with their slaves through the state. Therefore, he believed it best to look to the slaveowner's intent in determining whether or not Illinois's constitution had been violated.[17]

In his opinion, Judge McGirk ruled that the constitution of Illinois did not seek to prevent persons from bringing their slaves from Kentucky through Illinois, but rather to prohibit persons from introducing slaves

15. Foley, "Slave Freedom Suits," 19–23. 12 U.S. Rep. 507–10. Benjamin F. Butler to Hamilton R. Gamble, 16 January and 6 March 1838, Gamble papers.

16. 3 Mo. Rep. 270–77.

17. Ibid.

as residents of Illinois. And, in fact, actions of the Illinois legislature and judiciary, perhaps reflecting the sentiments of many who had immigrated there from slave states, demonstrated little inclination to prevent travelers from coming through Illinois with their slaves. McGirk also thought it impractical for the court to set a time limit for travel through the state. Instead, each case must be considered on its own merits. However, he believed that delay in bringing slaves through a free territory must result from necessity, not convenience, otherwise the slave would become free. Moreover, he held that not only must an emergency be shown to have delayed the immigrants' journey, but that "due diligence [was] used to remove them." McGirk believed that Mrs. Carrington had unnecessarily kept Julia with her and thereby had imprudently introduced slavery into Illinois.[18]

In his dissent Judge Wash agreed in part with the majority that the lower court had mishandled the law and the facts of the case, but also believed that a one-month stay and the hiring out of Julia for a couple of days was too insignificant to change her status. Moreover, he agreed with Gamble's proposed legal test of the slaveowner's intention in considering these cases. According to Wash, "the intention with which a thing is done gives color and character to almost every transaction."[19]

During the June 1836 term, in his final freedom suit as a lawyer before the Missouri Supreme Court, Gamble represented William Walker, who had purchased Rachael from J. B. W. Stockton, an army officer. Gamble's representation of Walker demonstrates the challenges that often confronted lawyers in arguing weak cases for clients. Moreover, many years later *Rachael v. Walker* would provide a very important precedent in arguments presented in *Scott v. Emerson.*[20]

Apparently, "having just married," Stockton, then stationed at Fort Snelling in the territory of Iowa, had purchased Rachael in St. Louis and brought her with him. Later, Stockton was posted at Fort Crawford in the territory of Michigan. According to court testimony, while she was at Fort

18. Ibid., 272–73. Finkelman, *Imperfect Union*, 96–100 and 155. David Zarefsky, *Lincoln, Douglas, and Slavery: In the Crucible of Public Debate* (Chicago: University of Chicago Press, 1990), 25–26. Finkelman demonstrates through his analysis of Illinois Supreme Court cases that not until the 1840s did the court have a definite bias against slavery.

19. 3 Mo. Rep. 276–77.

20. 4 Mo. Rep. 350–54 and 15 Mo. Rep. 576–92.

Snelling and Fort Crawford, Rachael never worked outside of the Stockton household and only as "a private servant." Afterward, Walker purchased and returned her to Missouri, where she sued him for her freedom.[21]

Having won the lower court case, Gamble was confronted with the difficulty of persuading the judges of the Missouri Supreme Court that Rachael's residence in free territory should not entitle her to freedom. In his favor was the fact that no similar case involving a military officer had yet been adjudicated, although he must have known the probability for success was low. However, making the best argument possible, he agreed that Rachael's "residence was such that in ordinary cases, would under the decisions of this court, entitle the plaintiff to her freedom—but in this case, she was taken to that territory as the servant of an officer of the United States' army, and was never otherwise employed there than as the servant of that officer." Moreover, Gamble asserted that a military officer could have no "domicil, in any other than the State of which he was an inhabitant, when appointed." The main question, then, Gamble contended, was whether Stockton could bring his property with him to the duty station to which he had been ordered.[22] Rachael's counsel and Gamble's good friend, Josiah Spalding, largely relied on precedent to support her case for freedom. In direct answer to Gamble's argument that an exception should be made for military officers, Spalding replied that Stockton, although stationed where slavery was not allowed, was not forced to bring Rachael with him.[23]

In his decision for a unanimous court, McGirk first reflected on the persistence of slaveholders in flaunting the prohibition of slavery from the Old Northwest and in fighting their suits. "It seems that the ingenuity of counsel and the interest of those disposed to deal in slave property, will never admit any thing to be settled in regard to this question. The ordinance of 1787, for the government of the north western territory, declares that neither slavery nor involuntary servitude shall exist in the same." After reviewing past decisions of the court, McGirk then turned to the heart of Gamble's argument regarding the "necessity" of Stockton introducing slavery where it was prohibited. As a military officer, McGirk

21. Ibid.
22. Ibid., 350.
23. Ibid.

conceded, Stockton was required to report where ordered; however, no requirement was imposed on him to bring his slaves with him, nor indeed, was any authority granted to him to violate the prohibition of slavery in the Northwest Territory. In this way, McGirk disposed of Gamble's argument, reversed the lower court's decision, and remanded the case for a new trial. No contemporary record of Gamble's reaction to the loss of the case is extant. As a lawyer his responsibility was to represent the best interests of his client. Perhaps he had advised Walker that Rachael's case for freedom was strong and that he would incur unnecessary expense by pursuing the matter in the courts. Walker may have rejected this advice and decided to pursue it anyway. Perhaps the calculation of Gamble and his client was that they could win before the lower court and then hope that the case would not be appealed to the Missouri Supreme Court.[24]

THE SLAVERY CONTROVERSY IN MISSOURI

After its decision in *Rachael v. Walker*, the Missouri Supreme Court increasingly drifted toward a policy less congenial to blacks' rights and more strongly proslavery in outlook. The court's evolution was gradual and reflected societal and political changes then occurring in antebellum Missouri and the rest of the country. While a small minority considered the gradual emancipation of Missouri's slaves desirable, a substantial majority opposed the plan for several reasons. One objection was that emancipation would create a severe shortage of labor, for almost all white Missourians were strictly opposed to allowing a large number of free blacks to remain among them. Another objection concerned the strong possibility that Southern immigration to the state would end. And finally, recognizing that any plan to emancipate slaves would be gradual, great concern was expressed that slaves, knowing that they would someday be free, would become restless and impatient for their freedom.[25]

Throughout Missouri's territorial period and afterward, whites had sought the restriction of the activities and travel of free blacks, the maintenance of slave discipline, and the prevention of abolitionists' interfer-

24. Ibid., 353–54.
25. Trexler, *Slavery in Missouri*, 114–17.

ence "in our social relations." Many provisions of the territorial code of 1804 were adopted by the first General Assembly and in later revisions of the law in 1835, 1845, and 1855. Most of the laws were left unchanged, for the difficulty was in enforcing the statutes already on the books. The code punished slaves with beatings for traveling from home without permission. Moreover, whites were fined for allowing another's slave to remain on their property without a master's consent. Except on the frontier, it was illegal for slaves or free blacks to carry weapons. Another prohibition concerned slave assemblies, which were legal only when their owners consented to them. Night patrols enforced these provisions and during the day slaves sent on errands were required to carry a pass.[26]

In attempts to address the concerns of whites, the General Assembly intermittently passed measures designed to protect slave property and prevent social unrest and insurrections. Passed in 1835, one measure punished a slave with thirty-nine lashes for concealing a fugitive slave. In 1843 slaves violating a curfew in St. Louis were given lashes and their master fined. The effectiveness of these measures is probably impossible to determine, but their passage and enforcement reflected the anxiety that whites felt about the black population living among them.[27]

By the mid-1830s the increase of the free black population of St. Louis caused concern among whites. A grand jury impaneled for the St. Louis circuit court sent a memorial to the General Assembly in which they complained of the difficulties free blacks were causing in St. Louis. According to the grand jury, free blacks caused disaffection among "the slave population," leading to insubordinate behavior and criminal activity. Because the state had done little to prosecute the existing laws, the city had employed one of its officers with the responsibility of arresting free blacks who were regarded as troublemakers. Moreover, the grand jurors asserted that slaves' interaction with free blacks caused many slaves to become insubordinate and unruly, much to the consternation of many whites.[28] The grand jury recommended that the legislature take action to ensure the enforcement of laws regulating the entrance of free blacks into the state, that masters control their slaves and not treat them as free persons, and that the legislature prevent cruelty to slaves. Moreover, they urged the

26. *Laws*, vol. 1, 27–33. Trexler, *Slavery in Missouri*, 179–81.
27. Trexler, *Slavery in Missouri*, 181–84.
28. St. Louis *Missouri Republican*, 22 August 1834.

authorities in St. Louis to do more to regulate drinking establishments, especially with a view toward preventing slaves from frequenting them.[29]

Possibly in response to the grand jury's memorial, the General Assembly passed an ordinance criminalizing the entrance of free blacks into Missouri after January 1840. All free blacks residing in the state before then were required to register themselves and obtain a license. Free blacks without a license were arrested and fined. Those without the means to pay their fines were beaten and given three days to leave the state.[30]

Not long after the grand jury had expressed its concerns about free blacks and slaves in its memorial, Gamble and some of St. Louis's most prominent citizens, understanding the strong animus felt toward those who spoke out against slavery, advised Elijah P. Lovejoy not to write against slavery in his newspaper, the St. Louis *Observer*. In a letter they warned him that "the public mind is greatly excited, and owing to the unjustifiable interference of our Northern brethren in our social relations, the community are perhaps, not in a situation to endure sound doctrine on this subject." Despite this friendly advice Lovejoy soon stirred up a great deal of trouble for himself when he criticized a St. Louis mob for murdering a free black man, Francis McIntosh, who had attempted to prevent the arrest of a fellow sailor. When McIntosh was taken into custody and told he would spend five years in prison for his interference, he attempted to escape and killed one of the officers. While awaiting trial, a mob took McIntosh from his cell, tied him to a tree, and burned him to death. Lovejoy soon moved across the Mississippi River to Alton, Illinois, where he continued to publish his newspaper until he was killed by a mob. Although no record of his reaction to these events exists, the killings of both McIntosh and Lovejoy may have surprised and shocked Gamble, and may explain his later attempts as a judge and governor to prevent the radicalization of the slavery issue.[31]

Unfortunately, the intolerance of many white Missourians did not abate

29. Ibid. For an excellent study of slavery in the cities see Richard C. Wade, *Slavery in the Cities: The South, 1820–1860* (London: Oxford University Press, 1964), 101–2 and 111–42.

30. Jefferson City *Jefferson Inquirer*, 22 December 1846. St. Louis *Missouri Republican*, 1 and 8 May 1850.

31. Trexler, *Slavery in Missouri*, 117–19. Michael Kent Curtis, "The 1837 Killing of Elijah Lovejoy by an Anti-Abolition Mob: Free Speech, Mobs, Republican Government, and the Privileges of American Citizens," *UCLA Law Review* 44 (1997): 1135–37.

during the 1840s and was exacerbated further by a series of state and national events that led to a hardening of proslavery attitudes. In 1841 three Illinois abolitionists were arrested and accused of attempting to aid slaves in Marion County to escape from Missouri. These men were convicted and sentenced to the penitentiary.[32] In the mid-1840s, the Texas annexation issue also created a great deal of excitement in Missouri and the rest of the country. Most Whigs, including Gamble (see chapter 2), feared that the annexation of Texas by the United States would lead to war with Mexico and cause further sectional strife over slavery. After the United States had acquired new territories at the end of the Mexican War, Missouri's General Assembly passed resolutions supporting the extension of the Missouri Compromise line to the Pacific. The Jackson Resolutions, named for Claiborne F. Jackson who had introduced them, also instructed Missouri's congressmen to combine with Southerners to fight "anti-slavery fanaticism."[33]

U.S. Senator Thomas H. Benton's refusal to follow the instructions of the Jackson Resolutions led to a split in the Democratic Party between Benton's supporters and opponents. In 1849 Benton traveled the state speaking to large crowds. In his speeches he argued that Congress had the power to restrict slavery and provoked outrage among many proslavery Missourians by stating that "if there was no slavery in Missouri today, I should oppose its coming into Missouri; if there was none in the United States, I should oppose its coming into the United States; as there is none in New Mexico or California, I am against sending it to those territories." Evident from this controversy is the power of the slavery issue, for it ended Benton's thirty-year career in the U.S. Senate and split the Democratic Party into two camps, one for and the other against Benton.[34]

A NEW COURT AND THE DRED SCOTT CASE

At the same time that Missouri was undergoing social and political change, the judiciary experienced a similar evolution in its handling of freedom

32. Trexler, *Slavery in Missouri*, 121–22.

33. Ibid., 138–44. Perry McCandless, *A History of Missouri*, vol. 2 (Columbia: University of Missouri Press, 1972), 237–38 and 247. William Nisbet Chambers, *Old Bullion Benton: Senator from the New West, Thomas Hart Benton, 1782–1858* (Boston: Little, Brown, 1956), 341.

34. Chambers, *Old Bullion Benton*, 345. For a full discussion of Benton's appeal and the controversy see Boman, *Abiel Leonard*, 145–49.

suits, although at first the differences were subtle, suggesting only the possibility of a coming revolution in its jurisprudence. A change in personnel on the court was a very important step in the court's transformation. Notwithstanding Justice George Tompkins's continued presence on the Missouri Supreme Court until 1845, the appointments of William B. Napton and William Scott by the May 1841 term established a strong proslavery majority on the court. This new court decided only one freedom suit in a slave's favor and this because the slaveholder's counsel had made a critical error on appeal.[35]

In his majority opinions, Judge Napton was particularly pointed in his statements about slavery and the principles on which he and Judge Scott intended to rule in freedom suit cases. Slaves "are in truth a species of property *sui generis* [Latin for "of its own kind"], to be held, disposed of, and regulated according to the laws of each particular state where slavery exists. In all slaveholding states *color* raises the presumption of slavery, and until the contrary is shown a man or woman of color is deemed to be a slave." In *obiter dicta* written to justify this principle, Napton argued that a master could only free a slave if the state allowed it. Moreover, he expressed the opinion that it was a dangerous policy to allow free blacks to reside in a slave society. This statement and the rulings they made demonstrated that Napton and Scott did not share Judge Tompkins's presumption that slavery was evil and should be restricted. Instead, Napton's principles presumed that slavery would continue indefinitely in Missouri and the South, and that freedom among blacks must be limited. And yet to that time the court had overturned no freedom suit precedent, although it soon took a bolder course.[36]

During this time of intensified proslavery sentiment in society and on the court, Dred Scott, a St. Louis slave, on April 6, 1846, petitioned the St. Louis circuit court for the right to sue his owner Irene Emerson for his

35. 7 Mo. Rep. 2 and 9 Mo. Rep. 2. William B. Napton diary, August 1850, William B. Napton papers, Missouri Historical Society, St. Louis, Missouri; hereinafter cited as Napton papers. The freedom suit referred to was *Randolph v. Alsey*. Randolph's counsel had failed to challenge the judge's instructions to the jury and therefore could not appeal the jury's decision upon that basis. 8 Mo. Rep. 656–57.

36. The freedom suits decided during Napton's tenure as judge on the court were *Rennick v. Chloe* (1841), 7 Mo. Rep. 197–205; *Randolph v. Alsey* (1844), 8 Mo. Rep. 656–57; *Chouteau v. Pierre* (1845), 9 Mo. Rep. 3–10; and *Charlotte v. Chouteau* (1847), 11 Mo. Rep. 193–201.

freedom. This petition was granted and the case came to trial on June 30, 1847. However, after his first case was lost, Scott's lawyers appealed, noting variances in the witnesses' testimony from their pretrial depositions. When Judge Alexander Hamilton agreed to hear Scott's case, the lawyers of Emerson appealed to the Missouri Supreme Court to prevent the suit from being retried.[37] However, because no final judgment had been rendered in the case, the supreme court refused to hear Emerson's appeal and the case was retried in circuit court on January 12, 1850. The jury found in favor of Scott and this time it was Emerson's lawyers who sought a new trial. After this motion was rejected, they appealed again to the Missouri Supreme Court.[38]

By the time Scott's case was argued before the Missouri Supreme Court in October 1850, four years had elapsed since Scott's original petition for his freedom. Some historians, noting the hardening of the proslavery element in Missouri and the South during this time, have credited the delay with being an important factor in Scott losing his case before the Missouri Supreme Court. However, the court of the 1840s had stated in unequivocal terms a new policy not to rule in favor of freedom for slaves. Given the intensity of Napton's and Scott's proslavery bias, little question exists that they would have ruled against Dred Scott whenever the case came before them. Certainly, according to Napton, this was their intention: "I had previously frequently canvassed with Judge Scott on the subject, and he and I had often declared our determination to overrule the old decisions of our court."[39]

37. Dred Scott's petition, 6 April 1846; John M. Krum's approval of petition, 6 April 1846; Irene Emerson's not guilty plea to the charge of assault and battery and false imprisonment, 19 November 1846; affidavit filed by Samuel M. Bay, 10 July 1847; George W. Goode's appeal to the Missouri Supreme Court to overturn Judge Hamilton's decision for retrial; and legal documents of *Dred Scott v. Emerson*, Missouri State Archives, Jefferson City, Missouri; hereinafter cited as Dred Scott documents. For a helpful discussion of the possible involvement of Irene Emerson's brother John Sanford in the case and his connection to the prominent, proslavery Chouteau family in St. Louis see Kenneth Kaufman, *Dred Scott's Advocate: A Biography of Roswell M. Field* (Columbia: University of Missouri Press, 1996), 168–71.

38. Fehrenbacher, *Dred Scott Case*, 132. Hugh A. Garland's and Lyman D. Norris's motion for a new trial, 19 January 1850; motion for retrial overruled, 13 February 1850; and the transcript of *Dred Scott v. Emerson* in the St. Louis Circuit Court, 23 February 1850, Dred Scott documents. 11 Mo. Rep., 413.

39. Fehrenbacher, *Dred Scott Case*, 133. Finkelman, *Imperfect Union*, 222–23. The likelihood that the court would have ruled against Scott is bolstered by the later behavior of both

Once again, by 1850 the Missouri Supreme Court's personnel had changed, leaving only Judge Napton from the former court. His new colleagues were James H. Birch and John F. Ryland. Both of these men were native Southerners, but of the two Birch was the more staunchly proslavery. Moreover, while Ryland was a Benton Democrat, Birch was a very partisan anti-Benton Democrat who in 1849 had sued Thomas H. Benton for slander.[40]

Because there was no new issue to consider in the freedom suit—the case was almost identical to *Rachael v. Walker*—the decision to review Scott's case indicated that at the very least the court wanted to reconsider the decisions of its predecessors. Observers of the court, with a knowledge of the precedent established in the 1840s and the strong proslavery views of both Napton and Birch, probably recognized that some modification of the law was imminent. However, few could have known that Napton and Birch intended to hand down a decision that would end all freedom suits and irreversibly politicize the issue in a dramatic way. One observer, Edward Bates, suspecting that something was up, asked Judge Ryland about the case. What he learned concerned him very much.

> Judge Ryland, last afternoon told me that the majority of the Court—Judges Napton & Birch—were about soon to give an opinion overruling all former decisions of the Supreme Court, declaring negro slaves emancipated by a residence Northwest of the Ohio, in virtue of the Ordinance of 1787. They assume, he says, that Congress has no power to legislate upon the subject of slavery in the Territories, and consequently, all the enactments on that subject are merely void! Judge Ryland expects to write a counter opinion. And thus we see how dangerous it is to put upon the Bench, mere partizan politicians, especially the bench of the highest courts. These two judges will undertake to nullify all the acts of Congress, on this subject, from the ordinance of '87 down to the Oregon bill; and to overrule the dozens of decisions by this same court, and a regular train of decisions to the like effect, by the supreme Court of Louisiana.[41]

Judge Napton and Judge Scott, who demonstrated their willingness to overturn precedent in freedom suits.

40. Fehrenbacher, *Dred Scott Case*, 134. 26 Mo. Rep., 153–63.

41. Bates diary, 26 October 1850, Bates papers. Fehrenbacher, *Dred Scott Case*, 133–34. Finkelman, *Imperfect Union*, 222–23.

As will be seen, in overturning precedent in freedom suits, it was unnecessary for the court to hand down so radical a decision. It is clear, however, that the charged political atmosphere of state and national politics had prompted Napton and Birch to toss aside all pretense of making a judicial decision. In addition to the Benton controversy in Missouri politics, the state had just endured one of its most volatile elections for representatives to the state legislature and Congress. Because of the split in the Democratic Party, for the first time the Whig Party had a very good chance of electing a large number of candidates to Missouri's General Assembly. Benton Democrats, who were in agreement with the Whig Party that Congress had the power to restrict slavery in the territories, worked together with Whigs to defeat anti-Benton Democrats. For these reasons, much bitterness existed between the two factions of the Democratic Party.[42]

Once again events intervened to delay a decision in *Scott v. Emerson*, for Missouri's constitution was amended, ending the term of the justices then on the supreme court and making the office elective. Although Napton and Birch also stood for reelection, the voters retained only Judge Ryland and elected Gamble and former judge Scott to join him. These events prevented Napton from delivering his controversial decision.[43]

To this time, except for the brief interval when he had served as a state legislator, Gamble had sought to remain apart from the turmoil and controversy of public life. As has already been noted, his membership in the American Colonization Society demonstrated his support for a moderate and gradual solution to the slavery problem. At the same time, Gamble owned a small number of slaves, usually from three to six, primarily to assist his wife in maintaining their home. In 1827 he had purchased his first slave, Abraham, who was then twelve years of age. His largest purchase was of six slaves in 1833 for $1,600. According to Gamble's financial records

---

42. Boman, *Abiel Leonard*, 149–53. According to Fehrenbacher, Napton was reluctant to overturn the Missouri Compromise. Here Fehrenbacher relies on an 1857 entry in Napton's diary. However, the contemporary testimony of Bates in his diary contradicts Napton's recollections. Moreover, other entries in Napton's diary demonstrate his very strong animus against the Missouri Compromise. Fehrenbacher, *Dred Scott Case*, 134. Napton diary, August 1850, 1854, and 1857, Napton papers.

43. Fehrenbacher, *Dred Scott Case*, 134.

and the Census, some of these slaves were sold to others. However, because Gamble's records are incomplete, it is difficult to determine whether these slaves were bought for others or were unsatisfactory to him for some reason. Moreover, he occasionally hired slaves for temporary needs. By 1850 Gamble owned six slaves, two of whom were women ages twenty-four and thirty-nine, two girls ages thirteen and four, and two boys ages thirteen and eight.[44] Despite this, his actions later during the Civil War indicate that his greatest concern was not the preservation or the abolition of slavery, but rather the preservation of the country's constitutional system and peace between the slave states and the free states. Slavery, therefore, was of secondary importance to him, even though throughout his life he had lived in the South and was himself a slaveholder.[45]

During Gamble's tenure on the Missouri Supreme Court, most slavery cases were noncontroversial, involving issues of slave hire, sale, debt collection, or the settlement of estates. Because most of these suits were heard after the *Dred Scott* case (which had determined conclusively how freedom suits would be adjudicated), the issues decided were largely routine in nature, hardly touching on any factious matter. For this reason, most of these cases were decided unanimously, including a freedom suit that followed the precedent established in *Scott v. Emerson*. However, Gamble and his colleagues did clarify certain aspects of slave property law, the regulation of slave assemblies, and free black rights. In a suit involving the hire of a slave who was killed, Gamble ruled that the hirer was liable to the owner for the slave's value if he failed to inform the owner about the dangerous nature of the work the slave would be doing. In other suits, the court ruled on slave property issues concerning insurance to cover "slave cargo," slaves used as security in loans, slaves as dowers, and warranties

44. Bill of sale for Abraham from George W. Atchison and William G. Pettus to Gamble, 18 July 1827; bill of sale for Sarah from Abraham B. Dewitt to Gamble, 3 April 1829; slave hire accounts with Sam Merry, 29 October 1832; bill of sale for six slaves from Samuel Merry to Gamble, 27 July 1833; bill of sale for Dorcas from John Hempstead to Gamble, 3 March 1834; bill of sale for three slaves from Yeats family to Gamble, 8 January 1835; bill of sale for Simon Bolivar from Archibald Gamble to Gamble, 25 August 1847; bill of sale for Sukey and her daughter Ellen from John Lay to Gamble, 10 September 1847; and bill of sale for woman and two children from Gamble to B. M. Lynch, 31 October 1849; Gamble papers. 1830 St. Louis Census, 359. 1840 St. Louis Census, 142. 1850 St. Louis Census, 511.

45. In subsequent chapters, these issues will be explored fully.

guaranteeing slaves' good health in their sale. One of Gamble's decisions ruled that a white man could not be indicted for attending or allowing an unlawful slave gathering unless indictment stated why the meeting was illegal. Finally, in a very unusual slave property suit, Judge Scott ruled that Margaret Davis, who had been freed by her master Evans, had no title to her daughter Patsey, even though Evans until then had allowed Davis to raise Patsey without any interference. Davis's lawyer argued that Evans's behavior indicated that Patsey was also free, but Scott ruled otherwise. He also asserted that under Missouri law a free black could not own a slave. While concurring in most of Scott's opinion, both Gamble and Ryland stated their opinion that a free black under Missouri law could own a slave.[46]

While these slave cases established important precedents regarding matters of slave property and the regulation of slaves and free blacks in Missouri, their importance is minimal in comparison to that of the *Dred Scott* case, which was argued before Gamble and his colleagues during the March 1852 term of the court. However, on the surface at least, nothing about this freedom suit was unusual, so that when Lyman D. Norris stood to represent Irene Emerson, most lawyers attending the court that day probably expected a routine argument and an eventual decision based on the facts of the case and precedents established in previous cases. Nevertheless, some indication of the imminent change in freedom suit jurisprudence was foreshadowed in Norris's argument, which was quite remarkable for its tone and criticism of former justices of the Missouri Supreme Court. First, Norris, apparently giving full vent to his proslavery beliefs, ridiculed Justice George Tompkins as "the great apostle of freedom at that day." Norris also stated that Tompkins "was deeply tinged with sentiments and opinions dangerous to the existence of that 'peculiar institution,' known as domestic slavery."[47] Norris then reviewed the court's previous decisions in freedom suits until he came to *Rachael v. Walker*, of which he took particular notice because of its similarity to *Scott v. Emerson*

46. For these suits see 15 Mo. Rep. 191–93, 240–44, 400–403, 494–99, and 595–97; 16 Mo. Rep. 98–101, 114–24, 411–16; 17 Mo. Rep. 58–64 and 359–62; 18 Mo. Rep. 249–52, 411–15, and 481–85; 19 Mo. Rep. 40–42, 204–11, 312–16, 379–80, 404–6, 453–54; and 20 Mo. Rep. 146–49. The freedom suit heard by the court after *Scott v. Emerson* was *Sylvia v. Kirby*, 17 Mo. Rep. 434–35.

47. 15 Mo. Rep. 577.

and Gamble's involvement in it as a lawyer. He noted that Walker, like Dr. Emerson, had been a military officer ordered to a post where slavery was prohibited, and that both men, nevertheless, had brought their slaves with them. He then stated candidly that there was no great difference in the facts of both cases and if Judge McGirk's precedent was allowed to stand his client's case would fail.[48]

In the main part of his argument, Norris contended that the early court under Tompkins's leadership had wrongly ruled that the Ordinance of 1787 was still in force after the ratification of the U.S. Constitution, unaware of or ignoring the fact that Congress under the new Constitution had also passed the ordinance making it law. "The dictum, 'once a free man, always a free man,' though founded about as deeply in law, history and reason as, that 'all men are born free and equal,' was received with equally blind faith, and these two points, which presented, in fact, the principal issues, were considered (if at all) as unimportant and ineffectual to protect the rights of citizens of slave States."[49]

In his concluding remarks, Norris argued that whenever the Missouri Compromise interfered with the laws of Missouri, it should be disregarded. He also asserted that Missouri's courts should not enforce the laws of other states when their enforcement resulted in Missouri's citizens losing their property. Moreover, he believed that the court was wrong to rule that slaves remained free once they returned to slave soil. In support of this contention, Norris cited the then recent U.S. Supreme Court decision in *Strader v. Graham* and ended his case with Judge Napton's "words of wisdom" concerning the inadvisability of encouraging emancipation in a slave state.[50]

In D. B. Hill's response to Norris in support of Scott's case for freedom, he focused on the facts and precedent in the case. Moreover, he did not respond extensively to the innovations of Norris's argument and the proslavery opinions he expressed, understanding correctly that the court's decision whether or not to follow its own precedent would determine Scott's status.[51]

In their explication of the court's decision in *Scott v. Emerson*, scholars

48. Ibid., 576–78.
49. Ibid., 579.
50. Ibid., 580–81.
51. Ibid., 581–82.

have not accounted for the fact that Judge William Scott's opinion was not as far-reaching as the one Napton had prepared. Given his strongly held proslavery and states' rights views, it is at first surprising that Judge Scott did not rule, as Napton had intended, that the Ordinance of 1787 and the Missouri Compromise were unconstitutional. Moreover, scholars have not accounted for Ryland's concurrence despite his intention to write a dissenting opinion to Napton's earlier decision. However, with Gamble's determination to rule according to law and precedent in freedom suit cases, Judge Scott, unlike his predecessor Napton, did not have a colleague to support his more radical decision. All of these facts point to a Scott-Ryland compromise in conference. This interpretation best explains Scott's "restraint" in not addressing the issue of congressional power and Ryland's agreement to overturn almost three decades of precedent in freedom suits.[52]

Judge Scott's majority opinion consisted of a legal and a moral argument. The first was founded on the important issue of the conflict of laws. As noted above, previous to this the Missouri Supreme Court had freed slaves whose masters had brought them into free territory or states to reside where slavery was prohibited. Scott, however, was unwilling to enforce free state statutes he considered "hostile" to Missouri law. While he paid lip service to the notion of cooperation between states in upholding the laws of another jurisdiction, Scott stated that he was unwilling to go so far as to allow the property rights of Missouri's citizens to be violated. Such decisions of the court had provided "a humiliating spectacle" in which, according to him, the courts treated slaveowners and their rights with contempt. Scott also argued that the enforcement of free state law was inconvenient and thereby unreasonable for those living along Missouri's border near free territory.

> If one of our slaves touch that soil with his master's assent, he becomes entitled to his freedom. Considering the numberless instances in which those living along an extreme frontier would have occasion to occupy their slaves beyond our boundary, how hard would it be if our courts should liberate all the slaves who should thus be employed. How unreasonable to ask it. If a master sends his slave to hunt his horses or cattle beyond the boundary, shall he thereby be liberated? . . . Laws operate only within the territory of

52. See Fehrenbacher, *Dred Scott Case*, 121–39.

the State for which they are made, and by enforcing them here, we, contrary to all principle, give them an extra-territorial effect.[53]

By introducing this worst-case scenario, Scott had two purposes in mind. The first was to prejudice the readers of his decision against extending comity in freedom suits and to divert attention away from the fact that slaveholders had lost their slaves only after having illegally introduced slavery into free territory. It is apparent that Judge Scott did not consider it humiliating for a free state to have slavery forced on it in this way. Moreover, the scenario was very misleading, for no slaveholder had ever lost a slave in a freedom suit in such a manner. In fact in *La Grange v. Chouteau* (1828), the supreme court had ruled that a slave's presence in Illinois for a few days to unload a boat did not make him free. Likewise, the right of transit to slaveholders bringing their slaves through free states and territories had been maintained by both free and slave states to this time.[54]

In support of his denial of comity, Scott agreed with Irene Emerson's lawyer that if a slave returns with his master after having been in a country that does not permit slavery, he remains a slave. In support of this, Scott cited *Strader v. Graham*, a case decided recently by the U.S. Supreme Court. In this Kentucky case slave musicians had been allowed to travel in Ohio and other states giving concerts. In January 1841, the slaves escaped from a steamboat owned by Strader. Graham, the owner of the slaves, sued Strader for the loss of his property. Strader claimed that the slaves were made free through their frequent travels into free states. The Kentucky court of appeals disagreed, ruling that the slaves' travels had not made them free. Strader appealed the case to the U.S. Supreme Court, which ruled that it did not have jurisdiction. In *obiter dicta* Chief Justice Roger B. Taney, who would later write the majority opinion in Dred Scott's case before the nation's highest tribunal, argued that a slave state must determine for itself the status of a slave returning from a free state.[55] Referring to this decision, Judge Scott asserted that while cooperation between slave states and free states had occurred in the past, circumstances had changed over the years, making it impossible any longer for Missouri to free slaves

53. Ibid., 583–84.
54. 2 Mo. Rep. 20–23.
55. Fehrenbacher, *Dred Scott Case*, 135–36.

in order to please those hostile to the important and vital institution of slavery in the South. Having thus explained his reasons for rejecting freedom suit precedent, Scott vented his wrath, blaming Northerners for the establishment of slavery in the United States. "Although we may, for our own sakes, regret that the avarice and hard-heartedness of the progenitors of those who are now so sensitive on the subject, ever introduced the institution among us, yet we will not go to them to learn law, morality or religion on the subject." [56] In the final part of his opinion, Judge Scott followed the lead of John C. Calhoun and other Southern writers who argued that slavery was beneficial to slaves and was "much more hurtful to the master than the slave." According to Scott, slaves were much better off than their counterparts in Africa, where they lived in ignorance and without God. [57]

As noted in the previous chapter, Scott sometimes strayed from precedent to rule in a manner he thought "best tended to subserve the ends of justice." It is not surprising, then, given his strong proslavery beliefs, that he ruled against Dred Scott and overturned very clear precedent in freedom suits. However, one cannot help but remember his own statement seven years before when in another freedom suit he had argued that Missouri's laws should not be "openly set at defiance . . . under the pretence of administering justice." [58]

GAMBLE'S DISSENT

In his decision Judge Scott blamed Northern criticism of slavery for making it impossible, or at least undesirable, for him to uphold almost thirty years of precedent in freedom suit jurisprudence. To him and other proslavery ideologues, accommodation or compromise with abolitionists and other critics of slavery could no longer be maintained. To Gamble, Judge Scott's proposition was dangerous to the country's political and legal system. Without respect for the opinions of others and for legal principles and precedent, Gamble believed that societal order and stability would be undermined, setting the country on a course to dissolution of the Union and possible destruction of the government. Such forebodings required

56. 15 Mo. Rep. 586–87.
57. Ibid., 587.
58. *Chouteau v. Pierre*, 9 Mo. Rep. 3–10.

no special prescience or wisdom, for by the spring of 1852, when the court's decision was announced, the country had already been through several years of turmoil over the slavery issue. Beginning with the Texas annexation issue, the crisis had gathered momentum with the acquisition of new territories at the conclusion of the Mexican War. Hoping to change the balance of slave and free states in Congress, Northerners and Southerners struggled to bring these new territories into the Union with their own favored labor system. This struggle would continue in the halls of Congress almost without interruption until the beginning of the Civil War. While a temporary respite from the sectional conflict was gained through the passage of a series of bills that came to be known as the Compromise of 1850, the question of the status of the newly acquired territories was not resolved, for the legislation addressed the issue ambiguously, allowing both Northern and Southern congressmen to proclaim the matter resolved victoriously for their side. Despite these claims, the sectional conflict soon heated up again thanks to the publication of *Uncle Tom's Cabin* and increasing friction between the North and South over the enforcement of one element of the compromise, the Fugitive Slave Law. From these disputes emerged others, providing a certain momentum to the bitterness and hostility between the sections over which Gamble and many of his moderate countrymen became increasingly concerned.[59]

Another important issue raised by Judge Scott's decision concerned the nature of the judiciary and its relationship to the other branches of government. Through the years Gamble's faith in limited government and clearly defined spheres of authority apparently had never wavered. This balance of power, he believed, was threatened by Scott's decision, which infringed on the prerogatives of the legislature. All three branches of the government must maintain these boundaries scrupulously, for without them the balance and limitations on governmental power are eroded, leading ultimately to the loss of the liberty and rights of citizens. As a judge, Gamble believed his responsibilities included not only protecting the judiciary from encroachments by the executive and legislative branches, but also in refraining from exercising the powers of the other branches of government. As a legislator a few years before, he had sought to main-

59. For a more complete account of the circumstances and aftermath of the Compromise of 1850 see David M. Potter, *The Impending Crisis: 1848–1861*, completed and edited by Don E. Fehrenbacher, the New American Nation Series (New York: Harper and Row, 1976), 90–144.

tain these same boundaries, demonstrating a consistency and attention to principle that would characterize his later duties as governor of the state as well. Noting these responsibilities in his dissent to Judge Scott's decision, Gamble stated that in considering the law and precedent of freedom suits, he was no "more at liberty to overturn them than [he] would any other series of decision." Without such judicial discipline, he believed the courts would soon become an increasingly legislative and partisan body, undermining the public's confidence in the faithful execution of its functions.[60]

While it is unknown what transpired in conference between the judges during their discussion of *Scott v. Emerson*, it is clear from his dissent that Gamble believed an important principle was at stake and that any decision straying from the facts and the law of the case could further strain the political situation in Missouri. Judge Scott probably sought to convince his colleagues that a decision similar to the one Napton had written earlier was the proper ruling. However, given Ryland's opposition to Napton's opinion declaring the Northwest Ordinance and the Missouri Compromise unconstitutional, Scott worked out the alternative, fall-back rationale for overturning freedom suit precedent that became law. While such a decision did not have the dramatic impact that Chief Justice Roger B. Taney's opinion on the U.S. Supreme Court would have, Scott's opinion, nevertheless, had the desired effect in advocating a strong proslavery position and bringing to an end the adjudication of most freedom suits in Missouri. Although a slaveowner and native Southerner himself, Gamble was unwilling to indulge his own predilections for a proslavery ruling, if he had any, believing that Judge Scott's decision would lead to further agitation of the slavery issue. To underscore his disapproval and to reiterate his commitment to the legal principles and precedents he believed were being undermined, Gamble thought it important to explain his dissent.[61]

---

60. *Journal of the House of Representatives of the State of Missouri of the First Session of the Thirteenth General Assembly, Begun and Held at the City of Jefferson, On Monday, the Eighteenth Day of November, in the Year of our Lord One Thousand Eight Hundred and Forty-Four* (Jefferson City: James Lusk, printer to the state, 1845), 111 and 212–14. *Hamilton and Treat v. St. Louis County Court*, 15 Mo. Rep. 28; *Bryson v. Bryson*, 17 Mo. Rep. 590–95; and *Smith v. Smith* and *Scott v. Emerson*, 20 Mo. Rep. 166–70 and 576–92. For a fuller discussion of these jurisprudential principles see the previous chapter.

61. Bay, *Bench and Bar*, 288. See also Fehrenbacher, *Dred Scott Case*, 137–39.

The first of these principles—and the one on which much depended—was the issue of comity, the cooperation of courts in implementing and enforcing the laws of other jurisdictions. In an effort to demonstrate that comity in freedom suits was not tendered to free states only, and thereby defuse Scott's South-versus-North rhetoric, Gamble explained that all slave states regulated emancipation, although they did so in different ways. These manumission laws in all slave states were founded on the principle that slaves, although property, were different from real estate or stock animals, for they were also persons with legal rights, including the right to gain their freedom under special circumstances. Here Gamble was answering the argument of Emerson's counsel Norris, who scoffed at the natural rights ideology on which freedom suit statutes were founded. Gamble believed that these statutes, having been passed by representatives of the people in each state, should be enforced. Therefore, although he did not state the matter explicitly, Gamble believed Judge Scott was denying the people the right to regulate slavery through their representatives. Moreover, to Gamble more was involved in the case than simply the protection of the property of slaveholders—something that Judge Scott had forgotten or ignored—for the legislatures of slave states had tendered the right, whether derived from natural or positive law, to slaves under limited circumstances to sue for their freedom.[62]

Another important principle Gamble defended was the right of any state to prohibit or foster slavery within its territory as it saw fit. This right was important, for it was the basis on which comity was founded and ensured that the sovereignty of each state was given proper respect. Therefore, it made no difference whether a slaveholder emancipated a slave by will, by some other means in his own state, or by voluntarily taking his slave to a free state or territory, for in every instance by law the slave was free. A slaveholder, Gamble believed, could not possibly be unaware of these facts. Such cooperation between slave and free states also enabled the free flow of commerce and immigration to an extent otherwise impossible.[63]

Finally, in rendering judicial decisions, Gamble considered it impera-

62. 15 Mo. Rep. 588.
63. Ibid., 589.

tive to make them apart from the controversies of the day, for otherwise the courts would be swayed to and fro by the temporary winds of change and disturbances. For this reason, regardless of whether he "doubted or denied the propriety" of former decisions, Gamble did not consider himself or anyone else free to deviate from the text of the law and precedent established by the court. Moreover, he could detect "nothing in the law relating to slavery which distinguishes it from the law on any other subject." The only difference was "the temporary public excitements" that clouded people's judgment and excited the passions of those on both sides of the dispute. In spite of such disturbances,

> it is proper that the judicial mind, calm and self-balanced, should adhere to principles established when there was no feeling to disturb the view of the legal question upon which the rights of parties depend. . . . The cases here referred to are cases decided when the public mind was tranquil, and when the tribunals maintained in their decisions the principles which had always received the approbation of an enlightened public opinion. Times may have changed, public feeling may have changed, but principles have not and do not change; and, in my judgment, there can be no safe basis for judicial decisions, but in those principles which are immutable.[64]

Throughout his dissent, Gamble registered a measured and mild rebuke to his colleagues for allowing themselves to surrender to what he hoped would be only a temporary disturbance of public discourse. Hardly "a stinging dissent," as one scholar has described it, instead Gamble sought to calm the passions of his fellow Missourians and to remind everyone that they should obey the law and that judges should enforce it. Moreover, he correctly anticipated the danger that such excitements posed to the Union. A few years later during the secession crisis, first as a private citizen and then as governor, he would again attempt to calm the stormy waters of Missouri politics and prevent a much more serious breach of the public peace. However, this circumstance was still in the future and unknown to Gamble and his contemporaries.[65]

64. Ibid., 590–92.
65. Finkelman, *Imperfect Union*, 227.

Chapter Five

A New Beginning

After serving three years on the Missouri Supreme Court as chief justice, Hamilton R. Gamble resigned in October 1854. Believing that the arduous nature of his duties had harmed his health, he wished for more time to supervise his children's educations and interests. Moreover, at fifty-five years of age and with a sizeable fortune accumulated, Gamble desired a quiet retirement during which he could indulge his interest in literature and history. Unfortunately, to the detriment of his personal predilections and well-being, the period of Gamble's semiretirement would be brief and ended in the most arduous and trying labors of his life as governor of Missouri during the Civil War.

In making his decision to resign, Gamble apparently consulted his colleagues on the court, John F. Ryland and William Scott, and suggested his successor be Abiel Leonard, a fellow Whig well-respected by the state bar for his profound legal knowledge and integrity. Justices Ryland and Scott and lawyers across the state received this suggestion enthusiastically, leading to Leonard's election on January 1, 1855, by a large majority against his opponent, former supreme court justice William B. Napton. Apparently delighting in his newfound freedom from the duties of the Missouri Supreme Court, Gamble joked with others on election day about electing such a "fishy Whig" as Leonard to the court.[1]

1. 18 Mo. Rep. 381–400, 410, and 416–80. See also Charles D. Drake to Abiel Leonard, 21 October 1854; and John C. Richardson to Abiel Leonard, 30 October 1854; members of the St. Louis bar to Abiel Leonard, 1 November 1854; and Jo. Davis to Abiel Leonard, 1 January 1855, Leonard papers. For an account of Abiel Leonard's election to the Missouri Supreme Court see

Gamble's resignation from the Missouri Supreme Court, however, did not leave him completely idle. Although considering himself a full-time lawyer no longer, Gamble continued to represent clients on a limited basis, taking only important and lucrative cases. Most of these were controversies over the rightful heirs or owners of valuable land. One of the first cases he took after his resignation was *Cutter v. Waddingham*, in which the ownership of very valuable land in St. Louis was disputed. The difficulty and importance of the case led Roswell M. Field, one of the foremost experts on land law in Missouri, to request Gamble to provide an opinion on legal questions in the case. Moreover, by employing Gamble, Field ensured that he did not represent the other side in the suit. Gamble's expertise in land cases was well known and led to his arguing three suits before the U.S. Supreme Court during the December terms in 1858 and 1859. Gamble was successful in two of these.[2]

In the period prior to the Civil War, several cases on which Gamble had written opinions came before the U.S. Supreme Court. All of these were upheld, although an attempt was made in the newspapers to misrepresent the facts in *Kissell v. St. Louis Public Schools*. In response to this effort, Gamble wrote to William Thomas Carroll, clerk of the U.S. Supreme Court, Missouri Congressman Luther M. Kennett, and U.S. Senator Henry S. Geyer, who was arguing the case for the St. Louis public schools. In his letter to Carroll, Gamble included an editorial published in the St. Louis *Missouri Republican* on December 28, 1855, correcting the misrepresentations published in the New York *Herald* and the *National Intelligencer*. Carroll replied to Gamble's letter assuring him that the justices were aware of the errors and would not be swayed by them. Congressman Kennett arranged for the publication of an editorial in the *Missouri Republican* to be included in the *National Intelligencer* and also wrote a cor-

---

Dennis K. Boman, *Abiel Leonard: Yankee Slaveholder, Eminent Jurist, and Passionate Unionist*, Studies in American History, vol. 38 (Lewiston: Edwin Mellen, 2002), 176–79.

2. 22 Mo. Rep. 206–91. Roswell M. Field to Hamilton R. Gamble, 19 March 1855; John Wickham to Hamilton R. Gamble, 28 March 1855, Gamble papers. *Easton v. Salisbury* and *Fenn v. Holme*, 62 U.S. Rep. 426–32 and 481–88; and *Berthold et al. v. McDonald et al.*, 63 U.S. Rep. 334–41. For a fuller understanding of the particulars of *Cutter v. Waddingham* see Kenneth C. Kaufman, *Dred Scott's Advocate: A Biography of Roswell M. Field* (Columbia: University of Missouri Press, 1996), 126–37. Boman, *Abiel Leonard*, 182, 209–10.

rection for the New York *Herald*. Moreover, Kennett had arranged for Reverdy Johnson, counsel representing Kissell, to write a letter correcting all errors.[3]

After his resignation from the Missouri Supreme Court, Gamble intended never again to run for political office, although others, recognizing his personal popularity and high reputation among voters, sought to change his mind. Leaders of the American Party—among whom were many of Gamble's former Whig friends—urged him to join their party. By this time the Whig Party had lost its vigor and many of its former adherents wished to establish a new political party to rival the Democrats, who had dominated Missouri and national politics for three decades. Nationally, the American Party exploited anti-Catholic and anti-immigrant sentiment and the dissatisfaction of many Northern Democrats with Presidents Franklin Pierce and James Buchanan, who respectively had supported the Kansas-Nebraska bill and the Lecompton Constitution. In Missouri the American Party, with most of its support in St. Louis, was not nativist or anti-Catholic, for such positions were inimical to the large German and Irish immigrant population there. Additionally, in the rest of the state the appeal of the American Party was limited, for most Missourians supported the Kansas-Nebraska bill and the Lecompton Constitution, which made possible the extension of slavery into Kansas.[4]

In 1857 calls came for Gamble to run as the American candidate for governor. The following year friends sought to persuade him to run for mayor of St. Louis and later nominated him for Congress. He declined all of these nominations. His refusal to seek political office stemmed from his dislike of the rough and tumble of Missouri politics and his concern that his opponents would misrepresent him as an abolitionist, a prospect that

3. William Thomas Carroll to Hamilton R. Gamble, 3 January 1856; Luther M. Kennett to Hamilton R. Gamble, 4 January 1856; and Henry S. Geyer to Hamilton R. Gamble, 7 January 1856, Gamble papers. St. Louis *Missouri Republican*, 28 December 1855. Gamble's other decisions appealed to the U.S. Supreme Court were *Gamache et al. v. Piquignot et al.*, 57 U.S. Rep. 451–69; and *Ham v. State of Missouri*, 59 U.S. Rep. 126–34.

4. Some of Gamble's Whig friends who had joined the American Party were John C. Richardson, Samuel T. Glover, and Samuel M. Breckinridge. For the development of the American Party in Missouri see Perry McCandless, *A History of Missouri*, vol. 2 (Columbia: University of Missouri Press, 1972), 265–70. John V. Mering, *The Whig Party in Missouri*, University of Missouri Studies, vol. 91 (Columbia: University of Missouri Press, 1967), 203–5.

he found particularly distasteful. Apparently, he also feared that the American Party was founded more on political expediency than principle and he recommended that the American and Whig parties cooperate to elect "conservatives." In this way the two parties could combine their strength to defeat Democratic nominees.[5] Moreover, Gamble was reluctant to seek and fill political office for personal reasons. Having accumulated a large estate over three decades, much of his time was occupied with its management. This estate, with an estimated value of over $117,000 at his death, consisted of stock investments, five-and-a-quarter city lots in St. Louis, two lots in St. Anthony Falls, Minnesota, where he planned to build a summer cottage, and agricultural land in St. Charles County totaling 426 acres.[6]

Adding to his other holdings in 1856, Gamble purchased 829 acres in Franklin County. During the spring and summer of 1857, he spent most of his time supervising the construction of buildings and the cultivation of crops. Gamble believed his personal supervision of these improvements was necessary to ensure that the enterprise was successful, for his son and namesake, who was then coming of age, would eventually take over management of the farm and was "without any experience, and the negroes who are to be put upon it are young and require training and control."[7]

Another matter of considerable interest to Gamble was the establishment of excellent educational institutions for his children and the community. Over the years he had supported different schools both monetarily and professionally. In 1848 Gamble had sent his son Hamilton to the St. Louis English and Classical High School, where he remained for several years in preparation for college. In 1854 Gamble wrote to Thomas H. Benton, who was then serving in the U.S. House of Representatives, seek-

5. Charles S. Rannels to Gamble, 9 February 1857; and Gamble to Charles S. Rannels, 17 February 1857; Gamble papers. See also the Liberty *Weekly Tribune*, 12 February 1858; and the Jefferson City *Inquirer*, 12 June 1858.

6. Probate record 6711, Civil Courts building, St. Louis, Missouri. Wilbert Henry Rosin, "Hamilton Rowan Gamble: Missouri's Civil War Governor" (Ph.D. diss., University of Missouri-Columbia, 1960), 34–37. In the 1860 Pennsylvania Census Gamble listed himself a "gentleman" with a personal net worth of $150,000 and real estate estimated at $275,000; 1860 Pennsylvania Census, Borough of Norristown.

7. J. W. Wilson to Hamilton R. Gamble, 27 September 1856; J. F. Smith to Hamilton R. Gamble, 10 February 1857; and Hamilton R. Gamble to Charles S. Rannels, 17 February 1857, Gamble papers.

ing a West Point commission for his son Hamilton. However, in this he was unsuccessful.[8]

Sometime in 1859 Gamble moved to Norristown, Pennsylvania, where he believed his two youngest children, Mary and David, who were then sixteen and fifteen years of age, would benefit from the region's superior schools. However, he intended to return to Missouri when his children reached maturity. Therefore, Gamble retained his family and professional ties to Missouri and occasionally visited during the short interim of his departure from Missouri until the Civil War. During this period Gamble observed with increasing alarm the tumultuous condition of state and national politics. In Missouri, after passage of the Kansas-Nebraska bill and the controversy surrounding the Lecompton Constitution, the Benton Democrats and Whigs united temporarily, taking control of the legislature and preventing the passage of strongly proslavery legislation. However, the national debate following the U.S. Supreme Court's decision in the *Dred Scott* case caused a rupture within the Benton faction of the Democratic Party. From the start this faction was held together by its devotion to Benton, some who held proslavery views, and others, concentrated in St. Louis, who nurtured antislavery and abolitionist views. Because of the *Dred Scott* controversy, some of the proslavery Benton Democrats sided with the anti-Benton faction while most of the antislavery and abolitionist Bentonites joined the Republican Party. The result of these realignments was the reassertion of the anti-Benton Democrats' control of the legislature and the governorship in 1858. During the 1859–60 legislative session this control led to the passage of a bill expelling all free blacks from the state. Fortunately for free blacks, most of whom lived in St. Louis, Governor Robert M. Stewart pocket-vetoed the bill.[9]

After this members of the Whig, American, and Republican parties

8. Accounts with the St. Louis English and Classical High School, 1848 and 1851; subscription to the Linden Wood Female College, 24 May 1854; Thomas H. Benton to Gamble, 6 November 1854; George Sleeter to Gamble, 9 December 1855; Gamble to Peter Lindell, undated letter concerning Gamble's subscription to City University, Gamble papers.

9. 1850 Census, 511. Howard K. Beale, ed., *The Diary of Edward Bates, 1859–1866* (Washington, D.C.: U.S. Government Printing Office, 1933), 94. Christopher Phillips, *Missouri's Confederate: Claiborne Fox Jackson and the Creation of Southern Identity in the Border West* (Columbia: University of Missouri Press, 2000), 220–22. Galusha Anderson, *The Story of a Border City During the Civil War* (Boston: Little, Brown, 1908), 11–14. *Proceedings of the Missouri State Convention Held in Jefferson City, June 1863* (St. Louis: George Knapp, 1863), 82–83.

established a new coalition to combine all opposition to the Democratic Party during the 1860 state and national elections. To bring and keep this coalition together was a difficult task, requiring the cooperation and tact of the leaders of these disparate groups. In February 1860 the Opposition Party held its state convention in Jefferson City. Before the convention some Whig members had balked at cooperating with Republicans, but more pragmatic members of the Opposition convinced the conservatives that it was in Missouri's and the nation's best interests to overcome their dislike for Republicans. Only the leadership and influence of longtime Whig Abiel Leonard kept the Whigs in the coalition. Because the delegates agreed on little else, the convention's accomplishments were modest: nominating Edward Bates for president and James S. Rollins for governor and passing a resolution calling for the preservation of the Union. When Bates unambiguously announced his opposition to slavery, the Opposition Party was weakened a good deal, and it broke apart completely after the Republican National Convention in Chicago, Illinois, did not nominate Bates as its presidential candidate and instead chose favorite son Abraham Lincoln.[10]

Concurrent with the Opposition Party's struggles to maintain unity, the Democratic Party struggled with its own centrifugal forces threatening to spin it asunder. Claiborne F. Jackson, the Democratic gubernatorial candidate, did not have the same standard of forthrightness in expressing his views as did Bates, and felt no compunction to present his political views in an unambiguous manner, but instead took policy positions calculated to appeal to the widest sector of the electorate. Jackson's difficulties of maintaining party unity were complicated considerably after Sample Orr, an independent candidate, entered the race and challenged him to a series of debates. These confrontations, coupled with pressure from the editor of the St. Louis *Missouri Republican* and others, forced Jackson to take positions on issues he had wished to avoid. Although a strong Southern rights and antirailroad man, to gain the editor's support Jackson backed railroad construction and the candidacy of Stephen A. Douglas. While some from the radical proslavery wing of the party defected and promoted their own

---

10. Boman, *Abiel Leonard*, 212–14. Beale, *Bates Diary*, 78. Walter H. Ryle, *Missouri: Union or Secession* (Nashville, Tenn.: George Peabody College for Teachers, 1931), 127–32.

candidate, Jackson, nevertheless, won the election. Immediately after his election in October, Jackson changed his support to Breckinridge, demonstrating that his former allegiance to Douglas had been nothing more than the calculation of a political trimmer.[11]

How Gamble reacted to these events and how closely he followed them is unknown, although it is certain that he would have been disappointed by the gubernatorial election of Jackson and the Republican Party's failure to nominate his former legal partner Edward Bates. What Gamble's initial reaction was to Lincoln's election to the presidency is also unknown. However, it seems likely that Gamble wished for the election of a less controversial moderate such as John Bell, the constitutional unionist candidate who stood on "no political principle other than *the Constitution . . . the Union . . . and the Enforcement of the Laws.*" This conclusion tends to be confirmed by Gamble's later action in aligning himself with Bell's supporters in St. Louis. Whatever his thoughts, Gamble soon sought to steady the ship of state rocked by the Southern reaction to Lincoln's election. By February 1861, seven Southern states had seceded from the Union and would be followed soon thereafter by several more.[12]

Undoubtedly, Gamble's concerns were deepened upon reading the text of Governor Jackson's inaugural address on New Year's Day 1861. In it Jackson, while maintaining his unionist pose, also argued that Missouri was bound to the South by its common institutions, customs, and sentiments, and that Missouri must share the fate of its Southern sisters. More ominous was Jackson's call for a state convention "to determine Missouri's future standing in the union of states as well as asking for legislation to strengthen the state militia." By this means Governor Jackson hoped to bring Missouri out of the Union.[13]

11. Phillips, *Missouri's Confederate*, 224–26 and 228–30. Ryle, *Missouri*, 144–48 and 155. William E. Parrish, *Turbulent Partnership: Missouri and the Union, 1861–1865* (Columbia: University of Missouri Press, 1963), 4–6. Arthur Roy Kirkpatrick, "Missouri on the Eve of the Civil War," *Missouri Historical Review* 55 (January 1961): 99–100.

12. James M. McPherson, *Battle Cry of Freedom: The Civil War Era, The Oxford History of the United States*, vol. 6, ed. C. Vann Woodward (New York: Oxford University Press, 1988), 221–22 and 234–35.

13. Ryle, *Missouri*, 179–80. Phillips, *Missouri's Confederate*, 235–36. Boman, *Abiel Leonard*, 218–19.

Strengthening Jackson's hand with the state legislature was the continued disproportionate representation of less populous and rural counties, where most of the residents were strongly proslavery and often of Southern birth. For this reason the 1861 General Assembly was composed of a majority of Breckinridge Democrats in both houses. Lieutenant Governor Thomas C. Reynolds, a leading advocate for secession, worked with secessionist legislators to organize Senate committees to place them firmly in their control. The Speaker accomplished the same in the House.[14]

Jackson's measures to establish a convention and prepare for war were not unanticipated by leaders of the unionist opposition, who were well aware of Jackson's strong support for the South. To counter this, these men organized meetings in which they argued that slavery in Missouri was safer in the Union than out. As a member of the Confederacy, they argued, Missouri's geographical position with three free states on its border would expose it to attacks from the east, north, and west. Moreover, at present slaveowners enjoyed the federal government's protection of their rights, including the return of runaways from the North under the Fugitive Slave Law. This protection, of course, would no longer be available if they seceded. Furthermore, unionists accused secessionists of using the statements and "intermeddlings" of abolitionists and Northern politicians to foment treason among Southerners, knowing full well that the Lincoln administration had no intention of interfering with slavery where it then existed legally. Finally, unionists also pointed out that secession would sever useful and lucrative economic ties to the East. Without this association Missouri could not develop its mineral resources and would lose valuable markets then available.[15]

In St. Louis, where much of Missouri's commerce with the East was carried on, unionists and secessionists jockeyed for preeminence. In January 1861 both sides organized secret military organizations and held public meetings to rally their supporters. Gamble, who was in St. Louis to attend to legal and private business, spoke at a rally held on January 12. Fifteen

14. Ryle, *Missouri*, 176, 178, 181–83, and 193. Phillips, *Missouri's Confederate*, 236. Kirkpatrick, "Eve of the Civil War," 100, 102–3.

15. Ryle, *Missouri*, 171–74 and 208–9. Boman, *Abiel Leonard*, 216–21.

hundred people attended, most of whom were Douglas and Bell men; a few Breckinridge supporters and Republicans were there as well. Gamble stated unequivocally his belief that nothing justified "the tearing down of the only fabric of constitutional liberty ever erected" and that secession could only bring ruin on Missouri and the country. Similarly, in 1832 he had opposed South Carolina's theory of nullification and its threat to secede. Throughout his speech Gamble "was interrupted . . . by loud and enthusiastic applause, and at the conclusion, the shouts . . . were perfectly deafening." This rally was the largest in St. Louis and represented the city's conservatives, who wished to quiet the rancor that extremists on both sides had fomented. Gamble's stand against secession manifested his fundamental disagreement with Southerners, who held strong traditional notions about personal and regional honor. Many secessionists argued that Northerners' criticism of slavery was an affront against their sense of honor and that now was the appropriate time to defend themselves against this calumny by withdrawing from their political association with the North and establishing a new nation where they would be respected. As a young man Gamble had shared this sense of outrage when Northerners had attached amendments to statehood legislation prohibiting slavery in Missouri. In a toast given at a public meeting in April 1821 Gamble had stated: "John Randolph; too firmly our friend to consent to our admission trammeled with any condition—a true Virginian." However, in the intervening decades to 1861, Gamble no longer considered the issue of honor to be of great importance. In place of these temporal concerns Gamble focused on eternal matters, as perhaps he might have stated it, and therefore strove to gain a deeper appreciation of the spiritual, an understanding that transformed his thinking. This transformation led him to mediate rather than to excite disputes, to find solutions to problems rather than to exploit them for personal or political advantage. In the hope of resolving the slavery issue peacefully, Gamble, while still a young man, had joined the American Colonization Movement. Similarly, his concern for the public peace had led him to support the suggestion to Elijah Lovejoy, the editor of the St. Louis *Observer*, that he refrain from commenting on the issue of slavery. This same concern had strengthened his resolve as chief justice of the Missouri Supreme Court to maintain legal precedent in the *Dred Scott* case, although from other decisions it is clear that this was a first principle of his jurisprudence.[16]

Despite Gamble's and others' efforts to rally support for the Union, Missouri's legislature moved inexorably toward passing measures that they hoped would sever its attachment to the government of the United States. Unionists in the General Assembly, unable to prevent the passage of a bill to create a state convention, maneuvered to limit its power by including a provision requiring a statewide vote before Missouri could secede. This was vigorously opposed by secessionist legislators and Jackson, but to no avail. Nevertheless, no other restrictions limiting the convention's power were imposed. Jackson and other secessionists soon regretted this.[17]

Once the convention bill had been signed into law both sides quickly mobilized their supporters and nominated candidates for the election of delegates to the state convention. Gamble, who had hoped to enjoy his retirement without the distraction of politics, soon found himself a candidate for the state convention on two different tickets: the Constitutional Union Ticket and the Citizens' Union Ticket. The Constitutional Union Ticket was supported by Bell and Douglas Democrats and some Republicans, while the Citizens' Union Ticket was backed almost exclusively by Republican voters. According to Nicholas Paschall, the editor of the St. Louis *Missouri Republican*, Gamble preferred that the nominees on the Constitutional Union Ticket be elected and that he would "not suffer his name to be used in any way to prevent the election of his associates on that ticket." Paschall also claimed that the only reason the Citizens' Union Ticket had nominated Gamble was to lend his popularity and prestige to

16. St. Louis *Missouri Republican*, 18 January 1861. Rosin, "Gamble," 51–52. *In Memoriam: Hamilton Rowan Gamble, Governor of Missouri* (St. Louis: George Knapp, 1864), 7–9. Ryle, *Missouri*, 203–4. Broadhead, "St. Louis During the Civil War," 18–21, 23–31, 40, 47, and 52–54. Christopher Phillips, *Damned Yankee: The Life of General Nathaniel Lyon* (Columbia: University of Missouri, 1990), 143–44. Thomas L. Snead, "The First Year of the War in Missouri," in *Battles and Leaders of the Civil War*, vol. 1 (Secaucus, N.J.: Castle, n.d.), 262–64. Boman, *Abiel Leonard*, 216, and 221–23. Gamble's spiritual transformation, his membership in the American Colonization Society, his advice to Elijah Lovejoy, and his decision in the *Dred Scott* case are covered in chapters 1, 2, and 4 of this book. For an excellent discussion of the issue of honor and its influence on individuals and history see Bertram Wyatt-Brown, "Honor's History Across the Academy," *Historically Speaking* 3, no. 5 (June 2002): 13–15.

17. Anderson, *Border City*, 42. Boman, *Abiel Leonard*, 219. Ryle, *Missouri*, 181–83.

their ticket. In his formal acceptance of the Constitutional Union Ticket nomination, Gamble stated his belief that at present no reason for secession existed and that any attempt to bring Missouri out of the Union would be disastrous to the interests of the state. Moreover, he argued that there could be justification for coercing a state not to secede, although he thought in most instances this would be unwise.[18]

Perhaps finding it difficult to support a former slaveowner and supporter of slavery, the German Wards printed up ballots for the Constitutional Union Ticket without Gamble's name. When the Bell men learned about this they printed a broadside the day of the election warning their voters about this. "The Anzeiger clique have given instructions that Judge GAMBLE's name should be stricken from the ticket, and it is being done in all the German Wards in the City. The intention is to beat Gamble at all hazards. Will you permit this act of treachery to be consummated? It is yet in your power to rebuke this insolence, and to elect the whole 'CONSTITUTIONAL TICKET,' upon which Judge Gamble's name appears."[19]

Despite this trick Gamble was easily elected to the state convention. The election results had turned out very favorably for unionist candidates and revealed that a large majority of Missourians were against secession, electing only union candidates to serve in the convention. Of 140,000 votes cast, antisubmission or states' rights candidates received only 30,000 votes. This result reflected the increasing influence of commercial, mining, and railroad interests of the state, which relied heavily on Northern and eastern capital, and were very much against secession. In the interior of the state where agriculture predominated, federal tariffs protected some Missouri crops and cooled the ardor of many farmers for secession who, being predominately of Southern nativity, might otherwise have been enthusiastic for the Confederate cause. Only in the regions along the Missouri River and the Kansas border did strong secessionist sentiment exist, and even there this support was far from unanimous.[20]

While the majority of Missourians supported the Union, most were

18. St. Louis *Missouri Republican*, 10, 11, and 16 April 1861.

19. Beale, *Bates' Diary*, 174.

20. Ryle, *Missouri*, 208–10. Parrish, *Turbulent Partnership*, 8–9. Anderson, *Border City*, 48. Kirkpatrick, "Eve of the Civil War," 104.

also proslavery and harbored a strong animus against the Republican Party and President-elect Lincoln. Most of the convention delegates reflected these views and only differed about the circumstances under which they would be willing to maintain the Union. As has already been noted, some conditional unionists were against the federal government enforcing its authority or forcing seceding states back into the Union. Any attempt to coerce the South was considered unconstitutional at worst, or unwise at best. However, another group, of which Gamble was a part, did not dismiss the possibility of coercing the South under extraordinary circumstances. This group would be most responsible for preventing secession in Missouri. These men were able to develop effective measures without allying themselves with abolitionists and Republicans, a political nonstarter in most of Civil War–era Missouri, St. Louis being the only prominent exception. While these measures prevented Missouri from becoming part of the Southern Confederacy, these efforts largely failed to prevent war because the secessionist minority was determined to precipitate the crisis to help the South. These efforts were aided unwittingly by the sometimes clumsy attempts of unconditional unionists to support the Union.[21]

In March 1861 the convention gathered together in Jefferson City in cramped and inadequate quarters, and where strong secessionist sentiment prevailed. Ostensibly to make use of more commodious quarters, some unionist delegates proposed that the convention adjourn to reassemble in the Mercantile Hall in St. Louis. In reality, unionists feared that some delegates might be influenced by secessionist lawmakers and Governor Jackson. Upon passage of this measure, a Missouri railroad transported the delegates free of charge to St. Louis. As described by a contemporary privy to the details of this arrangement, unionists in St. Louis hoped to influence the convention by its new surroundings.

When the Convention met for the first time in its new quarters, its members found themselves in a beautiful hall, such as some of them had never before seen. Each member was provided with a desk, and pages were at hand to do

21. St. Louis *Missouri Republican*, 12 and 14 June 1861. *Proceedings of the Missouri State Convention* (St. Louis: George Knapp, 1861), 64, 67, 84–93, 113–23, 172, 178–80, 183–84. For a different perspective arguing that Francis P. Blair Jr. as leader of the unconditional unionists was the moving force behind the convention see Ryle, *Missouri*, 198–208, 217, and 223–32.

his bidding, all at the expense of the loyal men of the city. The free use of the Mercantile Library and Reading Room, with its papers and periodicals from every part of the Union, and also of the Law Library of the city, was also tendered them. Then, by a secret prearrangement, in companies of from six to twelve, the members of the Convention were daily invited by Union men to dine with them; and, so long as the Convention continued its sessions, in the most conservative and kindly way, at the tables and in the parlors of the best and most intelligent men and women of the city, the whole question of secession in all its phases was thoroughly discussed.[22]

After the convention had finalized rules for debate, Gamble moved to establish a committee to consider Missouri's relationship to the federal government. The Committee on Federal Relations was charged with providing a report and recommendations. Gamble was named chairman of the committee that included six others, who deliberated for five days before presenting their work to the convention.[23]

The majority report, which Gamble wrote, reviewed the circumstances and crisis from the perspective of Missourians and Southerners on both sides of the secession issue. Gamble agreed that Southerners had a valid complaint about Northerners' criticism of slavery and interference in the recovery of fugitive slaves, but also asserted "that at present there is no adequate cause to impel Missouri to dissolve her connection with the Federal Union." Furthermore, he argued that legal remedies were available through the federal courts, which had never failed hitherto "to maintain the rights of Southern citizens, and to punish the violators of those rights." Moreover, he asserted that no state had the right to secede and that such a remedy would be worse than the evil it sought to correct. This was especially true of Missouri, which was surrounded by three free states to which slaves might escape. With Missouri out of the Union, no recourse for the recovery of fugitive slaves would be available, a circumstance that would force slaveholders to migrate to the South or to sell their slaves. What, Gamble wondered, could be more ironic than for Missouri to secede to

22. Anderson, *Border City*, 45. For a different perspective on the move of the convention to St. Louis see Kirkpatrick, "Eve of the Civil War," 104–5.

23. *Journal of the Missouri State Convention, Held at Jefferson City, July 1861* (St. Louis: George Knapp, 1861), 19 and 34–37. *In Memoriam*, 6. John F. Philips, "Hamilton Rowan Gamble and the Provisional Government of Missouri," *Missouri Historical Review* 5 (October 1910): 1–6.

protect slavery, and having entered "into a slaveholding confederacy," to find itself without slaves in a few years?[24]

In place of secession, Gamble offered the alternative remedy of amending the U.S. Constitution to guarantee slave property rights to the South. To achieve this goal, he called for a national convention to draft appropriate amendments to defuse the controversy and argued that the compromise measures presented by John J. Crittenden in Congress were a good starting point. By coming together in good faith with Northerners, the South could gain its rights without destroying the Union.[25]

In explaining his plan to the convention, Gamble stated that his purpose was to prevent a collision between the North and the South, and to maintain for Missouri a position of strict neutrality to mediate the dispute and prevent civil war. To understand this plan, it must be remembered that the convention's deliberations were held before Fort Sumter was fired on and while hope of resolving the dispute peacefully still remained. According to him the crisis was caused more by "the alienated feelings existing between the Northern and Southern sections of the country, than in the actual injury suffered by either; rather in the anticipation of future evils, than in the pressure of any now actually endured."[26]

While Gamble's report reflected the opinions of a majority of the committee, the convention, and the state, the perspective of a vocal and prominent minority was presented in a report by two members of the committee, John T. Redd and Harrison Hough. In their report, they complained of Northern interference with slavery and the publication of abolitionist literature, which they believed gave the South "some adequate cause" for secession. Instead of a national convention, Redd and Hough wanted a border states convention held to formulate the interests of the South before going into national convention. These interests would be presented as an ultimatum to the North, which, if rejected, would trigger the border states' departure from the Union.[27]

As debate unfolded and amendments were offered to Gamble's report, it became evident that while most members believed that it was best for

24. *Journal, March 1861*, 34–37.
25. Ibid.
26. *Journal, March 1861*, 34.
27. Ibid., 38–40.

Missouri and the slave states to remain in the Union, a significant minority was unwilling to take a neutral position in the dispute. Instead, these members sought to support the seceding states and to insist that the federal government remove its troops from forts and arsenals in the South. Moreover, they sought to place Missouri in a position to secede if the federal government took any military action against the South or if the border states seceded.[28]

Convention debate was sometimes acrimonious, revealing a good deal of animosity for the North. An issue generating a considerable amount of debate concerned the nature of the compact agreed on by the thirteen states in ratifying the U.S. Constitution. Some members of the convention agreed with radical secessionist leaders that states were sovereign and could unilaterally break away from the Union. Such a position indicated a strong leaning toward secession if Missouri was forced to take sides.[29]

Gamble and those members of the convention opposed to secession argued from historical, economic, and constitutional grounds. James O. Broadhead, an unconditional unionist and one of the founding members of Missouri's Republican Party in St. Louis, disagreed with many of the delegates' characterizations of the Republican Party as sectional, divisive, and abolitionist. He argued that a government, not "*a league of sovereign, independent States,*" was established under the U.S. Constitution. Regarding the matter of coercion, or as he restated it, the enforcement of the laws, Broadhead noted that President George Washington had not hesitated to lead troops into western Pennsylvania to put down the Whiskey Rebellion in 1794. It was important, if the government was to be preserved, "that it should have power to protect itself against the insubordination of its citizens." Furthermore, rebellion would bring economic ruin to the state and cause the loss of $45 million in slave property.[30]

The convention votes overwhelmingly supported Gamble's proposal of placing Missouri in a position to mediate the dispute between the North and the South. In convening a national convention, Northern and Southern states could consider how best to amend the Constitution and settle

28. *Journal, March 1861*, 40, 41, and 45–49, and *Journal of the Missouri State Convention, Held in Jefferson City, June 1862* (St. Louis: George Knapp, 1862), 13, and 17–18.

29. *Proceedings, March 1861*, 89, 108, 110, and 123–36.

30. Ibid., 114–23.

once and for all the divisive issue of slavery and its extension. For those nominally unionist members who were leaning strongly toward support- ing the South and secession, the plan was appealing as well, for it recom- mended no forceful action supporting the Lincoln administration. Antici- pating possible troubles ahead, Gamble also proposed that a committee be selected with the power after adjournment to reconvene the convention if circumstances intervened. This and Gamble's other resolutions passed.[31]

After the convention Gamble left Missouri, probably returning to Norristown, Pennsylvania, to see his family before traveling to Wash- ington, D.C., to consult with his brother-in-law, Attorney General Ed- ward Bates. During this period before his return to Missouri, Gamble undoubtedly still harbored the hope that he could retire "to spend his last days in the quietude of his home, undisturbed by the rude tumults of the world." This desire would soon be shattered, however, by the press of fast- changing and revolutionary events.[32]

After the convention events moved swiftly toward war. Having al- ready formed paramilitary and secret organizations, supporters of both the federal government and the Southern Confederacy maneuvered for advantage in case of war, which certainly looked imminent after the sur- render of U.S. troops at Fort Sumter. In response to Lincoln's call for soldiers, Governor Jackson refused to support the Union effort. Instead, he called state militia troops into camps of instruction. One of these was established in St. Louis and was named Camp Jackson. Building a strong military force there, Jackson authorized its commander Brigadier Gen- eral Daniel M. Frost to capture the St. Louis Arsenal in the event of a crisis. Jackson probably hoped to seize St. Louis as well, enabling him then to secure the rest of the state for the Confederacy. However, in this he was disappointed, for unionists in St. Louis led by Frank P. Blair Jr. and the St. Louis Safety Committee thwarted Jackson's plans. Unionists convinced Lincoln to appoint Captain Nathaniel Lyon as commander of the St. Louis Arsenal. Lyon, who was strongly committed to the Union, took vigorous action to protect the arsenal, strengthening the defenses

31. Ibid., 46, 47, 49, and 59.
32. Charles Bates to Onward Bates, 31 March 1861, Bates papers. *In Memoriam*, 88–89.

and seizing the high ground nearby. Moreover, arrangements were made to send most of the arsenal's weapons to Illinois to prevent their falling into the enemy's hands.[33]

After securing the St. Louis Arsenal and learning that weapons from the new Confederate government were hidden there, unionists moved to capture Camp Jackson. Captain Lyon, disguised as the elderly mother-in-law of Blair, was driven in a carriage through the militia encampment to gather intelligence about the number of troops, how well they were armed, and the topography of the land. Afterward, Lyon reported to the St. Louis Committee of Safety that Camp Jackson was "a nest of secessionists" and that he intended to capture it immediately. The committee supported Lyon's plan, leading to Frost's surrender of the camp on May 10, 1861. Lyon then marched the prisoners through town and was attacked by a pro-Southern crowd into which some of the troops discharged their weapons, killing approximately twenty-five people. The legislature, which had been deliberating on a militia bill at the time, on learning of Camp Jackson's surrender immediately passed a bill diverting all treasury funds to the militia, raised property taxes, and authorized Governor Jackson to secure a $500,000 loan for defense. Moreover, the legislature provided Jackson with the authority to put down any insurrections.[34]

These events caused many to despair of any peaceful resolution of the differences between unionist and secessionist leaders. In St. Louis, just two days after the Camp Jackson affair, a rumor circulated among supporters of the South that "the murderous Dutch (Germans) . . . were about to kill them and loot and burn their houses." In response, some barricaded

33. Broadhead, "St. Louis During the Civil War," 9–16, 32–35, 39–41, 43–46. Phillips, *Lyon*, 140–42, 150–52, 154, 159–64. John M. Schofield, *Forty-Six Years in the Army*, with a foreword by William M. Ferraro (New York: Century., 1897; reprint, Norman: University of Oklahoma Press, 1998), 33–34. Anderson, *Border City*, 73–75 and 84–85. Arthur Roy Kirkpatrick, "Missouri in the Early Months of the Civil War," *Missouri Historical Review* 55 (April 1961): 251 and 253.

34. Anderson, *Border City*, 92–93, 97, and 102–3. Snead, "First Year of the War," 265. Phillips, *Lyon*, 177–94. Schofield, *Forty-Six Years in the Army*, 36–37. Broadhead, "St. Louis During the Civil War," 49–52 and 54–55. James W. Covington, "The Camp Jackson Affair," *Missouri Historical Review* 55 (April 1961): 197–212. William Parrish, *Turbulent Partnership: Missouri and the Union, 1861–1865*, with an introduction by Robert L. D. Davidson (Columbia: University of Missouri, 1963), 21–25.

themselves in their homes, determined to fight desperately for life and hearth. The vast majority, however, filled

carriages and wagons . . . with trunks, valises, hastily made bundles, and frightened men, women, and children were flying along the streets towards every point of the compass. Some scared souls, unable to obtain a vehicle of any kind, were walking or running with breathless haste, carrying all sorts of bundles in their hands, under their arms or on their shoulders. All these were fleeing from imaginary danger. But the fancied conflagration and slaughter which they believed themselves to be escaping were to them awful realities, enacted, with all their attendant horrors, over and over again in their minds.[35]

Into this situation returned General William S. Harney, commander of the Department of the West, who had previously prevented Lyon from taking forceful action to protect the St. Louis Arsenal. Fearing that Harney, although loyal, was unequal to the emergency of the circumstances, Blair had asked the administration to replace him. Harney was ordered to Washington and Lyon had been placed in command, leading to his action to protect the arsenal and capture Camp Jackson. Harney on his way to Washington had been captured by Confederate forces but released after the leadership in Richmond realized that he would not join their cause. Upon his release, Harney finished his journey to Washington, where he was then able to persuade the Lincoln administration that he was loyal and should be returned to his post.[36]

On May 13, a day after the turmoil in St. Louis and two days after his return, Harney stated in a proclamation that civil order must be maintained, censured the legislature's passage of the military bill, and approved of the capture of Camp Jackson. In the aftermath of these events, moderate unionists sent James E. Yeatman to Washington and telegraphed Gamble to join him there. At the same time, despite Harney's vigorous action to preserve federal authority in Missouri, Blair sent Franklin A. Dick to Washington asking Lincoln again to remove Harney. Gamble and Yeatman, with Attorney General Bates's help, supported Harney, be-

35. Anderson, *Border City*, 108–10.
36. Parrish, *Turbulent Partnership*, 17–19 and 25.

lieving he would follow a more cautious and conciliatory course of action than would Lyon, who was Blair's choice for the command. On May 16, Lincoln reluctantly sent to Blair an order providing for Harney's removal. In a letter, however, Lincoln made it clear that Harney should receive the order only if in Blair's judgment "it is *indispensable*" to do so.[37]

On May 21, Harney met with General Sterling Price, commander of Missouri's militia forces, to work out an arrangement to prevent any further military confrontations between federal and state forces in Missouri. Out of this conference came the Harney-Price agreement, in which both parties agreed to keep the peace. According to James O. Broadhead, Harney had promised the St. Louis Safety Committee that he would demand the resignation of Governor Jackson and Lieutenant Governor Thomas C. Reynolds. Harney's failure to keep his promise led to his ouster when it became clear that Price and Jackson were actively preparing for armed conflict with the U.S. government.[38]

Lyon, now in command of federal forces in Missouri, quickened the recruitment of the State Guard. However, before open conflict erupted between state and federal forces, conservatives attempted to arrange an agreement between Lyon and Jackson and Price to avert violence. On June 12 the meeting took place and proved disastrous, for Lyon, who was in an uncompromising mood, refused to prevent the recruitment of U.S. troops and insisted on the strict enforcement of the laws and the Constitution within the boundaries of Missouri. This led to the hurried departure of Jackson and Price from St. Louis and the evacuation of Jefferson City with the militia forces they could pull together to meet Lyon's expected attack. Lyon did not disappoint, for he pursued Price's makeshift army through the central and western parts of Missouri, thereby cutting

37. Ibid., 25–28.
38. Ibid., 29–30. Kirkpatrick, "Early Months," 236–39. Boman, *Abiel Leonard*, 222–23. Abiel Leonard to James O. Broadhead, 3 June 1861, James O. Broadhead papers, Missouri Historical Society, St. Louis, Missouri. James O. Broadhead to Abiel Leonard, 5 June 1861, courtesy of William Everett, private collection of descendant of Abiel Leonard. Albert Castel's interpretation of this meeting is the soundest, *General Sterling Price and the Civil War in the West* (Baton Rouge: Louisiana State University Press, 1968), 14–22. Robert E. Shalhope argues that because Price was an honorable man dedicated to republican principles, he would not have acted in a "devious manner." See *Sterling Price: Portrait of a Southerner* (Columbia: University of Missouri Press, 1971), 160–64.

off the Confederacy from the pro-Southern counties in the central and northwestern parts of the state. This action also made available to federal forces the Missouri River and railroads for the rapid transport of troops and supplies. Lyon continued his vigorous campaign against Jackson and Price until his death at Wilson's Creek.[39]

The departure of Jackson and the legislature left Missouri without a state government. As noted above, the convention had followed Gamble's recommendation to establish a committee with the authority to reconvene the convention to meet any future emergency. On July 6, five members of this committee called the state convention back into session to meet later that month. Many conservatives were relieved when Gamble decided to return to Missouri to participate in the convention's meetings, fearing that radical and precipitous action could lead to warfare within the state. Others, such as the editor of the St. Louis *Missouri Republican*, warned the convention it "should not attempt to revise the Constitution nor to provide a Provisional Government." Instead, the convention should call a special election for a new governor and legislature.[40]

Arriving in St. Louis after the state convention had already convened, Gamble was appointed to the committee deliberating about what action was appropriate after Missouri's government had fled from Jefferson City. The committee had already recommended that the convention appoint a new governor, lieutenant governor, and secretary of state and that an election be held for these offices in August 1862. Moreover, the committee proposed that the state constitution be amended to increase the number of judges on the state supreme court to seven and to repeal the military acts passed during the special May 1861 session of the legislature. Arriving sometime after the debate had begun, Gamble successfully convinced the committee to remove the measure increasing the number of judges on the Missouri Supreme Court and persuaded them to move up the state elections to November 1861.[41]

39. Parrish, *Turbulent Partnership*, 31–31. Phillips, *Lyon*, 210–14. Kirkpatrick, "Early Months," 243–44, and 247.

40. St. Louis *Missouri Republican*, 7 and 24 July 1861. Edward Bates to Gamble, 16 July 1861; and James S. Rollins to Gamble, 17 July 1861, Gamble papers.

41. St. Louis *Missouri Republican*, 30 July 1861. Parrish, *Turbulent Partnership*, 33. *Journal of the Missouri State Convention, Held at Jefferson City, July 1861* (St. Louis: George Knapp, 1861), 9–12.

While a majority of the convention's members supported the committee's report, a minority vigorously opposed it. Debate focused on the intentions of the legislature in creating the convention, the nature and powers of conventions, and the constitutionality of deposing the state government and repealing legislation. Those opposed to the resolutions argued that the legislature had intended to provide the convention with very restricted and limited powers only. The debate in the legislature revealed, however, that the supporters of the bill had fought hard to provide the convention with unlimited powers, and that opponents had withheld their support until it was agreed that any secession ordinance passed must be submitted to the people. The convention was otherwise unlimited in its authority.[42]

Led by St. Louis lawyer and orator Uriel Wright, the minority also claimed that the convention did not have the power to depose state officers, asserting that only the legislature could oust an official by impeachment and conviction. Gamble, who took the lead in the debate for the majority, in style and substance was the very opposite of Wright, who was brilliant, prolix, and mercurial. Gamble, on the other hand, was described by one of the members of the convention as a speaker who relied on logic and "sincere eloquence." His response to Wright was that impeachment and conviction was the only *constitutionally* prescribed manner to remove state officials. However, he believed the convention did not derive its powers from the constitution, explaining that the convention was an "extra, and supra constitutional" body, and in all respects held the same authority as would all the people gathered together "in one vast plain." In the most dramatic exchange of the debate, Gamble challenged Wright's interpretation of the ordinance creating the convention. Moreover, Gamble demonstrated from the language of the ordinance that Wright was incorrect in his assertion that the convention must submit its work to the people. Evidently, Wright had hoped to prevent the convention from taking any forceful action.[43]

42. *Proceedings of the Missouri State Convention Held at the City of Jefferson, July 1861*, 44, 71, 69, 88, 102, and 109–11. For section ten of the ordinance restricting the convention from bringing Missouri out of the Union without submitting the matter to a vote see *Journal, March 1861*, 4.

43. St. Louis *Missouri Republican*, 2 August 1861. *Proceedings, July 1861*, 73–74, 86–87, 95, 109. Philips, "Gamble," 6 and 8–9.

Expanding on the theme of the convention's powers, Gamble extensively delved into the nature of republican government and the history and purpose of conventions. He argued that the state convention had extraordinary powers to amend, or even to abolish and replace the state constitution, so long as the new document did not conflict with the U.S. Constitution. To sustain this assertion, he reviewed the powers and actions of conventions held in different states, and cited as evidence for their wide-ranging powers those conventions that had assembled to ratify the U.S. Constitution and state constitutions without submitting their actions to the people. This certainly supported the position of those who held that a convention was equal in authority and power to the people gathered together "in one vast plain." Moreover, the thirteenth section of Missouri's constitution supported the idea that the people during emergencies might take drastic action, even so far as "altering their Constitution and form of Government, whenever it may be necessary to their safety and happiness."[44]

In the end, the arguments for deposing the state government and establishing a provisional government prevailed. Having taken the lead in these debates, Gamble was asked to draft a proclamation from the convention announcing their decision to oust the Jackson administration and the legislature, replacing it with a provisional government. In his proclamation Gamble stated that despite the convention's attempt to maintain peace in March, the actions of a treasonous governor and his administration had brought civil war to Missouri. Since then battles had been fought and blood shed. The governor had sought to bring Missouri out of the Union and now had fled the state. Because of this, there was no state government at a critical moment in Missouri's history.[45]

While Gamble prepared the convention's proclamation, other members worked to find acceptable choices for governor, lieutenant governor, and secretary of state. The consensus was almost unanimous in the selection of Gamble as governor. His nomination, along with the choice of Willard P. Hall for lieutenant governor and Mordecai Oliver for secre-

44. *Proceedings, July 1861*, 20–22, 24, 36–39, 44, 55, 62–63, and 118–19. Parrish, *Turbulent Partnership*, 212. For a different perspective on the debate on removing the state government see ibid., 31–47.

45. *Proceedings, July 1861*, 51–56.

tary of state, demonstrated the convention's intention to establish a strong unionist government that would be acceptable to most supporters of the Union. Several factors recommended Gamble to the convention as the best choice for governor. Many editorials of Missouri newspapers noted his lack of political ambition, his long residence and acquaintance with many leaders throughout the state, and his solid character and strong intellect. Probably another factor in the decision was Gamble's close, long-running personal and professional relationship with his brother-in-law Edward Bates, who was then attorney general of the United States. Bates trusted and respected Gamble and could be expected to aid him in his negotiations with the Lincoln administration for military and financial support. Of course, dissenting voices were heard from those favoring secession and from abolitionists. Secessionists sought to foment discord with Gamble's administration and prepare for Jackson's return to power. Abolitionists sought to use the war to emancipate the slaves and resented Gamble's intention to preserve the status quo in black-white relations in Missouri. Thus began Gamble's tenure as governor of Missouri during the most trying period in the state's history, a time that would require all his ingenuity, resourcefulness, and steadiness of character.[46]

46. Editorials concerning Gamble's election as provisional governor from the Columbia *Missouri Statesman*, the St. Joseph *Journal*, the Louisiana *Journal*, the Frederickstown *Journal*, the Palmyra *Courier*, and the Chillicothe *Constitutional* were published in the St. Louis *Missouri Republican*, 1, 9, and 15 August 1861.

Chapter Six

Governor Hamilton R. Gamble

Upon assuming the office of provisional governor of Missouri in early August 1861, Hamilton R. Gamble faced the very difficult tasks of establishing himself as the legitimate governor of Missouri and of reestablishing peace throughout the state. Although ousted Governor Claiborne F. Jackson had been driven from the state, a significant minority of Missourians still considered him to be the duly elected governor. Because this minority supported, or were sympathetic to, the goals of the secessionists, they were willing to overlook the most egregious type of behavior by Jackson, including his deceptive unionist pose during the first five months of his governorship, his secret negotiations with President Jefferson Davis and other Confederate leaders, and his removal of the Missouri treasury and other state property, including military weapons. Moreover, Jackson had acted without a mandate from the state convention, something that no other state executive of the newly created government of the Southern Confederacy had attempted to do. Instead of blaming Jackson and his supporters, this minority blamed Gamble and the Lincoln administration for the many calamities that befell them with the advent of civil war. In accepting the provisional governorship at a time when the military contest was still in doubt, Gamble undertook a great personal risk, demonstrating once again his devotion to constitutional and republican government and his commitment to the union of states.

From the beginning, Gamble was confronted by many important, precedent-setting decisions for his administration. In his inaugural speech to the convention and his proclamation a short time later, Gamble expressed his determination to prevent Missouri's secession from the Union and to maintain law and order. Recognizing the primary significance of the slavery issue, he addressed it first by promising that he would not interfere with the institution, protecting it "to the very utmost extent of [his] Executive power." This statement, he hoped, might undercut secessionists' proslavery rhetoric used to recruit young men into the army led by Sterling Price. Gamble next rescinded ousted Governor Jackson's proclamation calling militia units into active service and announcing the state convention's repeal of the militia act giving his predecessor expanded military authority. Gamble ordered these militia units to disband and declared void the commissions of militia officers under the repealed militia act. Moreover, he ordered sheriffs and officers of the various courts to maintain the peace and to prosecute those violating the laws throughout the state. Gamble also instructed those situated where the civil authorities could not enforce the law to request support from the state and ordered all white men of military age to enroll in the militia forces that he was then organizing.[1]

During the period prior to Gamble's governorship, battles had been fought on June 17 at Boonville in the central part of Missouri and another on July 5 at Carthage in the southwest. Additionally, military activity increased significantly after the Battle of Carthage through a series of skirmishes and other actions occurring almost daily until the Battle of Wilson's Creek on August 10. After federal General Nathaniel Lyon's defeat there, many feared that Confederate General Price would march on the state capitol at Jefferson City, where Gamble was busily engaged in developing a state response to the threat. During this period for a brief time, General Ulysses S. Grant commanded the troops at Jefferson City. Upon his arrival he "found a good many troops in Jefferson City, but in the greatest confusion, and no one person knew where they all were." Upon his inspection of the various military camps about town, Grant discovered that the troops lacked rations, clothing, military equipment, ammunition, and artillery. The surrounding territory was in rebellion and "the city was filled with Union fugitives who had been driven by guerrilla

1. St. Louis *Missouri Republican*, 2 and 5 August 1861.

bands to take refuge with the National troops. They were in a deplorable condition and must have starved but for the support they received from the government."[2]

The major reason for the disorganized condition of the Union military in Missouri at the time was the necessity of employing inexperienced volunteer recruits to meet the emergency posed by Governor Jackson and his army. In order to put troops in the field as quickly as possible recruiters cut corners and violated army regulations, often providing inadequate records of the names of the officers and men, the time of their enlistments, and their terms of service. Moreover, regiments were frequently put into the field commanded by officers without the training to instill in them good order and discipline. Another problem complicating recruitment was Governor Jackson's unsurprising refusal to provide support to the government's efforts to raise the four-regiment quota of the president's initial call for 75,000 three-month men. For this reason the majority of troops raised in April and May came from St. Louis, where U.S. troops were garrisoned and a talented and vigilant group of unionists resided. In May federal authority was given for the recruitment of loyal citizens into a reserve corps, four-fifths of whom were German residents whose views were unrepresentative of the rest of the state. Therefore, when these troops were deployed in the field and garrisoned, a fair amount of distrust existed between them and the state's inhabitants who harbored strong nativist views. In all, the Missouri volunteer and reserve regiments totaled just more than 10,000 men. Because of the inadequacy of their numbers and the need for cavalry and artillery, General Lyon employed Home Guard units who had formed privately to protect themselves in their communities. Some of these units received arms from the federal government, although many provided their own weapons; they numbered around 15,000 men. The Home Guard troops received no pay or subsistence from the federal government and presented no reports to the Department of the West in the early months of the war. Of these, Lyon enlisted approximately 2,200 for three-month service to guard a portion

2. *The War of the Rebellion: A Compilation of the Official Records of the Union and Confederate Armies*, 128 vols. (Washington, D.C.: U.S. Government Printing Office, 1880–1902), series 1, vol. 3, 1–3 and 452. Ulysses S. Grant, *Personal Memoirs of U. S. Grant* (New York: Library of America, 1990), 170–71.

of his "lines of communication" to enable the largest part of his volunteer
and reserve forces to serve in the field against General Price's army. Later
that summer many of these Home Guard units were absorbed into the
U.S. military as three-year volunteers. By the end of 1861 the total number of three-year troops from Missouri numbered almost 24,000 infantry,
just over 3,000 artillery, and 5,900 cavalry.[3]

Not long after Gamble became governor, General Charles C. Fremont
was appointed to command the Department of the West, which included
Missouri. He and federal commanders under him worked to reestablish
order in Missouri, while Gamble sought to influence policy and to establish a loyal state militia which, he hoped, would eventually replace the
Home Guard regiments and out-of-state federal forces. Unfortunately,
through heavy-handed and often unlawful tactics, these forces had undermined the authority of the provisional government and Missouri's military security. Many of these regiments' officers and men believed slavery
the cause of the war and sought to destroy it wherever they could. Some
regiments quickly became notorious for aiding the escape of slaves and
taking extraordinary measures against civilians, especially slaveholders.
Soon after becoming governor, Gamble received numerous reports that
federal troops from neighboring free states were entering private homes
and stealing property. In response he promised Missourians "to stop the
practices on the part of the military which have occasioned so much ir-
ritation throughout the State—such as arresting citizens who have neither taken up arms against the Government, nor aided those who are in
open hostility to it, and searching private houses without any reasonable
ground to suspect the occupants of any improper conduct and unnecessarily seizing of and injuring private property."[4]

One of these incidents concerned a Home Guard regiment's alleged

3. Chester Harding Jr. to Lorenzo Thomas, 7 July 1861; and Chester Harding Jr. to Gamble,
1 January 1862, *Official Records*, series 1, vol. 3, 391–92; and series 3, vol. 1, 794–96.

4. St. Louis *Republican*, 5 August 1861. James T. Matson to Gamble, 13 September 1861 and
J. W. Wilson to Gamble, 23 May 1862, Gamble papers. J. T. K. Hayward to J. C. Fremont, 10
and 12 August 1861; Speed Butler to General Stephen A. Hurlbut, 10 and 14 August 1861; and
John S. Phelps to G. M. Dodge, 2 December 1861, *Official Records*, series 2, vol. 1, 204–9 and 781.
See also Dennis K. Boman, "Conduct and Revolt in the Twenty-fifth Ohio Battery: An Insider's
Account," *Ohio History* (Summer–Autumn 1995): 170–74.

murder of James Lightner, and the wounding of another man for firing into a steamboat near Lexington. Gamble sent Samuel G. Sawyer to investigate the matter but received no cooperation from Colonel Charles G. Stifel, who refused to meet with Sawyer and prevented the performance of an autopsy on Lightner's body. Sawyer reported that witnesses, fearing for their safety, refused to testify without Colonel Stifel's permission.[5]

A second incident concerned the arrest of former Speaker of the House John McAfee, who had cooperated with Governor Jackson in passing legislation to strengthen state militia forces to defend against the invasion of out-of-state troops. After his capture, General Stephen A. Hurlbut put McAfee to work digging ditches in the hot sun for an entire day "when the mercury ranged about 100 degrees in the shade." When transporting McAfee from Macon to Palmyra Hurlbut vindictively intended to strap him "on the top of the cab on the engine" of a train, but this was prevented when the railroad personnel started before McAfee could be marched to the front of the train, giving him and his escorts "barely time to get on the cars." Fremont, upon hearing of McAfee's treatment, demanded that Hurlbut report the reason for and the circumstances of the arrest. In his explanation Hurlbut stated that although McAfee "commits no act himself" he is known to be "a dangerous and subtle enemy . . . [who] encourages and advises others." Hurlbut explained further that he had offered to release McAfee "if he would give his pledge not to resist by force the 'Gamble Government.' He refused so to do." This obstinacy, coupled with his part in causing the current conflict in Missouri, Hurlbut argued, justified his action. Fremont agreed and ordered McAfee to be held "not only [until he] pledges himself to keep the peace but will use all his influence in so doing in his immediate vicinity of country." Perhaps reconsidering the wisdom of such a course, Fremont later ordered McAfee released. These and other incidents convinced Gamble that creating a state militia force to

---

5. St. Louis *Missouri Republican*, 3 June 1862. Gamble to Samuel G. Sawyer, 5 August 1861; L. W. Burris to Gamble, 8 August 1861; George Brown to Gamble, 10 August 1861; Anonymous to Gamble, 13 August 1861; Samuel G. Sawyer, 15 August 1861; E. B. Dobyns to Gamble, 18 August 1861; J. G. Chiles to Gamble, 23 August 1861; Gamble to Abraham Lincoln, 26 August 1861; Gamble to Chester P. Harding, 27 August 1861; Gamble's aide to E. B. Dobyns, 27 August 1861; and William P. Lewright to Gamble, undated, Gamble papers. General Stephen A. Hurlbut to Colonel J. M. Palmer, 14 July 1861; J. T. K. Hayward to J. W. Brooks, 13 and 14 August 1861, *Official Records*, series 2, vol. 1, 185; and series 1, vol. 3, 458–60. Grant, *Memoirs*, 163–64.

protect their own communities was preferable to garrisoning federal and Home Guard units throughout Missouri.[6]

On August 17, Gamble proclaimed the creation of a state militia to combat "bands of armed men . . . engaged in lawless enterprises against their fellow citizens. The ordinary civil process is insufficient to secure the peace of the State and it has become necessary to provide a military force sufficient for the purpose." He also appointed "division inspectors" to organize the militia units according to the 1859 militia act. These inspectors mustered in troops and established barracks and parade grounds. Gamble next issued a call for 42,000 men to enlist for six months, to which only slightly more than 6,100 enlisted. The tepid response, which Gamble anticipated, resulted from a preference of most loyal men to serve in federal regiments that the U.S. government subsisted, outfitted, and paid. Without a means to raise revenue, most loyal men feared that the state government could not adequately support its new force. To overcome this problem Gamble wrote to Lincoln requesting funds and reminding him that the federal government was bound constitutionally to repel the invasion of Price's army. Part of this responsibility included providing funding and arms for the militia. Although Lincoln readily recognized this constitutional duty, the federal government's resources were stretched, and without enough money and arms then available to provide for everyone, the administration was forced to prioritize their distribution. For this reason Gamble's efforts met with few results, despite sending an agent to Washington and writing letters to Lincoln, Bates, and Postmaster General Montgomery Blair.[7]

6. To Francis P. Blair, 22 May 1861; report of Nathaniel Lyon, 16 May 1861; report of Captain Nelson Cole, 16 May 1861; J. T. K. Hayward to Fremont, 10 and 12 August 1861; Speed Butler to Stephen A. Hurlbut, 10 and 14 August 1861; Stephen A. Hurlbut to John Pope, 13 August 1861; J. T. K. Hayward to J. W. Brooks, 13 August 1861; and John Pope to Stephen A. Hurlbut, 15 August 1861, *Official Records*, series 1, vol. 3, 9–11, 378, 433–35, and 459–59; and series 2, vol. 1, 207–10.

7. St. Louis *Missouri Republican*, 21 and 26 August 1861. James H. Birch to George R. Smith, 17 September 1861, Missouri Militia Records, Duke University Library, Durham, North Carolina; hereinafter cited as Militia Records. Chester Harding Jr. to Gamble, 1 January 1862, *Official Records*, series 3, vol. 1, 794–96. Gamble to Abraham Lincoln, 26 August 1861, and 13 and 28 September 1861; Gamble to Edward Bates, 17 September 1861; Gamble to Montgomery Blair, 5 October 1861; and Gamble to William G. Elliot, 15 October 1861, Abraham Lincoln papers, Library of Congress, Washington, D.C.; hereinafter cited as Lincoln papers.

Through these first endeavors and contacts Gamble and Lincoln developed an important relationship forged by their common goal of preserving the Union and returning peace to Missouri and the country. During his service as provisional governor on several occasions Gamble traveled to Washington and met with Lincoln, cabinet members, and War Department officials to coordinate the war effort in Missouri. Both men corresponded with one another directly and through their staff and others. Having conservative philosophies and both being former Whigs, Gamble and Lincoln had similar outlooks regarding the role of government and their devotion to the Union. While their views concerning slavery differed, Lincoln holding antislavery and free soil notions opposite to Gamble's proslavery ideas, both agreed that for policy and constitutional reasons the federal government should not interfere with slavery in the states. In their efforts to restore the Union, attempts to abolish slavery, they believed, would further reduce the probability that the country could soon be reunited.[8]

Gamble, although unsympathetic to secession, understood the motivations of many Missourians to join Price's army or otherwise to support the South. The strong prejudice of many against Northerners in general, and their outrage for what many Missourians considered to be unwarranted interference with the institution of slavery, had intensified after federal and Home Guard troops' actions seemed to verify the warnings of "fire-eating" politicians and orators, who for the past decade had sought to convince Southerners to secede from the Union. Furthermore, many young men were then serving in Price's army in response to former Governor Jackson's request for volunteers to prevent the federal government under the "Black Republican" Lincoln from subjugating the state government. As an individual explained to Gamble: "All this is because our citizens some of them at least obeyed the call of our Governor which was thought to be lawful." Recognizing such extenuating circumstances, Gamble consulted with Lincoln and Secretary of War Simon Cameron before issuing a special order on August 13 in which he offered pardon to all members of Price's army who had joined under Jackson's orders and would return

---

8. The correspondence between Gamble and Lincoln can be found primarily in the Gamble and Lincoln papers.

home to live as peaceful citizens. However, this amnesty would not protect those who had committed crimes. Moreover, each person accepting pardon must take an oath to remain faithful to the national and state governments. This policy had the advantage of providing an added incentive to desert for those in Price's army who were wearied with the war and wished to return home. However, it also created problems for Gamble and commanders in the field who were confronted with determining who genuinely wished to remain at home peacefully and those who instead returned to spy or to recruit new soldiers into Confederate service. Later, when the state convention assembled, the delegates supported this policy, although they also provided severe penalties for those who did not keep their oath and acted to undermine the provisional government.[9]

Martial Law and Civil Government during Wartime

Gamble struggled to bring peace to Missouri by implementing measures to stop the abuses of federal military forces and to offer amnesty to Missourians who would lay down their arms and return home peacefully. Violations of the rules of war had occurred largely because most of the conflict's participants on both sides were amateur soldiers who were not under the firm control of their equally amateur commanders. Moreover, unionist civil and military leaders had no experience in the administration of a region where a portion, sometimes a large segment, of the population was in rebellion, often making normal law enforcement measures and civil law ineffective. In considering their subsequent actions, therefore, this inexperience must be kept in mind. Furthermore, their motives must be considered and distinctions made between action taken for revenge and that meant to diminish or deter imminent danger. Ideally, for the constriction of civil liberties to be justified, the policy should affect only those causing the danger and should have no unintended consequences; but of course, an ideal policy was often impossible to develop and frequently the innocent suffered along with the guilty. While it was important for com-

9. Robert N. Smith to Gamble, 12 August 1861, Gamble papers. Simon Cameron to Gamble, 3 August 1861; Special Order, 13 August 1861; Ulysses S. Grant to Speed Butler, 27 August 1861, *Official Records*, series 1, vol. 3, 463; series 1, vol. 53, 498; and series 2, vol. 1, 208. Edward Bates to Lincoln, 24 August 1861; and Gamble to Lincoln, 31 October 1861, Lincoln papers.

manders to limit the constriction of civil liberties, loss of life had to be prevented, or at least minimized. In the end, there was a necessary trial-and-error period during which some measures were rejected while others proved effective.[10]

In July, before the convention elected Gamble as governor, General John Pope was placed in command of the region north of the Missouri River, which soon thereafter became part of the Department of the West under the command of Fremont. Pope, who later briefly commanded the Army of Virginia at the Battle of Second Bull Run, demonstrated a good deal of promise in his first major command of the war. Pope faced multiple challenges, as many of the communities were strongly secessionist and had provided men and materiel to Price's army. Moreover, many inhabitants formed guerrilla bands to destroy railroad bridges, shoot into trains carrying troops, and cut telegraph lines. For this reason, Pope and regiments from neighboring Illinois were sent to restore peace. Immediately, Pope instituted a system of summary military justice "without awaiting civil process" and made each community, especially its most vocal secessionist members, responsible for maintaining the peace. This was accomplished through the establishment of safety committees in every town. These committees were composed of "parties who have social, domestic, and pecuniary interests at stake," were to be no larger than five persons, and were to represent every political party including secessionists, for Pope believed that security could be achieved only by making everyone responsible for their communities' safety. The members of these safety committees were given the power "to call out all citizens of the county, to assemble at such times and places, and in such numbers as may be necessary to secure these objects," but were also held liable for any breach of the peace. If it became necessary for the military to return to restore

10. The issue of the proper balance of civil liberties and safety during wartime is a very controversial and difficult problem as evidenced from the wide spectrum of disagreement among scholars. See, for example, Mark E. Neely Jr., *The Fate of Liberty: Abraham Lincoln and Civil Liberties* (New York: Oxford University Press, 1991). William H. Rehnquist, *All the Laws but One: Civil Liberties in Wartime* (New York: Alfred A. Knopf, 1998). Zechariah Chafee Jr., *Free Speech in the United States* (Cambridge, Mass.: Harvard University Press, 1942). Frank L. Klement, *Dark Lanterns: Secret Political Societies, Conspiracies, and Treason Trials in the Civil War* (Baton Rouge: Louisiana State University Press, 1984). Dean Sprague, *Freedom Under Lincoln* (Boston: Riverside Press Cambridge, 1965).

order, a levy on the community would be collected by the commanding officer. Furthermore, the troops would be quartered and billeted on the people. To carry out this order, and possibly to find guerrilla bands in his district, Pope sent troops to nineteen county seats simultaneously with copies of the order and directions on how to implement it.[11]

Soon, however, Pope's General Order No. 3 came under scrutiny more for its indiscriminate punishment of the entire community than for the levy itself. Apparently, this issue came to Gamble's attention when unionists wrote to him soon after his election complaining about the unfairness of the order in making them responsible for the actions of secessionists. Believing that it was still possible to conciliate many who had originally taken up arms against the provisional and national governments, Gamble objected to Pope's order and to the harsh methods of some of the federal and Home Guard units then stationed in Missouri. In a letter to Lincoln on August 26, Gamble expressed his reservations about the wisdom and fairness of the policy. He also noted the difficulties presented by the presence of "troops from other states" who completely misunderstood the circumstances in Missouri. The actions of these regiments had harmed the Union cause when upon putting down violence, they "attempted to introduce a system of law by which citizens without regard to the question whether they participated in the violence or not were made responsible for the expenses of military expeditions undertaken for the purpose of punishing those guilty of the outrages." Gamble feared that friends of the Union would become estranged from the government and he noted that these actions had

> done much to embarrass and cripple me in my attempts to restore peace and fidelity to the Union throughout the State. In fact I very little hope that peace can be restored while the friends of the Constitution are unable to defend the acts of the military officers of the government. Those friends are

11. Report of Colonel Robert F. Smith; John Pope to Chester Harding Jr., 15 July 1861; John Pope to John C. Fremont, 16 and 17 July and 5 and 25 August 1861; Fremont to Colonel Townsend, 18 July 1861; John Pope to the people of North Missouri, 19 July 1861; General Orders, No. 3, Pope to Colonel J. D. Stevenson, 2 August 1861; Pope to J. H. Sturgeon, 3 August 1861; Pope to John C. Kelton, 4 and 17 August 1861; Pope to commanding officer at Boonville, 9 August 1861, *Official Records*, series 1, vol. 3, 40–41, 395–96 and 398, 417–19, 420–21, 423–24, 426–27, and 447–48; and series 2, vol. 1, 187 and 201–3.

first silent and then lukewarm. I am not ignorant of the fact that in all wars there are violations of private rights, but it is seldom in modern times that such abuses have the express sanction of officers high in command. I leave this subject to your consideration merely remarking that I am continually embarrassed by the complaints of real union men against the action of the military whose conduct I can neither excuse nor control. While I have become hardened against complaints of secessionists I have a deep interest in the protection of real union men. If it were possible to subject the military in acting upon unarmed citizens to any control of a civil officer or of a body of civilians much of the cause of present complaint would be removed.

The protests of Gamble and others led to the repeal of General Order No. 3 on August 30, when Pope stated through another published order his willingness to cooperate with Gamble and his hope "that peace and quiet should be re-established in North Missouri." Nevertheless, Pope warned the district of "far more severe and difficult" consequences if "this leniency" was used as an opportunity to perpetrate more outrages and violence.[12]

Of course, violence was not isolated to Pope's command, for numerous reports of guerrilla bands and the destruction of property were received from all parts of the state. Increasingly it became evident that a large segment of the population, although a minority, supported secession actively, while still others supported or opposed the rebellion, but really were noncombatants seeking to avoid becoming involved in the conflict. Furthermore, many of the communities lost their strongest supporters of the Union when men responded to the president's and Governor Gamble's call for troops. Faced with these circumstances in St. Louis, where he had located his headquarters, on July 28 Fremont appointed Colonel John McNeil as "military commandant of Saint Louis." His duties were to protect the city, keep the peace, provide a body guard for Fremont and security at headquarters, and pen a daily report. On August 14, concluding that the situation was still dangerous, Fremont established martial law. These decisions seemed warranted to suppress the violence that had occurred

12. L. W. Burris to Gamble, 8 August 1861; Charles Gibson to Gamble, 8 and 19 August 1861; George Brown to Gamble, 10 August 1861; J. T. K. Hayward to Gamble, 17 August 1861; E. B. Dobyns to Gamble, 18 August 1861; and Gamble to Lincoln, 26 August 1861, Gamble papers. Special Orders, No. 13, 30 August 1861, *Official Records*, series 2, vol. 1, 220–21.

sporadically since the capture of state troops at Camp Jackson in May. One contemporary estimated that 8,000 secessionists resided in St. Louis. These men constituted a serious menace, especially if the city should be threatened by Price's army. Under martial law passes were required for persons to enter or leave St. Louis and these could not be acquired without taking an oath of allegiance to the U.S. government. Provost-Marshal Justus McKinstry also prohibited all persons, except military and law enforcement, from carrying concealed weapons and required permits for the sale of weapons. Although he stated his determination not to interfere with the adjudication of civil law, McKinstry arrested the president of the police commission for holding secessionist views. Later he released him on the condition he resign from the commission and promise to leave the city to reside in the free states and not to return "without the consent of the military authorities." At the end of August Fremont declared martial law statewide, giving military commanders in his department a good deal of latitude in their maintenance of the peace.[13]

FREMONT'S ADMINISTRATION

Lincoln's appointment of Fremont as military commander of the Department of the West, which included Missouri, complicated the task of maintaining peace in Missouri. Unfortunately, Fremont's strong support for emancipation conflicted with the view of the majority, whose values were represented in Governor Gamble's policy to preserve slavery, and therefore undermined unionist support throughout the state. German immigrants in St. Louis, along with some native Missourians, supported Fremont, who increasingly was influenced by their animosity and distrust

13. Justus McKinstry to Colonel S. Burbank, 21 August 1861; John McNeil to Simon Cameron, 16 October 1861; and John McNeil to William Seward, October 1861; Fremont to John McNeil, 28 July 1861; and J. T. K. Hayward to Fremont, 10 August 1861, *Official Records*, series 1, vol. 3, 410; series 2, vol. 1, 128, 134, and 204–6; and vol. 2, 117. Galusha Anderson, *The Story of a Border City During the Civil War* (Boston: Little, Brown, 1908), 213–14 and 217–18. For a secessionist and a unionist account of the Camp Jackson incident see Thomas L. Snead, "The First Year of the War in Missouri," in *Battles and Leaders of the Civil War*, vol. 1 (New York: Century, 1887; reprint, Secaucus, N.J.: Castle, n.d.), 264–65. William Tecumseh Sherman, *Memoirs* (New York: The Library of America, 1990), 190–92.

of Governor Gamble and proslavery unionists. During this difficult and dangerous time Fremont's mistrust of Gamble led to misunderstandings between them.[14]

Unfortunately, Lincoln was unable to secure cooperation between Fremont and Gamble. Learning that Gamble was raising a state militia, Fremont naturally sought to influence the selection of its officers. The governor promptly replied that under state law officers were elected "within their respective commands," although he was empowered to appoint an adjutant-general and a quartermaster general. Gamble promised to appoint anyone Fremont wished, an offer of which he never availed himself. Not long after, Fremont requested the removal of the police commissioners in St. Louis. Once again Gamble explained the limitations of his authority. Apparently Fremont's suspicion of Gamble only deepened, for complaints filtered back to Lincoln, leading him to request that Bates write to Gamble and urge consultation with Fremont in the appointment of officers to Missouri's federal regiments. Fremont, probably influenced by emancipationists in St. Louis where he was headquartered, mistrusted Gamble enough to ask Lincoln not to allow him to raise a state militia.[15]

Consistent with his understanding of the causes of the conflict and his mistrust of Missouri's provisional government, Fremont issued a proclamation on August 30 promising to shoot all persons captured in arms against the United States, and stating his intention to confiscate the property of those in arms and those who had aided the enemy. Fremont also declared the slaves of disloyal men free.[16]

14. St. Louis *Missouri Republican*, 11 September 1861 and 2 June 1862. In his article about Fremont's tenure as departmental commander, Robert L. Turkoly-Joczik apparently does not understand the nature of support for the Union in Missouri and the other border states, emphasizing the favorable reaction of abolitionists and Northerners to Fremont's emancipation proclamation, instead of noting the deep unpopularity in Missouri for emancipation in any form. See "Fremont and the Western Department," *Missouri Historical Review* 82, no. 4 (July 1988): 363–85. For a different interpretation of Fremont's actions see Wilbert Henry Rosin, "Hamilton Rowan Gamble: Missouri's Civil War Governor" (Ph.D. diss., University of Missouri, 1960), 214.

15. J. C. Kelton to Gamble, 2 August 1861; Fremont to Gamble, 3 and 18 August 1861; and Edward Bates to Gamble, 12 August 1861, Gamble papers; and Fremont to Lincoln, 3 September 1861, *Official Records*, series 1, vol. 3, 470.

16. Proclamation of John C. Fremont, 30 August 1861; General Orders, No. 6, J. C. Kelton, 30 August 1861; *Official Records*, series 1, vol. 3, 466–70.

While approving of Fremont's declaration of martial law, Lincoln objected to the proclamation's provisions regarding the shooting of prisoners of war, confiscation, and emancipation. He believed the first of the provisions unwise—not to mention inhumane—for it would provoke similar treatment of Union prisoners of war. To prevent the policy from being implemented, Lincoln required his approval before any sentences of death could be executed. Furthermore, the provisions concerning the confiscation of property and emancipation were in violation of Congress's confiscation act of August 6, 1861, and therefore, must be repealed.[17] Fremont replied that he preferred that Lincoln write a public letter ordering him to rescind the objectionable provisions of the proclamation. Fremont argued that his own revocation of them would be an admission that he had not considered the matter fully and had made a mistake. More probably, Fremont feared alienating Radical Republicans in Missouri and the rest of the North by moderating his severe-war stance. Concerning the provision of the proclamation promising to shoot enemy prisoners, Fremont stated: "I do not think the enemy can either misconstrue or urge anything against it, or undertake to make unusual retaliation. . . . The article does not at all refer to prisoners of war." However, the reaction of two Confederate commanders demonstrated that, regardless of Fremont's intentions, they believed he was ordering the execution of Confederate prisoners of war.[18]

Fremont's proclamation became a huge political headache for Lincoln as well, for it undermined his policy of leaving slavery alone and focusing the war effort on reuniting the South with the United States. Those who wished to make the conflict a war for abolition now had someone around whom to rally. Moreover, this effort posed a significant threat to the war effort, for a large number of unionists in Missouri and the other border states conditioned their support of the Lincoln administration on the promise that slavery would be left alone. The proclamation also helped

17. Lincoln to John C. Fremont, 2 and 11 September 1861; and Fremont to Lincoln, 8 September 1861, *Official Records*, series 1, vol. 3, 477–78, and 485–86.

18. Ibid. and proclamation of M. Jeff. Thompson, 2 September 1861, and of Ben McCulloch, 10 September 1861, *Official Records*, series 1, vol. 3, 693 and 700. T. Harry Williams, "Fremont and the Politicians," *Journal of the American Military History Foundation* 2 (Winter 1938): 181–82 and 188.

Confederate recruiters for Price's army and probably inspired many to provide aid and comfort to his invading army. John B. Henderson, who lived in northeast Missouri and soon would become one of Missouri's U.S. senators, explained the negative impact of Fremont's proclamation to James O. Broadhead, one of Lincoln's friends in St. Louis. The letter, which was forwarded to Lincoln, demonstrated the frustration of many with Fremont. "You know the sensitiveness of our people on the question of *nigger* and especially *free nigger* and there is no use of losing Union strength by threatening anything but *death* to these men. . . . Again I find that the idea is busily being created in Illinois adjoining to us that this proclamation shows the true object of the war to be the emancipation of slaves. This foolish and accursed notion came near ruining our county, the soundest in the State, but I sincerely hope I have it now checked for a time."[19]

At the time of this controversy, the military situation in Missouri had quickly deteriorated. Despite the frequent requests of Gamble and others to reinforce Lyon, who was in command of a Union force near Springfield, Fremont, without taking any action, had allowed a superior enemy force under Price to defeat Lyon's army on August 10. Following this disaster Fremont proved to be incapable of energetic leadership. His incompetence became increasingly evident as Price operated in Missouri with impunity, defeating another Union army on September 20 at Lexington. The danger to the garrison was evident to Gamble and commanders in the field a week before Lexington's surrender; nevertheless, Fremont made no move to concentrate his forces in the region to meet Price's larger force. Despite his later protestations that he did not have transportation to move troops to the Lexington area, just days later Fremont found a way to move a force of 38,000 men into the field after he realized he must act or lose his command. Nevertheless, Fremont's pursuit was leisurely at best, allowing General Price's army the opportunity along the way to take advantage of

19. J. O. Davis to Gamble, 22 August 1861, Gamble papers. St. Louis *Missouri Republican*, 10 and 15 September 1861. U. S. Grant to Speed Butler, 27 August 1861, *Official Records*, series 1, vol. 3, 463. Joshua F. Speed to Lincoln, 1 and 3 September 1861; Montgomery Blair to Lincoln, 14 September 1861; and John B. Henderson to James O. Broadhead, 7 September 1861, Lincoln papers.

the hospitality of the prosecession residents, who provided supplies and entertainment as they retreated toward Pineville, Arkansas. Price hoped that Fremont, who was in Springfield in late October, would pursue him into Arkansas, where he believed the terrain favored his army. However, after the Union army's evacuation of Springfield and retreat to the Sedalia region, Price moved his army toward Newtonia, eventually encamping near Osceola on the Sac River.[20]

After the capture of Lexington the St. Louis *Evening News* criticized Fremont for failing to relieve Colonel James A. Mulligan in time. The proprietor Charles G. Ramsay was arrested by the provost-marshal, interrogated, and imprisoned. Moreover, the military seized the building where the paper was published. Although this was not the first time that the military had violated freedom of the press, it was the first time a unionist paper had been suppressed. This series of events, as might be expected, eroded unionist support for Fremont's leadership. Even after this Lincoln decided to give Fremont another opportunity to redeem himself, while at the same time placing more pressure on him to act quickly to protect the state. Lincoln also hoped that the influence on Fremont of General David Hunter, whom Lincoln had sent to serve as Fremont's chief of staff, would lead to a reversal of the dismal situation. Undoubtedly, he also desired to

20. S. M. Breckinridge to Gamble, 3 August 1861; John M. Richardson to Gamble, 10 August 1861; and Charles Gibson to Gamble, 27 September 1861, Gamble papers. Samuel T. Glover to Montgomery Blair, 2 September 1861; James O. Broadhead to Montgomery Blair, 3 September 1861; Winfield Scott to Lincoln, 5 September 1861; Lincoln to David Hunter, 9 September 1861; John B. Henderson to James O. Broadhead, 7 September 1861; John M. Shaffer to Winfield Scott, 14 September 1861; Francis P. Blair Jr. to Lincoln, 15 September 1861; Samuel T. Glover to Lincoln, 20 and 21 September 1861; and John How to Montgomery Blair, 3 October 1861, Lincoln papers. Parrish, *Turbulent Partnership*, 52 and 66–68. Nathaniel Lyon to Chester Harding Jr., 2 July 1861; M. Jeff. Thompson to Joseph Tucker, 16 July 1861; John M. Schofield to Chester Harding Jr., 26 July 1861; Ulysses S. Grant to William H. Worthington, 26 August 1861; Jefferson C. Davis to Fremont, 12 and 19 September 1861; Gamble to Fremont, 13 September 1861; Benjamin M. Prentiss to Fremont, 22 September 1861; W. E. Prince to James H. Lane, 23 September 1861; and Report of Lorenzo Thomas, October 1861, *Official Records*, series 1, vol. 3, 171–72, 174, 178, 183–84, 388, 407–8, 543–49, and 608–9; series 2, vol. 1, 217. Albert Castel, *General Sterling Price and the Civil War in the West* (Baton Rouge: Louisiana State University Press, 1968), 56–60. Robert E. Shalhope, *Sterling Price: Portrait of a Southerner* (Columbia: University of Missouri Press, 1971), 184–89. Williams, "Fremont," 182–83.

avoid the political fallout and subsequent harm to the war effort in the border states that might result from Fremont's dismissal.[21]

Just prior to the loss of the garrison at Lexington, Gamble again traveled to Washington. His purpose was to gain funding for weapons, a promise that Gamble secured. Before returning to Missouri, he discussed the critical military situation with Lincoln, who requested that Gamble carry a letter to Fremont. Hoping to foster cooperation between the two men, Lincoln also wished to gain fresh insights about Fremont's character and command style when Gamble reported to him on the meeting. After returning to St. Louis, on September 13 Gamble first handed Lincoln's letter to Fremont, who immediately read it. Gamble explained that the president had read the letter to him and had mentioned "a want of cordiality between us" concerning which Gamble claimed he was unaware. He also stated that he had made the decision to travel to Washington the day before Fremont had issued his proclamation, so it was not true, as some editorialists in the newspapers had asserted, that he had met with Lincoln to urge the repeal of the August 30 proclamation declaring slaves free in Missouri. Fremont explained his disappointment with Gamble for not cooperating with him in the appointment of officers to the state militia. Gamble patiently reminded him that under state law he could not appoint officers. In an effort to clear the air completely, Gamble mentioned that he had heard Fremont's complaint that he had "not promptly remove[d] the police commissioners of St. Louis." Gamble explained that state law allowed him to remove commissioners only for "official misconduct." Furthermore, he explained that as soon as a commissioner had resigned he had named one of Fremont's nominees. Gamble had then requested that the new commissioner examine the records of the commission's proceedings. When the commission heard of Gamble's inquiries, they sent their records to him for his personal inspection. "I examined them, found the cause I sought, & removed them forthwith—I exercised the power as soon as I could." Moreover, Gamble promised cooperation in military operations, assuring Fremont "that the state troops would be subjected to

21. For Fremont's defense of his actions in Missouri see Fremont, "In Command in Missouri," in *Battles and Leaders of the Civil War*, vol. 1 (New York: Century, 1887; reprint, Secaucus, N.J.: Castle, n.d.), 278–88. Bruce Tap, *Over Lincoln's Shoulder: The Committee on the Conduct of the War* (Lawrence: University of Kansas Press, 1998), 81–91. Williams, "Fremont," 183 and 185–88.

the command of those carrying on the military operations of the United States." At the end of the interview Fremont requested Gamble to remain in St. Louis for further consultations. After some delay without accomplishing much of anything, Gamble, frustrated and disillusioned by the interview and its aftermath, observed that he expected immediate military disaster under Fremont's leadership.[22]

These disappointments, however, apparently spurred Gamble to redouble his efforts to procure arms for the state militia; recruiting had continued despite the empty state treasury. In a letter to Attorney General Bates he wrote the terse statement: "For God's sake get me arms for infantry & cavalry." Next, Gamble commissioned William M. McPherson to Washington to obtain what military supplies he could for the state. Gamble also sought to purchase muskets on bonds guaranteed by the federal government. Lincoln agreed to provide $200,000 and promised a bond guarantee to Gamble enabling the state to raise revenue through their sale. While these ad hoc arrangements helped to improve the circumstances of the militia, Gamble recognized that reform of the militia law was necessary and that some formal agreement with the Lincoln administration and the War Department must be made to make the militia an efficient, well-supplied, and well-paid organization.[23]

To address the problem of militia law and other pressing matters, Gamble called together the state convention on October 10. Most of the delegates were able to attend, although one notable absentee was Sterling Price, who had presided over the March assembly but was then commander of the invading Confederate army. Other members with sentiments favoring the administration of ousted Governor Jackson and secession still remained, but the vast majority was unionist, although they differed on many other matters. The most prominent and talented of the secessionist delegates was Uriel Wright, a St. Louis lawyer and popular stump speaker. During the previous meetings of the convention Wright, who often spoke

22. Williams, "Fremont," 185 and 185–88. Gamble to Charles Gibson, 19 and 20 September 1861, Gamble papers.

23. William M. McPherson to Gamble, 23 and 28 September 1861; Edward Bates to Gamble, 27 September and 3 October 1861, Gamble papers. Gamble to Edward Bates, 17 September 1861; Gamble to Lincoln, 13 and 28 September 1861; and Gamble to Montgomery Blair, 5 October 1861, Lincoln papers.

at great length, tested the patience of many of the unionist delegates, who found it difficult at times to counter Wright's arguments, for in debate he often made subtle and vague assertions from which, when challenged, he retreated. While these disagreements often amounted to unimportant side issues, when one considered the overall themes of his speeches it became evident that his purpose was to undermine the convictions of some, to tie up the convention's deliberations, and to prevent, or at least minimize and delay, any action that might support the Union. For this reason, during the July session Wright had argued that the convention should not declare Price's seat vacant, did not have the power to oust Jackson and the legislature, and that Lincoln, through his unconstitutional call for federal troops, as Wright characterized it, was more responsible for the national and state crisis than anyone else.[24]

During the October session, Wright again sought to hinder and delay convention action. Tiring of these tactics, unionist delegates attempted to limit debate to thirty minutes and then to five minutes, but these efforts were unsuccessful. In very lengthy addresses to the convention Wright defended Jackson's administration and criticized unionist efforts to prevent secession. As was inevitable, during the early months of the war both sides had committed excesses in their struggle to gain supremacy over the other, but Wright presented a one-sided analysis in debate and argued that Lincoln and the provisional government had violated the U.S. Constitution and the rights of Missouri and the South. Ignoring the threat of Price's army and many guerrilla bands present, Wright argued that the best policy for the convention was to do nothing. In this he was supported by two or three others who admitted their commitment to maintaining Missouri's close attachment to the South. These delegates and Wright also criticized Fremont's emancipation proclamation of August 30 and derided many of the unionist delegates for being antislavery, a charge untrue of the vast majority and made to prejudice the public against them. Despite their efforts, Wright and the others were unsuccessful in preventing the convention from taking forceful action to protect the state from insurrection. Soon after the convention, Wright was arrested by the pro-

24. *Proceedings of the Missouri State Convention, Held at Jefferson City, July 1861* (St. Louis: George Knapp, 1861), 5–12, 25, 61–68. *Journal of the Missouri State Convention Held at the City of St. Louis, October 1861* (St. Louis: George Knapp, 1861), 3.

vost-marshal and paroled and later exchanged for a prisoner held by Price. During the next session of the convention in June 1862, the decision was made to expel Wright and seven other members after reviewing each of their cases individually. By then Wright had removed to Virginia and was using his oratorical skill to recruit soldiers for the Confederate army.[25]

Despite the determined opposition of a few members, the convention quickly got down to business by establishing committees to consider matters regarding the militia, finances, civil officers, and elections. Perhaps the most important work accomplished by these committees was reform of the militia. The reform bill sought to strengthen the state's ability to defend itself by giving Gamble greater powers and more latitude in recruiting, organizing, commanding, and subsisting the militia. Reported out of committee by Jacob T. Tindall, who was then commander of the Twenty-third Missouri Infantry and would later be killed at the Battle of Shiloh, the bill made all white males between the ages of eighteen and forty-five liable for military service in the Missouri State Militia, which would be subject to the same rules and regulations as the U.S. Army. To boost recruitment these troops would receive the same pay as their counterparts in volunteer federal regiments. The bill also prescribed that Gamble as governor and commander-in-chief would appoint chiefs of staff in the militia's different departments, staff aids, and all officers down to the rank of major with the consent of the state senate. Moreover, demonstrating the delegates' respect for his judgment, the convention gave Gamble the responsibility of establishing the rules for court-martial proceedings and modifying the U.S. Army's regulations as needed to conform them to the special circumstances of the militia. Finally, the convention passed a resolution asking Gamble to negotiate with Washington to coordinate the efforts of the state government and military forces with those of the federal government.[26]

25. *Proceedings of the Missouri State Convention Held at the City of St. Louis, October 1861* (St. Louis: George Knapp, 1861), 8, 16–17, 20–33, 40–41, 46–49, 50–51, 53, 60–66, 71–72, 84–85, 87, 90–93, and 166–68. *Proceedings, July 1861,* 3 and 29–33. *Proceedings of the Missouri State Convention Held in Jefferson City, June 1862* (St. Louis: George Knapp, 1862), 40–43. Gamble to Henry W. Halleck, 27 November 1861, *Official Records,* series 2, vol. 1, 137.

26. *Journal, October 1861,* 17–20 and 110. Report of Quinn Morton, 1 December 1862 and Benjamin M. Prentiss, 17 November 1862, *Official Records,* series 1, vol. 10, part 1, 277–80 and 291.

Another matter of importance considered by the convention was a proposal to postpone the state elections scheduled for that fall. In the July session a committee was established to determine the convention's best course following Governor Jackson's and the legislature's flight from the capitol. Initially, the committee had scheduled the election for governor, the legislature, and other state officers for August 1862, but after Gamble returned from the East and was appointed to the committee, he worked to change different aspects of their proposal. Believing that the convention's work should be presented for approval to the people as soon as possible, Gamble persuaded the committee to hold an earlier election. However, in the October session of the convention the delegates reversed this decision and postponed the election again until August 1862. Gamble supported this decision because of the very unstable situation in Missouri, where civil law in many areas was disrupted and martial law was imposed. Moreover, Gamble considered it probable that General Price's army and roving bands of guerrilla forces would attempt to influence the election. Gamble also received advice from unionists he respected who resided in different parts of the state and provided him with information about the people's sentiments. From central Missouri where secession was strongest, former Missouri Supreme Court judge Abiel Leonard warned Gamble that an election in 1861 might end in the reelection of Jackson and the legislature. Leonard and other prominent unionists argued that without military victory it would be foolhardy to hold an election. Not unsurprisingly, Wright wanted the election held in 1861 but convinced no one else to vote with him, the vote to postpone being 49 to 1.[27]

Related to the issue of elections was how to ensure that officeholders and voters were loyal. A bill from the committee on civil officers sought to abolish some offices, reduce salaries, and test the loyalty of civil officers of the state. In the midst of civil war with an empty treasury and the state struggling to remain financially solvent, the committee decided to abolish the positions of the board of public works, superintendent of common

27. *Proceedings, July 1861*, 24, 73–76, and 131. William E. Parrish, *Turbulent Partnership: Missouri and the Union, 1861–1865* (Columbia: University of Missouri Press, 1963), 36–41. Abiel Leonard to Gamble, 2 August 1861; J. O. Davis to Gamble, 22 August 1861; and John S. Phelps to Gamble, 3 October 1861, Gamble papers. *Journal, October 1861*, 8. *Proceedings, October 1861*, 9–32, 39–41, 50–51, 60–66, and 72–74.

schools, county school commissioner, state geologist and assistant. Remuneration for the remaining positions was reduced by 20 percent. The bill also provided for every officer to take an oath of allegiance to the constitutions of the state and nation and never to aid the rebellion in any way. Refusal to take the oath caused the immediate dismissal of the official. One of the convention delegates, James O. Broadhead, however, wanted to take even more drastic action by vacating all civil offices and giving Governor Gamble the power to appoint replacements. This action had the advantage of ensuring that all civil officers would be loyal. This concern over the loyalty of persons in office had led to a similar measure proposed in the July session of the convention to add a number of new justices to the Missouri Supreme Court. As a former chief justice of the state supreme court, Gamble had opposed the committee's court-packing scheme. Passage of the loyalty-oath measure, nevertheless, had the desired effect, for proslavery and secessionist justices William B. Napton, Ephraim B. Ewing, and William Scott refused to take the oath and were ousted from their positions, providing Gamble with an opportunity to appoint loyal justices. Many other important offices were vacated similarly. One of the bill's unintended consequences, however, was that it placed a burden on Gamble to find loyal persons to fill offices in communities where the vast majority was disloyal. This left many important offices vacant throughout Missouri until Gamble or his lieutenant governor Willard P. Hall could find persons to fill them.[28]

During the first few months of the war many Missourians preferred to enlist in federal regiments rather than risk not being paid for service in the militia. Just prior to the convention Gamble had gained from the Lincoln administration a guarantee on state bonds issued for war purposes. These bonds could then be sold on the market to fund the militia. After some deliberation on issuing defense warrant bonds, the convention authorized Gamble to issue $1 million in bonds and an equal amount to the state au-

28. *Journal, October 1861*, 10 and 14. *Proceedings, October 1861*, 77–78. *Journal of the Missouri State Convention Held in Jefferson City June 1862* (St. Louis: George Knapp, 1862), 7 and 95. Parrish, *Turbulent Partnership*, 86. St. Louis *Missouri Republican*, 24 December 1861 and 3 June 1862. This problem had existed from the very beginning of Gamble's administration. See Buel Leopard and Floyd C. Shoemaker, eds., *The Messages and Proclamations of the Governors of the State of Missouri* (Columbia: The State Historical Society of Missouri, 1922), 450.

ditor. These bonds, not unlike other forms of currency then circulated by states and banks, depreciated to 75 percent of face value but rebounded by the summer of 1862 to 85 percent of their initial offering price.[29]

During the convention Gamble had corresponded with Montgomery Blair and Edward Bates seeking a commitment from Lincoln either to fund the militia or provide Missouri with the federal troops needed to restore peace. As requested by resolution, after the convention Gamble again traveled to Washington, where he met with Lincoln to discuss Missouri's security. From the administration Gamble successfully gained tentative approval of his plan to establish a large militia force that would operate exclusively in Missouri. By then Gamble had met with the president on at least three different occasions and had corresponded with him personally and through surrogates. Their relationship was cordial, although briefly the president had been angry with Gamble for failing to report promptly about his meeting with Fremont on September 13. Apparently, this minor episode was quickly forgotten and Gamble was able to present his funding plan to the president face to face. Lincoln, wanting to see the details and to gain advice from the military, asked Gamble to write a memorandum delineating his plan in broad outline. This memorandum was circulated among those at the highest levels of the War Department, including overall commander of the U.S. military General George B. McClellan, with whom Gamble discussed his plan at the White House.[30]

In his memorandum Gamble summarized the circumstances in Missouri, noting the suffering of unionists throughout the state. Quoting the resolutions of the state convention, Gamble noted the advantage of employing troops in Missouri well-acquainted with the people and the terrain. Moreover, far more Missourians—especially those with families to support—would enlist in the militia if they could remain in the state. In an effort to make his proposal more appealing to the military, he also

29. St. Louis *Missouri Republican*, 3 June 1862. *Journal, October 1861*, 10–11, 23–25. *Proceedings, October 1861*, 102–3 and 110. Gamble to Montgomery Blair, 5 October 1861, Lincoln papers.

30. Gamble to Lincoln, 26 August 1861; Gamble to Charles Gibson, 20 September 1861; William M. McPherson to Gamble, 23 September 1861; Edward Bates to Gamble, 3 October 1861; and Gamble to Dr. John R. Moore, 30 November 1861, Gamble papers. Gamble to Montgomery Blair, 5 October 1861; Gamble to William G. Elliot, 15 October 1861; Gamble to Lincoln, 31 October 1861; Gamble's memorandum on state militia plan, 31 October 1861; and Gamble to Henry W. Halleck, October 1862, Lincoln papers.

promised not to prevent any of the state militia regiments from becoming federal regiments if they preferred. Implementation of the plan was only possible if the U.S. government provided funds to subsist and pay the troops. Gamble suggested that this could best be accomplished by sending the funds through the military's regular channels, and in this way avoiding any real or imagined scandals that might result from employing state officials in the disbursement of federal money.[31]

One of the objections to Gamble's plan was the issue of command. With two separate military forces in Missouri, the possibility of conflict and a lack of coordination between the two commands was a real possibility. Fortunately, General McClellan as commander of the Department of the Ohio had confronted this issue already when he had served as major general of both the federal and state forces there. By making the commander of the Department of the West, or one of his subordinates, in charge of the state militia as well, coordination of the two forces' efforts could be expected. Having gained support for the plan from Montgomery Blair and Edward Bates, his two cabinet members from Missouri, and General McClellan, Lincoln agreed to Gamble's plan and directed that the militia be governed by army regulations and the Articles of War. According to their agreement the militia would serve only in Missouri, would be subject to U.S. military law with some modifications, and would be provided pay, weapons, and subsistence from the U.S. government. Lincoln also asked Gamble to draw up an order to ensure that only militia in actual service would receive support. In doing so, Lincoln recommended that he "conform exactly to the present U.S. volunteer laws and regulations, except when departures are indispensable." Another concern was to ensure that the militia cooperated with the U.S. military and its officers in its operations within Missouri. Finally, Lincoln instructed the secretary of war to issue orders to effect the arrangement and to subsist and pay the militia like federal regiments. This required regular army officers to "make the necessary provision in their respective departments for carrying into effect this agreement."[32]

31. Gamble's memorandum and letter to Lincoln, 31 October 1861, Lincoln papers.

32. Memorandum and letter of Lincoln to Gamble, 4 November 1861; memorandum to secretary of war, 4 November 1861, Gamble papers. Gamble's proposal, 5 November 1861; Lincoln to Gamble, 6 November 1861; and General Orders, No. 96, 7 November 1861, *Official Records*, series 1, vol. 3, 565–66; and series 1, vol. 13, 9.

The success of Gamble's negotiations was greeted with relief among most unionists and was detailed in newspaper stories in Missouri. To obtain weapons for the Missouri State Militia, Gamble designated his nephew and federal judge Charles Gibson as state agent in Washington, D.C. Gibson's task was difficult, for he was in competition for weapons with agents from other states and the federal government. Unfortunately, much of the weaponry available was of inferior quality and in the end the militia was outfitted with Austrian rifles and Hall's carbines. In particular, the carbines proved to be next to useless, for, according to a later adjutant-general's report, when fired they discharged a "gas from the breech causing the men involuntarily to start, thus affecting the accuracy of the aim."[33]

During the negotiations in Washington, D.C., Gamble probably discussed with Lincoln other matters related to Missouri, including the performance of Fremont as commander of the Department of the West. For some time Lincoln had received reports about Fremont's corruption and incompetence from various quarters. These reports prompted Lincoln to send others to investigate Fremont's command. Undoubtedly, Lincoln wanted to ascertain whether or not the reports he had received were accurate, both out of fairness to Fremont and to document his incompetence or corruption if it became necessary to remove him. This was especially important given Fremont's powerful friends, who were certain to protest his removal and characterize his detractors as disloyal and proslavery. One of the complaints of Fremont's critics was that he had secluded himself from everyone, even refusing to see those with important information about military affairs. Fremont's apparent indifference to the military situation and impractical measures taken to that point reinforced the opinion of most that he lacked a plan of action, common sense, and the requisite administrative and military skills necessary to command the military district competently. Most damning of all was his inaction in the face of military defeats and the mounting disasters suffered by unionists throughout Missouri. What emerged was a picture of Fremont the perfectionist, a man unwilling to act until he had considered and provided for every detail.[34]

33. Gamble to Charles Gibson, 7 November 1861, *Official Records*, vol. 8, 454. *Annual Report of the Adjutant General of the State of Missouri for the Year 1863* (St. Louis: n.p., 1864), 468–70.

34. J. O. Davis to Gamble, 22 August 1861, Gamble papers. St. Louis *Missouri Republican*, 10 and 15 September 1861. U. S. Grant to Speed Butler, 27 August 1861; Lincoln to Fremont, 2 and 11 September 1861; and Fremont to Lincoln, 8 September 1861; proclamation of M. Jeff.

The report of General Lorenzo Thomas probably convinced Lincoln that he could no longer delay action. Thomas detailed many irregularities in securing supplies, both in the method of contracting and in payment. He believed that many of the supplies purchased were unnecessary, that too much was paid for them, and that many of Fremont's friends had made huge profits. Moreover, many of the supplies purchased at exorbitant prices turned out to be worthless. Later in early 1862, a War Claims Commission investigated these allegations and found that most, especially those against Justus McKinstry, were true. Thomas also reported the conclusions of Generals Hunter and Samuel R. Curtis, and those of many prominent men in Missouri, including Gamble, that Fremont was incompetent and must be replaced. Lincoln concluded that they were correct, although he retained his belief that Fremont was a good man who had intended to support his country. Consistent with this conclusion, Lincoln sent General Curtis orders to relieve Fremont only if he was not then in the field conducting a campaign against the enemy. These orders reached Fremont on November 2. General Hunter was given temporary command until a new commander with the requisite military knowledge and ability to pacify Missouri could be found. Lincoln's selection was a good one and led to a turnaround in the military affairs of Missouri.[35]

Thompson, 2 September 1861, and of Ben McCulloch, 10 September 1861; Lorenzo Thomas to Simon Cameron, 21 October 1861, *Official Records*, series 1, vol. 3, 463, 477–78, 485–86, 540–49, 693, and 700. Joshua Speed to Lincoln, 1 and 3 September 1861; Montgomery Blair to Lincoln, 14 September 1861; and John B. Henderson to James O. Broadhead, 7 September 1861, Lincoln papers. For a different perspective on Fremont see Blanche C. Grant, ed., *Kit Carson's Own Story of his Life as Dictated to Col. And Mrs. D. C. Peters About 1856–1857* (Santa Barbara, Calif.: Narrative, 2001), 45–87.

35. Lorenzo Thomas to Simon Cameron, 21 October 1861; Winfield Scott to John C. Fremont, General Orders, No. 18, 24 October 1861; Lincoln to Samuel R. Curtis, 24 October 1861; General Orders, No. 28, 2 November 1861; David Hunter to adjutant-general of the U.S. Army, 3 November 1861, *Official Records*, series 1, vol. 3, 540–49, 553, 559, and 561. Elihu B. Washburne to Lincoln, 26 October 1861, Lincoln papers. Michael Burlingame and John R. Turner Ettlinger, eds., *Inside Lincoln's White House: The Complete Civil War Diary of John Hay* (Carbondale: Southern Illinois University Press, 1997), 123–24. See also Howard K. Beale, ed., *The Diary of Edward Bates, 1859–1866* (Washington, D.C.: U.S. Government Printing Office, 1933), 198–99. Williams, "Fremont," 183.

Chapter Seven

Gamble's Wartime Policy

*H*aving gained the Lincoln administration's agreement to finance the state militia, Governor Hamilton R. Gamble
returned to Missouri to work out various details and concentrate on any pressing business awaiting his arrival. Fortunately, even
during wartime, Gamble had no misgivings about leaving the state, for he
was confident in the judgment of Lieutenant Governor Willard P. Hall, a
trusted colleague and supporter. While Gamble was still in Washington,
D.C., John C. Fremont had been removed from command of the Department of the West, which had been reconstituted as the Department of the
Missouri. Lincoln most probably had consulted Gamble, his cabinet, and
General George B. McClellan before removing Fremont and temporarily
replacing him with General David Hunter. Having served as Fremont's
lieutenant, Hunter took command immediately and promptly repealed an
agreement between Fremont and Confederate General Sterling Price to
stop political arrests. Other provisions, such as calling for the disbanding
of irregular troops, were already covered by the laws and customs of war
and therefore, were superfluous, especially when it was clear that Price
exercised no real control in Missouri anyway.[1]

1. Proclamation of agreement between John C. Fremont and Sterling Price, 1 and 5 November 1861; Fremont to George B. McClellan, 6 November 1861; David Hunter to Lorenzo
Thomas, 7 November; and Hunter to Sterling Price, *The War of the Rebellion: A Compilation of the
Official Records of the Union and Confederate Armies*, 128 vols. (Washington, D.C.: U.S. Government Printing Office, 1880–1902), series 1, vol. 3, 561–65. Stephen W. Sears, ed., *The Civil War*

Just a few days after Fremont's removal from command, General Henry W. Halleck was assigned to the command of the Department of the Missouri and General Hunter was ordered to command the Department of Kansas. Apparently, Gamble was unacquainted with Halleck, for his brother-in-law, Attorney General Edward Bates, and his nephew, Charles Gibson, both assured him that Halleck was a "frank, straightforward man." Over the next few months, although occasional disagreements occurred between them, Gamble and Halleck worked well together and respected each other. In Halleck, Gamble found a sound judgment and professionalism wanting in Fremont's administration of the department. As governor, Gamble confronted numerous difficulties related to wartime realities, including the state's finances being near bankruptcy, the inability to collect taxes and other revenues throughout much of Missouri, the subsisting and sheltering of refugees driven from their homes by Price's army and guerrilla bands, and the need to fill numerous political offices that had been vacated when officeholders refused to take the oath of allegiance to the state and federal governments. These difficulties made Gamble anxious to disentangle himself from military matters as much as possible. Moreover, even without the great press of business on him then, his inclination was to leave to military men the business of fighting the war. Nevertheless, Gamble was unafraid of intervening whenever he believed it necessary for the good of the state, such as when he had sought to vivify Fremont's military movements to save Lexington from capture, or later when he protested a plan to remove troops from Missouri. Finally, Gamble also shared military intelligence with Halleck and other military men, and helped coordinate militia and federal operations.[2]

Upon arriving in St. Louis, Halleck found the circumstances of the de-

---

Papers of George B. McClellan: Selected Correspondence, 1860–1865 (New York: Ticknor & Fields, 1989; reprint, New York: Da Capo, 1992), 144–45.

2. Charles Gibson to Gamble, 10 November 1861, Gamble papers. Gamble to Halleck, 23 December 1861; Gamble to Bates, 10 January 1862; Francis P. Blair Jr. to Halleck, 12 August 1862; C. P. Buckingham to Gamble, 3 September 1862, *Official Records*, series 1, vol. 13, 562; series 2, vol. 1, 153; series 3, vol. 1, 788; and series 3, vol. 2, 510. St. Louis *Missouri Republican*, 22 August 1862. Gamble to Halleck, October 1862, Lincoln papers. Howard K. Beale, ed., *The Diary of Edward Bates, 1859–1866* (Washington, D.C.: U.S. Government Printing Office, 1933), 201 and 219.

partment every bit as bad as the reports sent to Lincoln had stated. However, unlike his predecessor, Halleck quickly set to work putting things in order. Of great concern to him was obtaining weapons—he estimated that 30,000 of his troops had none—surveying defenses in St. Louis and throughout the state, and gaining a firm control over the officers and men of regiments who had committed many outrages in Missouri. Because many of the regiments were not properly mustered into the service, he could not report accurately the number of troops under his command. Further complicating his task was the unreliable nature "of many of the troops heretofore raised in this State." In a letter to McClellan he explained that "some of these corps are not only organized in a manner entirely contrary to law. . . . On the contrary, being mostly foreigners, officered in many cases by foreign adventurers or perhaps refugees from justice and having been tampered with by political partisans for political purposes, they constitute a very dangerous element in society as well as in the army." When he used the terms *foreigners* and *political partisans*, Halleck had in mind the German troops and press. While this was an overly simplistic analysis, and probably revealed his own nativist prejudices, nevertheless, Halleck had quickly identified the difficulties that antislavery elements, both from other countries and from out of state, were causing. Governor Gamble may have warned him about the radical abolitionist faction in St. Louis, which was acting lawlessly and had influenced Fremont to issue the proclamation freeing slaves in Missouri. A majority of this faction was German, although one should remember that a minority, including some of the leadership, was composed of Americans.[3]

To ensure the proper muster of troops, and thus gain pay and subsistence for them, Halleck published a series of general orders commanding federal and militia forces to muster in officers and men according to military law. In these orders, he instructed his command concerning the circumstances that warranted the seizure of civilian property or services. Moreover, Halleck appointed a military board to examine the defenses of St. Louis to consider if they had been located properly according to a workable plan. The board also was given the task of investigating whether

3. Gamble to McClellan, 6 and 10 December 1861 and 14 January 1862, *Official Records*, series 1, vol. 8, 408–10, 500–502, and 818–19. Sears, *McClellan Papers*, 130–31 and 143–44.

or not the contractors had committed any fraud in the construction of the fortifications. The very necessity of issuing these types of general orders at the outset of Halleck's command was a strong indictment of Fremont's competence as an administrator and commander.[4]

Perhaps the most intractable problem with which Halleck and other commanders after him were faced was how to prevent troops from abusing their power. These abuses included murder, theft, and the humiliation of civilians through physical and verbal abuse and other unnecessary outrages that alienated many of Missouri's citizens from the federal government. Halleck explained to McClellan the seriousness of these abuses of power: "The conduct of our troops under Fremont's campaign, and especially the course pursued by those under Lane and Jennison has turned against us many thousands who were formerly Union men. A few more such raids, in connection with the ultra speeches made by leading men in Congress, will make this State as unanimous against us as is Eastern Virginia." For his part, Gamble wanted very vigorous action taken against the culprits responsible for the outrages, stating in a letter to Halleck: "I would like very much to see the shooting process begin and will undertake to provide you with suitable subjects (beginning with Jennison) until the service is purged from men who disgrace humanity and ruin the cause of our Government." However, Halleck found it very difficult to enforce discipline, for some commanders of regiments refused to enforce his orders and shielded their officers and men from court-martial. In the instance of the Fourth Missouri Volunteer Regiment, Halleck ordered several companies, which had formerly been part of the Third U.S. Reserve Corps, to perform hard labor on the fortifications under construction at Cairo, Illinois. He also ordered the officers of these companies to be cashiered for failing to enforce proper discipline. In particular, Halleck found the enforcement of discipline difficult among many German regiments, for some of their officers fomented disobedience to orders they thought unjust. In January and February 1862 Halleck, through the use of undercover police, discovered "secret meetings" in St. Louis in which

4. General Orders, No. 8, 26 November 1861; General Orders, No. 21, 9 December 1861; and Special Orders, No. 24, 2 December 1861, *Official Records*, series 1, vol. 8, 380–81, 401–2, and 418.

the German community and the press sought to undermine his authority by elevating General Franz Sigel to the rank of major general. This threat was potentially dangerous, for over 50,000 German immigrants had settled in St. Louis. Against Halleck's orders, many German officers were present at a meeting held on January 26, having left their commands without his permission. According to their plan, Sigel would lead an insurrection among the German regiments to force the Lincoln administration to restore Fremont to command in Missouri. In his report of the conspiracy to McClellan, Halleck expressed his concern that the administration might yield to the conspirators' demands and thus weaken his control over the department. McClellan replied that he had consulted with Secretary of War Edwin Stanton and had been assured that despite the truth of Halleck's intelligence, the German population did not have the means or power to effect its purposes. Furthermore, Stanton promised to support him completely in his efforts to maintain the peace.[5]

While Halleck struggled to restore order to the department, Gamble issued his first general order to institute the militia agreement with Lincoln, explaining the funding and subsistence arrangement, the organization of troops, and the handing over of the state forces command to Halleck as commander of the Department of the Missouri. This order announced the state's readiness to begin implementation of Halleck's General Order No. 96 and demonstrated the cooperation necessary to make the arrangement work. These orders benefited recruitment into the militia, for no question remained concerning how these forces would be funded. The United States would pay, outfit, and subsist militia troops the same as federal regiments. However, whenever officers of equal rank in the militia and U.S. regiments served in the field together, the agreement stipulated that U.S. officers would outrank their militia counterparts. Moreover, mi-

5. Halleck to McClellan, 10 December 1861 and 2 February 1862; Gamble to Halleck, 6 January 1862; Halleck to Francis P. Blair Jr., 6 January 1862; General Orders, No. 28, 2 February 1862; General Orders, No. 46, 22 February 1862, *Official Records*, series 1, vol. 8, 252, 542, 563–64, 818–19, and 828–29. *McClellan Papers*, 171–72. Virgil C. Blum, "The Political and Military Activities of the German Element in St. Louis, 1859–1861," *Missouri Historical Review* 42 (January 1948): 103 and 107–8. It appears that the administration had been fully informed of the plot by Francis P. Blair Jr., who had warned the conspirators that he would expose them if they moved forward with their plans. See John M. Schofield, *Forty-Six Years in the Army* (New York: Century, 1897; reprint, Norman: University of Oklahoma Press, 1998), 84–88.

litia forces were subject to the articles of war and each regiment had to conform to the organizational structure of the U.S. military.[6]

On November 29, to begin mustering in soldiers and recruiting others, Halleck placed General John M. Schofield in command of the militia. The choice of Schofield proved to be a good one, for he and Gamble respected each other and worked harmoniously in the execution of their arduous duties. Gamble, who had no experience in military administrative duties, relied heavily on Schofield's expertise in such matters. A few days later, Gamble learned from Halleck that Schofield might be ordered to duty in the East and telegraphed Attorney General Bates to prevent his transfer. On the telegram General George B. McClellan scribbled a note stating that he had no intention of removing Schofield from Missouri. Lincoln's personal secretary John G. Nicolay relayed this information to Gamble only four days after he had communicated his objection to Schofield's transfer.[7]

During this period, Gamble worked with both Halleck and Schofield to raise and supply troops. Schofield divided the state into districts and appointed officers to command the militia within them. He directed these commanders to bring together companies and detachments "into battalions and regiments as rapidly as they may be formed and mustered into service." This work continued until the summer of 1862, when most of the regiments were finally raised and outfitted as Missouri State Militia. Schofield also directed the district commanders to recommend to Gamble the appointment of competent individuals as field officers. Finally, he ordered district commanders to cooperate with the officers in command of U.S. troops in their areas and to detach troops for military operations under their direction whenever possible.[8]

While these preparations went on, the Confederate army under Sterling Price's command remained in central Missouri, from where he hoped

6. General Orders, No. 96, 7 November 1861 and General Orders, No. 1, 25 November 1861, *Official Records*, series 1, vol. 3, 565; and series 1, vol. 8, 378.

7. General Orders, No. 1, 29 November 1861, *Official Records*, series 1, vol. 8, 394. Gamble to Edward Bates, 7 December 1861, and John G. Nicolay to Gamble, 11 December 1861, Lincoln papers.

8. John M. Schofield to Benjamin Loan, 10 December 1861, *Official Records*, series 1, vol. 8, 422–23. Schofield, *Forty-Six Years in the Army*, 55.

to launch a campaign eastward, capture St. Louis, and ultimately sever the state from federal control. However, this objective proved to be overly ambitious, for Price struggled merely to maintain his army in the field. Without significant support from the Confederate government these efforts were very difficult, for Price's soldiers lacked sufficient clothing, arms, and food. These factors, combined with homesickness and the realization that military life was often bleak and dangerous, convinced many to desert. Apparently recognizing the critical circumstances of his command, Price promised his soldiers that those who remained would soon receive pay and subsistence from their government in Richmond. He also suggested that many of them return home for a short time where they could gather clothing and other supplies before rejoining the army.[9]

To those who hoped for an end to the conflict, the circumstances of Price's army appeared to be an opportunity to restore peace by persuading his soldiers to lay down their arms and accept an offer of amnesty. Dr. John R. Moore offered to act as an emissary to Price's army to seek an end to hostilities. Gamble was skeptical of the plan, believing that an offer of amnesty would be perceived as an act of desperation rather than one of "kindness." However, in the interest of not missing a chance for peace he sent Moore to the front to determine if some arrangement might be worked out with Price. Gamble did not want his motivation for agreeing to Moore's plan to be misunderstood, emphasizing that he and Lincoln both desired peace, not out of fear, but from their desire to redeem those willing to return home and live as law-abiding citizens. Of Lincoln Gamble explained to Moore that

> I can say to you with all frankness that while I differ from the President and his political party upon all questions which distinguish that party I was strongly impressed with the belief that he most earnestly desires for each one of his fellow citizens that he should be reconciled to the government and be secured in his person and property from all consequences of taking up arms. So great is my confidence in his disposition to afford security to all

9. Halleck to George B. McClellan, 29 November 1861; John Pope to Halleck, 29 November 1861; John Pope to G. W. Cullum, 10 December 1861; Earl Van Dorn to Sterling Price, 7 February 1862; and Confidential Circular of G. T. Beauregard, 21 February 1862, *Official Records*, series 1, vol. 7, 899–900; and vol. 8, 392–93, 420–22, and 748. Galusha Anderson, *The Story of a Border City During the Civil War* (Boston: Little, Brown, 1908), 168–69.

who are disposed to peace that I would willingly give my individual pledge
to any person from Gen. Price the leader of the army down to any private
that upon reasonable assurance of continuing loyalty the past will be forgotten. I certainly would not give such a pledge if I was not perfectly confident
that it would be fully redeemed. Upon any intimation coming to me from
any person who wishes to avail himself of the clemency of the Government
I will take measures to have him secured against trouble and if the time
should shortly come when bodies of men will desire in reality to become
peaceful citizens I will cause (as I think I can) a proclamation to be issued
from Washington giving security from molestation.[10]

When Moore arrived at his headquarters, General Pope recommended to
Halleck that Moore be allowed to present a letter from Governor Gamble
to Price explaining the conditions on which he and his army might be par-
doned for their past actions against the U.S. government. It is clear from
Gamble's statements later that he had consulted with Lincoln in this matter and had written the letter in conformity with the president's policy.
Unfortunately, Price rejected Gamble's proposal and the war in Missouri
continued.[11]

Over the next few months Price's army, although intact, presented
little serious threat to the militia and federal forces in Missouri. Shortly
after Gamble's offer of amnesty had been rejected, Halleck struck against
forces supporting Price along the Missouri River, a region on which he
relied for supplies and men. This campaign forced Price to retreat into
Arkansas, perhaps dampening some of the enthusiasm in Missouri for the
Southern cause. And yet, many real threats to supporters of the Union remained. The most immediate threat continued to be that posed by bands
of guerrillas who were willing to ambush Union troops, burn bridges,
and destroy railroad track. Working secretly under cover of night, irregular troops could do much good for the South by fixing many federal
regiments in Missouri that might otherwise fight elsewhere. And, in fact,
guerrilla actions and the possibility of Price's army again invading Missouri prevented the transfer of federal regiments from the department

10. Gamble to John R. Moore, 30 November 1861, Gamble papers.
11. John Pope to Halleck, 2 December 1861; and Halleck to Charles C. Whittelsey, 2 January
1862, *Official Records*, series 1, vol. 8, 399; and series 2, vol. 1, 249. St. Louis *Missouri Republican*,
22 August 1862.

for several months. Many of the members of these irregular forces had received written commissions from Price.[12]

MARTIAL LAW UNDER HALLECK

Recognizing that the civil authorities were no longer able to enforce the laws, Halleck demanded the authority to declare martial law in Missouri. This power was necessary, he believed, to strike at Price's civilian supporters who provided his army with the means for conducting war. In just a few days Lincoln granted Halleck the authority to suspend the writ of *habeas corpus* and to implement martial law. With this authority, men supporting the enemy or engaged in guerrilla actions against Halleck's command were no longer treated as civilians, but instead found themselves liable to the heaviest penalties under military law during wartime.[13]

On December 26, Halleck declared martial law in St. Louis and along all of the railroads in Missouri. However, he reassured the public that his intention was not "to interfere with the jurisdiction of any civil court which is loyal to the Government of the United States." Later, at the request of Gamble, the military began enforcing the ordinance passed by the state convention requiring all officeholders to take an oath of allegiance to the governments of Missouri and the United States. Halleck also ordered the mayor of St. Louis to ensure that all city officials met this requirement. While preferable to having disloyal persons holding office, finding suitable replacements was no easy task. Many unionists were already seeking appointments in the state militia or in the federal army and were unavailable. Most frustrating was the difficulty of finding loyal men in those parts of the state where secession was the dominant sentiment of the population.[14]

12. Halleck to George B. McClellan, 19 December 1861 and 9 January 1862; and William F. Switzler to Halleck, 26 December 1861, *Official Records*, series 1, vol. 7, 539–40, and vol. 8, 448–49; and series 2, vol. 1, 239–40.

13. Halleck to George B. McClellan, 30 November 1861; and Lincoln and William Seward to Halleck, 2 December 1861, *Official Records*, series 1, vol. 8, 395 and 401.

14. General Orders, No. 34, 26 December 1861; General Orders, No. 19, 7 December 1861; and General Orders, No. 55, 3 March 1862, *Official* Records, series 1, vol. 8, 414, 468, and 586–87. *Journal of the Missouri State Convention Held in Jefferson City, June 1862* (St. Louis: George Knapp, 1862), 7. *Proceedings of the Missouri State Convention Held in Jefferson City, June 1862* (St. Louis: George Knapp, 1862), 95 and 113.

Even in areas where civil authority was fully in place, Halleck regulated activities normally supervised by state or federal officials. Of particular importance was the regulation of commerce along the Mississippi, Missouri, Tennessee, and Cumberland rivers and overland routes into regions lately restored to the Union. This was necessary to prevent the smuggling of goods to the enemy. Steamboats and other vessels were required to carry special permits onboard and passengers' baggage was checked and sealed before departure. Soon these regulations were superseded by those promulgated by Secretary of the Treasury Salmon P. Chase. Travel by individuals was also closely watched, especially in regions near the enemy. Some provost-marshals, although far from the front, required persons entering their jurisdiction to obtain a passport. Demonstrating that he understood inconveniences to the public should be minimized, Halleck ordered that only commanding officers in war zones should issue passports and then "only for passing the lines."[15]

Another liberty restricted in Missouri was freedom of the press. Under Fremont the St. Louis *State Journal* and the Boonville *Patriot*, both of which supported secession, were suppressed. Ulysses S. Grant, then in command at Jefferson City, had ordered the press of the Boonville paper seized and its editor arrested. Later Fremont, reacting to accounts criticizing his inaction, suppressed two other newspapers. Soon after assuming command, Halleck also sought to control the press. He first ordered all newspapers outside of St. Louis to provide a copy of every issue to the provost-marshal general or suffer suppression. Not long after this, Edmund J. Ellis, editor of the Boone County *Standard*, was arrested and tried before a military commission. The *Standard* was published in Columbia, where much support for Price's army and guerrilla activity predominated. Ellis, who could hardly deny what he had published in his paper, argued that the military commission was an unconstitutional institution and therefore had no jurisdiction over his activities. The court rejected this argument and brought two charges against him: the first accused Ellis of publishing "information for the benefit of the enemy and encouraging resistance to the Government and laws of the United States"; the second charged him with the publication "of articles and information intended and designed to

15. General Orders, Nos. 52 and 53, 3 March 1862; General Orders, No. 16, 11 January 1862; and General Orders, No. 61, 12 March 1862, *Official Records*, series 1, vol. 8, 495, 584–86, and 607–8.

comfort the enemy and incite persons to rebellion." The court found Ellis guilty of both charges and sentenced him to be banished from Missouri and ordered the confiscation of the press, furniture, and other property of the paper. In confirming the sentence, Halleck warned Ellis that if he returned to Missouri during the war he would be imprisoned. Later, Secretary of War Edwin M. Stanton approved Halleck's action and published an order directing that any editions of newspapers publishing information valuable to the enemy were to be destroyed.[16]

After receiving expanded authority from the president, Halleck, who was an expert on military law, having published a treatise on the subject before the war, quickly implemented harsh policies to destroy guerrilla bands and to punish those who supported them. In a series of general orders and explanations to individual commanders, Halleck clearly defined to the officers and men under his command the extent of the new authority given to them. These general orders were also published in the newspapers as a warning to the public. Halleck explained that these measures were according to the law of war and were justified because a more "mild and indulgent course" had been ineffective in stopping individuals from helping the enemy. As a practical matter "we cannot at the same time extend to rebels the rights of peace and enforce against them the penalties of war. They have forfeited their civil rights as citizens by making war against the Government, and upon their own heads must fall the consequences." To implement and administer this authority, Halleck first appointed a provost-marshal general for the Department of Missouri and provost-marshals in St. Louis and elsewhere to enforce his orders throughout the state. Noting the wide-scale efforts of persons in some regions to assist the enemy, he warned that such activities were punishable by death. Such severity was necessary to restore peace. Commanding officers were to arrest all violators of the peace, to designate the charges against the accused,

16. Nathaniel Lyon to Chester Harding, 2 July 1861; M. Jeff. Thompson to Joseph Tucker, 16 July 1861; John M. Schofield to Chester Harding, 26 July 1861; and Ulysses S. Grant to William H. Worthington, 26 August 1861, *Official Records*, series 1, vol. 3, 388, 407–8, 608–9; and series 2, vol. 1, 217. Anderson, *Border City*, 214–16. St. Louis *Missouri Republican*, 10 January 1862. "Memorandum of Various Political Arrests"; "Trial of Edmund J. Ellis," 25–26 February 1862; Edwin M. Stanton to Halleck, 5 April 1862; General Orders, No. 48, 26 February 1862, *Official Records*, series 1, vol. 8, 568–69; and series 2, 276, 348, and 453–57.

to provide evidence gathered under oath, and to send this evidence to the provost-marshal general. Because many of the violations were not punishable by courts-martial, periodically Halleck designated persons to serve on "military commissions," judicial tribunals on which military officers sat as judges, to try individuals accused of supporting the enemy in some way, destroying bridges and other important infrastructure, and to confiscate the property of the disloyal. For persons acting as spies he promised arrest, trial, and firing squad, and warned women in particular that "the laws of war make no distinction of sex; all are liable to the same penalty." Halleck's resolve to punish women was demonstrated earlier when he had arrested and expelled from the department a woman who had been providing information to the enemy.[17]

A short time after receiving the authority to establish martial law, the action of guerrilla bands intensified, thereby complicating immensely Halleck's task of restoring peace in Missouri. By ambushing federal and militia forces and destroying bridges, railroad tracks, and telegraph wires, these guerrilla bands were disrupting his efforts to cut off Price's retreat and destroy his army. Believing that "examples of severe punishment are the only remedies," Halleck ordered those guerrillas caught destroying bridges, railroad track, and telegraph wires to be immediately shot without trial. Those suspected of these activities were to be arrested and tried by military commission and were to suffer death if convicted. He also ordered those failing to report these crimes to the military authorities be held financially responsible for the damages. These measures provoked Confederate General Price to protest the arrest of "individuals and parties of men specially appointed and instructed by me to destroy railroads, culverts, and bridges." He claimed that this was "heretofore recognized by the civilized world . . . as distinctly lawful and proper." Halleck bluntly replied that he would treat lawful combatant prisoners according to the rules of war, but that Price had acted unlawfully in sending persons posing as citizens to steal and destroy the property of many unionists. These actions were doubly offensive in Halleck's view, for they did nothing to further the cause of the Confederacy, but instead were simply acts of ven-

17. General Orders, No. 13, 4 December 1861, *Official Records*, series 1, vol. 8, 405–7. Anderson, *Border City*, 237–38.

geance. Such action on Price's part, Halleck added, was giving "immunity to crime." Moreover, he accused Price of mistreating Union prisoners of war, of driving supporters of the Union from southwestern Missouri, and generally promoting criminal acts by his soldiers.[18]

From Halleck's general order of January 1, 1862, establishing military commissions, and from the record of the cases, one gains an appreciation of the dangers then present to the military and civilians in Missouri. Military commissions were convened, he made clear, to try offenses untriable in civil courts and in courts-martial that were limited in their jurisdiction. Apparently, this authority was used along with arrests—by then unconstrained by the writ of *habeas corpus*—to intimidate individuals who were suspected of "aiding and abetting the enemy," spying, and other crimes. Halleck considered these military commissions a useful tool to protect the lives of peaceful citizens, but also recognized that they were liable to misuse. For this reason, he established rigid rules for their implementation. First, these tribunals could only be convened by himself or General McClellan. Second, each commission was to be composed of at least three military officers, one of these serving as judge-advocate and recorder of the proceedings. Third, although some differences would be permitted, the proceedings of the commissions were to be conducted like those of courts-martial. Moreover, from indictments made against persons arrested, Halleck ascertained that many officers in the field were not making the proper distinctions between offenses triable by civilian courts, courts-martial, and military commissions and informed them that only those persons guilty of violating "the general rules of war" could be tried before commissions.[19]

By instituting commission trials Halleck sought to deter others from committing crimes and participating in guerrilla activities. This purpose

18. General Orders, No. 32, 22 December 1862; Halleck to George B. McClellan, 26 December 1861; Sterling Price to Halleck, 12 January 1862; Special Orders, No. 14, undated; and Halleck to Sterling Price, 22 January 1862, *Official Records*, series 1, vol. 3, 593; vol. 8, 462–64, 496, and 514–15.

19. General Orders, No. 1, 1 January 1862; George E. Leighton to William H. Seward, 3 March 1862, and "List of political prisoners"; *Official Records*, series 2, vol. 1, 247–49; and vol. 2, 249–52.

required the execution of men convicted of bridge burning and murder. However, in his oversight of commission trials Halleck exercised a good deal of restraint, often commuting sentences of death to imprisonment during the war when mitigating circumstances demonstrated that the persons convicted were dupes of their neighbors or otherwise did not deserve the severest penalty. In February 1862 he ordered the commutation of death sentences to several individuals "in consideration of the recent victories won by the Federal forces, and of the rapidly-increasing loyalty of citizens of Missouri." This commutation was only provisional and the original sentences would be carried out if new uprisings and the destruction of communications resumed. In using the expanded powers provided to him, Halleck also punished those who failed to report guerrilla activities in their neighborhood by convening military commissions to assess damages against "disloyal" members of the community. This measure enabled him to punish conspirators who otherwise might help the insurrection without fear of retribution. In a similar way, Halleck appointed a civilian commission in St. Louis to make assessments against secessionists to provide aid and lodging to unionist refugees from southwestern Missouri. Later this policy was challenged, of which more will be written below.[20]

Organization of the Militia

At the time of their implementation, Gamble did not object to Halleck's policies. He believed in deferring to the judgment of professionals, although he reserved the right, which he had previously exercised, to protest when those measures harmed the war effort. Gamble also observed that during time of war it was inevitable that people's civil rights would be violated occasionally. This was not a trivial matter with him, but he considered some limitation of freedoms preferable to the great loss of life that had occurred so far. Gamble later explained the violence and extent of this anarchy in a message to the legislature.

20. Trial of William Hearst, 10–13 January 1862; General Orders, No. 20, 14 January 1862; General Orders, No. 44, 20 February 1862; Benjamin G. Farrar to Halleck, 1 March 1862; General Orders, No. 54, 3 March 1862; and General Orders, No. 13, 30 March 1862; *Official Records*, series 1, vol. 8, 411, 431–32, 561, and 586; and series 2, vol. 1, 170–71, 177, 285–92, 402–6.

The people of most of the loyal States know nothing of the species of war through which we have passed. They send their sons to distant battle fields, they bear the interruption of their ordinary pursuits and the burdens of taxation, but they know nothing of the horrors of a war in which families each night fear that before morning they may be aroused by bands of armed men coming to plunder their dwellings and probably murder their protectors. Such war has prevailed in Missouri and such has been the condition of many of her loyal people because of their fidelity to the Government.

For these reasons, as the war progressed Gamble increasingly favored harsh measures against guerrillas and before sending commanders into the field he instructed them to protect loyal citizens and to kill those they found "with arms in their hands." [21]

During Halleck's command of the Department of the Missouri, Gamble's duties as governor were primarily supportive of the military. At the time, because of the state convention's decisions in October 1861, no legislature convened and no elections were held throughout the state. The majority of Gamble's time was expended in his efforts to create a state militia force according to the arrangement he had made with Lincoln and military leaders in Washington. Although Gamble had asked for funding from the federal government for 42,000 troops, Congress authorized money to support only 10,000. Gamble's request was based on military necessity and the premise that the Missouri State Militia would allow the withdrawal of all or most federal troops from the state. One of the more difficult tasks he confronted was finding arms, clothing, and other supplies for the militia. As one might expect, at the beginning of the war these resources were scarce and the competition for them among the federal government and the Northern states was keen. To gain what they could, Gamble sent agents to Washington to purchase any available arms and supplies. Soon after his arrival in St. Louis, Halleck mentioned the circumstances of federal troops who were poorly sheltered and clothed, many of whom were then on the sick list. This want of supplies caused some

21. Gamble to Lincoln, 26 August 1861, Gamble papers. St. Louis *Missouri Republican*, 27 July and 22 August 1862. General Orders, No. 19, 22 July 1862, *Official Records*, series 1, vol. 13, 506. Buel Leopard and Floyd C. Shoemaker, eds., *The Messages and Proclamations of the Governors of the State of Missouri* (Columbia: The State Historical Society of Missouri, 1922), 431.

frustration for Gamble, for the outfitting of federal troops took priority over the militia. Nevertheless, by April 1862 his efforts were rewarded, for the militia, although not perfectly equipped with arms, were, according to General Schofield, "better supplied than the majority of volunteers."[22]

It is to the credit of both Gamble and Halleck that through this time of stress and strain they remained on friendly terms and shared their concerns honestly with one another. This cooperation and trust ensured that the militia and federal troops coordinated their efforts together well and maximized the response to any threat Price's army or guerrilla troops might present. A very important policy on which they agreed concerned slavery. Both men were unwilling to flaunt the judgment of Congress and the president who directed the military only to confiscate slaves if they were employed in the service of the Confederate army. Moreover, Halleck favored this policy because he feared that the enemy was learning important details about "the numbers and condition" of Union troops from fugitive slaves. Gamble supported the policy for a different reason, believing that the indiscriminate stealing of slaves would lead many Missourians to side with Price's army.[23]

During the winter of 1862, Price's army withdrew into Arkansas and as part of a larger force under the command of Earl Van Dorn participated in the Battle of Pea Ridge, where they were defeated on March 7 and 8 by federal troops under Samuel R. Curtis. Moreover, forces under Halleck's command outside of Missouri made progress in rolling back Confederate armies under General Albert Sydney Johnston. After General Ulysses S. Grant's capture of Forts Henry and Donelson on the Tennessee and Cumberland rivers in northern Tennessee, Johnston was forced to retreat south until his fateful decision to attack Union troops at Pittsburg Landing, where the Battle of Shiloh was fought on April 6 and 7. While these

22. William McPherson to Gamble, 23 and 28 September 1861; and Edward Bates to Gamble, 27 September and 3 October 1861, Gamble papers. Halleck to George B. McClellan, 3 December 1861; and John M. Schofield to James Totten, 7 April 1861, *Official Records*, series 1, vol. 8, 402–3 and 672–73. Beale, *Bates Diary*, 31 December 1861 and 3 January 1862, 219. Gamble to Lincoln, 13 and 28 September 1861; Gamble to Montgomery Blair, 5 October 1861, Lincoln papers.

23. General Orders, No. 3, 20 November 1861; Gamble to Halleck, 6 January 1862; Halleck to Gamble, 7 January 1862; Halleck to Colonel Carlin, 9 January 1862, *Official Records*, series 1, vol. 8, 370; series 2, vol. 1, 252 and 799.

Union victories ended Confederate dreams of retaking Missouri, danger still remained from invasion by Price's army and from guerrilla activity in Missouri.[24]

Just days after the victory at Shiloh, Halleck hastened to assume active command in the field, leaving Schofield in command of militia forces and most of the federal forces in Missouri. Schofield, with the help of Gamble, was just completing the organization of militia, which consisted of almost 14,000 men, most of whom were "mounted riflemen." These forces, comprising fourteen regiments of cavalry, one infantry regiment, and one battery of artillery, had been mustered into the militia where they would serve and were immediately useful as occupation troops in Missouri. These troops cooperated with federal troops from whom they learned military discipline and maneuver tactics. This proved to be an efficient means for putting new troops quickly into the field. This efficient formation of the militia was fortunate, for Halleck was anxious to concentrate as much of his command near Corinth, Mississippi, where he was then conducting a siege against Confederate forces. On May 6, Halleck ordered Schofield to forward to him almost all federal infantry still in Missouri. Having reduced his troops in this way, Schofield moved to protect General Curtis's lines of communications, which operated from Rolla, Missouri, all the way to just north of Little Rock, Arkansas. This stretched Schofield's forces too thinly and made them vulnerable to possible attack from guerrilla forces, some of which were organized and manned by troops from Price's army who had returned after their defeat in Arkansas.[25]

During this period, Gamble did what he could to support Schofield, authorizing him to organize the militia and arrange it as he thought best. Gamble also appointed and dismissed officers according to Schofield's recommendations and provided advice on the conduct of military judicial proceedings. In June, when Schofield's forces had been stretched to their thinnest, Gamble wrote to Secretary of War Edwin M. Stanton to request that he order two U.S. volunteer regiments, then stationed at Fort Scott, Kansas, and unemployed, to report to southwestern Missouri, where Con-

24. James M. McPherson, *Battle Cry of Freedom: The Civil War Era*, vol. 6, the Oxford History of the United States (New York: Oxford University Press, 1988), 403–14.

25. Schofield, *Forty-Six Years in the Army*, 55–56. "Report of Brig. Gen. John M. Schofield, U.S. Army of operations in Missouri and Northwestern Arkansas, April 10–November 20, 1862," *Official Records*, series 1, vol. 13, 7–21.

federate forces were concentrating. Gamble's request was granted, as was his later request to retain militia forces exceeding the number authorized by Congress.[26]

KANSAS-MISSOURI BORDER WARFARE

As was the case through the last half of the 1850s, border warfare between Missouri and Kansas continued throughout the war. The residents along the Kansas-Missouri border had fought one another for a number of years because of their disagreement over slavery. U.S. Senator David R. Atchison had organized and led Missourians into Kansas to fight and vote in elections held to determine whether the territory would become slave or free. Election fraud and intimidation had ensured the election of proslavery delegates to the constitutional convention. These delegates quickly drafted a document that did not reflect the opinion of a majority of Kansans, many of whom had recently immigrated to the territory to establish its free status. Next, recognizing that the majority of Kansas voters opposed slavery, the delegates of the convention refused to submit their work to the people, instead sending it to Congress with a petition for admittance into the Union as a slave state. This proposal was rejected by the House, where the majority of Northern congressmen, including twenty-two Democrats, rejected the Lecompton Constitution. This rejection, however, did not end the violence, and lawless individuals from both Kansas and Missouri continued to raid, steal, and kill one another.[27]

With the outbreak of war, Missourians and Kansans, the majority of whom were unionists, were unable to set aside their long-standing grievances against each other. In fact, evidence pointed to an intensification of the hatred and the violence, causing Gamble to seek aid in ending border conflict. During the first months of the war, having learned of a proposal to establish an independent military command in Kansas, he and Lieutenant Governor Hall wrote to Lincoln expressing their opposition to the

26. Ibid. Gamble to Edwin M. Stanton, 4 June, 7 and 15 August 1862; Assistant Secretary of War to Gamble, 19 June 1862; James Totten to John M. Schofield, 23 June 1862; Halleck to Gamble, 15 August 1862; and Edwin M. Stanton to Gamble, 22 August 1862, *Official Records,* series 1, vol. 13, 414, 438, 557–58; series 2, vol. 4, 55–56; and series 3, vol. 2, 319, 392, and 438.

27. McPherson, *Battle Cry of Freedom,* 145–69. Jay Monaghan, *Civil War on the Western Border, 1854–1865* (Lincoln: University of Nebraska Press, 1955), 45–106.

appointment of U.S. Senator James H. Lane to its command. There was mounting evidence that Lane and his chief lieutenant Charles R. Jennison were using the war as an opportunity to wreak vengeance on Missourians along the border. Having received a number of complaints about Lane's and Jennison's activities against Missourians, Gamble expected General David Hunter, who had been appointed to command Union troops in Kansas, to take vigorous action to prevent further depredations. If nothing was done, Gamble promised "as the chief executor of the State to see that the citizens are protected."[28]

Evidence of the brazen activities of the military leadership of Kansas came from Jennison himself, who in November 1861 published a proclamation to the inhabitants of the northwestern counties of Missouri in which he promised to protect the lives and property of all loyal citizens, but also threatened to punish all disloyal persons. Claiming that Missourians' "professed friendship has been a fraud; [their] oaths of allegiance have been shams and perjuries," Jennison stated that "traitors will everywhere be treated as outlaws—enemies of God and men—too base to hold any description of property having no rights which loyal men are bound to respect." While much guerrilla activity occurred in western Missouri, not unlike the situation throughout the state, it is evident that Jennison's response was often an excuse for him and his regiment to loot and destroy property. Apparently, soon after Halleck took command of the Department of the Missouri, Governor Gamble sought to make him aware of the problem by arranging an interview with O. G. Cates, a representative of citizens loyal to the Union in Jackson County in northwestern Missouri. Cates sought protection from Jennison and other Kansas "jayhawkers" and compensation for property stolen or destroyed. In response Halleck immediately ordered General Pope to prevent civilians and troops in Kansas from coming into Missouri. However, he also informed Cates that he did not have the authority to compensate persons for their losses and directed him to submit his claims to the War Department.[29]

28. Gamble to Lincoln and Willard P. Hall to Lincoln, 18 October 1861, Lincoln papers. Gamble to O. G. Cates, 21 November 1861, *Official Records*, series 1, vol. 17, part 2, 92.

29. Charles R. Jennison to the people of Jackson, LaFayette, Cass, Johnson, and Pettis counties, 27 November 1861; O. G. Cates to Halleck, 28 January 1862; O. G. Cates to Edwin M. Stanton, 26 February 1862, *Official Records*, series 1, vol. 17, part 2, 91–94; series 2, vol. 1, 231–32.

Unfortunately, despite his desire to help, it soon became evident to Halleck that stopping the violence in western Missouri would not be easy. In response to inquiry from Secretary of War Stanton about the matter, Halleck explained that he had two regiments "stationed or moving in Jackson County" to stop the violence against civilians. This action had effected little change and, he believed, would continue to be ineffective unless he distributed throughout the state the militia and at least 50,000 additional soldiers. To end the depredations was very difficult, if not impossible, for "the Kansas jayhawkers" were not under his command. Moreover, the commanders of volunteer troops often supported and participated in these outrages, and of course, shielded themselves and their men from prosecution by court-martial when accused. Under these circumstances, Halleck had requested and received authority from the War Department to muster out without court-martial those officers "shown to be guilty of this species of plunder and marauding." These dismissals had "the good effect" of purging regiments of some of the bad officers and serving notice to the rest that such conduct would not be tolerated.[30]

In May 1862, after it became evident that the intervention of Secretary of War Stanton and General Halleck had not stopped the border troubles, Gamble wrote directly to Lincoln about the Kansas border incursions. Gamble believed these invasions were undermining his authority, for they made him appear powerless, and asserted that he had a right to expect Lincoln to remove this difficulty, if it was within his power. Gamble, not wishing to provide a one-sided account, and to demonstrate his own restraint, explained that he had used his influence to prevent Missourians from retaliating against the inhabitants of Kansas. The same restraint, however, was not being exercised by the authorities in Kansas. In fact, they seemed to seize on any pretense to cross into Missouri and cause trouble. To prevent any further troubles, Gamble proposed that Lincoln prohibit the military in Kansas from entering Missouri unless General Schofield requested their help. To demonstrate his good faith in making this proposal, Gamble also thought that it would only be right to restrict Missouri regiments from entering Kansas.[31]

Despite Gamble's appeal to Lincoln, during the summer of 1862 the

---

30. Halleck to Edwin M. Stanton, 25 March 1862, *Official Records*, series 1, vol. 8, 641–42.
31. Gamble to Lincoln, 19 May 1862, Gamble and Lincoln papers.

troubles along the Kansas-Missouri border continued. Apparently, slavery continued to be the major point of contention between the border residents. Kansans complained that Missourians were crossing into their state and kidnapping "persons of color." Missourians protested the loss of their slaves and in some instances may have retrieved blacks taken from them. Whatever the reason, armed bands from both states crossed into the other and acted without military or civilian authority in taking or destroying property and committing other outrages. In September Gamble again protested these activities and offered the same proposal to Lincoln he had made in May. Nevertheless, the depredations never completely ended and they remained a source of concern for Gamble throughout his governorship. This conflict, however, was only the beginning of a dispute between unionists who disagreed about the issue of slavery and who increasingly distrusted one another.[32]

32. General Orders, No. 3, 7 May 1862; Edward M. Samuel et al. to Lincoln, 8 September 1862, *Official Records*, series 1, vol. 13, 372 and 618–19. St. Louis *Missouri Republican*, 7 July 1862. Andrew Brownlow to Gamble, 1 August 1862; Gamble to Lincoln, 8 September 1862; Schofield to Gamble, 2 February 1863; and Gamble to Lincoln, 2 May 1863, Gamble papers.

Chapter Eight

Gamble and the Politics of Slavery

By 1862, with the hope of a short war fading, the issue of slavery increasingly factored into unionists' consciousness and calculations concerning the war. Responding to this changing perception, Lincoln offered to Congress a gradual, compensated emancipation plan to end slavery in the loyal border states. The slavery issue and the question of how best to fight the war became the sources of major disagreements between conservatives and radicals in Missouri's convention and later in the legislature. In preparation for the first election held during wartime, opposition to Hamilton R. Gamble organized itself around these key issues. Moreover, the radicals argued that Gamble's performance of his duties had been ineffective, some critics going so far as to claim that he was disloyal. At first, Gamble ignored his critics, but increasingly he was stung by their criticisms, which he felt were unfair and undermined his authority, causing others to be less confident in him as a leader. Moreover, at the same time Gamble perceived a change in attitude toward him in Washington, D.C., perhaps in part because of his lukewarm response to the Lincoln administration's emancipation plan. Despite all of this, he endeavored to work with the administration for the good of the war effort in Missouri and the rest of the country.

In June 1862, Governor Gamble reconvened the state convention to decide a number of pressing matters. After providing a short history of the challenges of the previous ten months and the actions his administration had taken, Gamble noted various issues requiring the attention of the convention. Among this business was the need to finance the state's burgeoning war debt, to modify the loyalty oath required of all officers of the state, to restructure congressional districts, and to postpone elections for a short time to enable many of the state's federal troops to participate.[1]

The convention quickly took up Gamble's agenda. Because the state election would soon be held, the delegates sought to strengthen the loyalty oath required of each voter and candidate for office. In particular, the majority pushed for a modification of the oath that would require the swearer to attest that he had never taken up arms against the state and national governments. A strengthened oath, it was hoped, would prevent most disloyal persons from voting and running for office. This measure went hand in hand with other proposals modifying the election law of Missouri to arrange for soldiers serving in Missouri's volunteer regiments to vote. As the law then stood, because of their absence from home, these soldiers, who were the strongest supporters of the Union and the provisional government, could not participate in the statewide election. Although some delegates were against giving soldiers the right to vote, most believed that it would be unfair to deny to Missouri's troops the rights for which they were fighting. However, it was agreed that before voting, soldiers should be required to take the oath of allegiance as well. Moreover, the delegates voted to postpone the state election from August until November to provide time to make the necessary special arrangements.[2]

Another important election matter considered by the convention concerned whether the state executive offices would be contested in the fall election. A proposal to postpone the election for governor and lieutenant governor was defeated. Gamble, who had only reluctantly accepted the governorship, soon expressed his dissatisfaction with the vote, apparently considering it a vote of no-confidence. Reports of Gamble's displeasure reached the floor of the convention and led to a reconsideration of the proposal to continue Gamble and the other state executive officers in power. The overwhelming consensus of the delegates was that Gamble

1. St. Louis *Missouri Republican*, 3 June 1862.

2. *Journal of the Missouri State Convention Held in Jefferson City June 1862* (St. Louis: George Knapp, 1862), 10–12, 19, 21–24, and 27–29. *Proceedings of the Missouri State Convention Held in Jefferson City, June 1862* (St. Louis: George Knapp, 1862), 95–97, 117–19, 130–31, 200–201, 216–18, and 222.

had proven himself a loyal and effective governor under the most trying circumstances possible, and that the election of a disloyal or radical
individual could bring disaster to Missouri. Moreover, the advantage of
Gamble's good relationship with the Lincoln administration would be lost
with the election of someone else. After the debate the delegates voted
unanimously for a resolution stating "that this Convention has undiminished confidence in the patriotism, wisdom, and integrity of Governor
Gamble and the other officers elected by the Convention, and now continued in office for the rest of [their four-year] term."[3]

The delegates also proposed a number of special wartime measures
that were meant to diminish human suffering, to compensate those whose
property had been stolen or destroyed, and to exempt some counties from
the responsibility of paying their 1861 taxes to the state. The first delegates to request exemption were those from the western border counties. However, soon other delegates pushed for similar tax relief for their
constituents, leading to the realization that such measures would undermine the state government's ability to raise revenue to fight the war and
fund the debt. Instead, the delegates passed a resolution asking the U.S.
Congress to pay claims individuals might have against the government.
Moreover, the convention passed a small appropriation for the care of sick
and wounded soldiers. These measures were wholly inadequate to meeting Missouri's fiscal responsibilities. Therefore, at the end of the year in a
message to the state legislature, Gamble noted that the state's obligation
was just over $24 million and that interest and principal payments had not
been made. If this circumstance continued, he warned, permanent damage
to Missouri's credit could result. For this reason, as a temporary wartime
measure, Gamble proposed taxing all printed documents as a necessary
indirect tax, which he believed the people would pay more "cheerfully"
than they would a direct tax.[4]

If, when he accepted the office of governor, Gamble imagined that he
could quiet the controversy surrounding slavery, he was quickly disappointed. Radical leaders in Missouri, wishing to transform the war into

3. *Journal, 1862*, 32. *Proceedings, 1862*, 146, 174, 178–79, 200, 205–13, and 216.
4. *Journal, 1862*, 14–16, 35, and 44–45. *Proceedings, 1862*, 15, 24–26, and 223–25. Buel
Leopard and Floyd C. Shoemaker, eds., *The Messages and Proclamations of the Governors of the State
of Missouri* (Columbia: The State Historical Society of Missouri, 1922), 438–40.

a crusade against slavery, protested when Halleck and other commanders enforced federal and state laws protecting the institution. Moreover,
these commanders, who were under orders not to interfere with slavery,
were denounced in newspapers throughout the state and country. These
protests complicated both Gamble's and Lincoln's task of maintaining
support for the war and their administrations. These protests soon forced
Lincoln to reconsider his slavery policy and to seek a compromise. This
decision, in turn, made more difficult Gamble's own efforts to prevent a
schism from developing between proslavery and radical unionists.[5]

In formulating his emancipation policy, Lincoln did not abandon his
concerns about the preservation of slaveholders' constitutional rights.
Unlike his radical critics, he was unwilling to embrace immediate emancipation, believing such a course to be both unwise and unjust, although he
was also convinced that either immediate or gradual emancipation could
be employed as a military necessity. In devising his emancipation plan,
Lincoln sought to weaken the enemy without alienating the military leadership and rank-and-file soldier on whom the fate of the nation rested.
Having concluded that the border states were secure, Lincoln proposed in
March 1862 that Congress pass legislation to encourage them voluntarily
to end slavery gradually.[6]

In his message to Congress, Lincoln argued that the abolition of slavery
in the border states was "one of the most efficient means" of preserving
the Union available to him, for it deprived the Confederate leadership of
the hope that the loyal slave states might yet secede from the Union. His
proposal, Lincoln took pains to make clear, was voluntary, for the federal
government did not have the authority to interfere with slavery in the
loyal states. He believed it was best for each to work out the details, but
that he expected each state to submit the matter to its voters before adopting a plan of gradual and compensated emancipation. Moreover, Lincoln
asserted that by promoting a quicker end to the war, compensated emancipation was economical when one compared this to the great daily cost of
fighting the war. In a letter to Henry J. Raymond, editor of the *New York
Times*, Lincoln demonstrated that the cost of freeing all the slaves in the

5. Henry W. Halleck to Edwin M. Stanton, 12 July 1862, *Official Records*, series 1, vol. 17,
part 2, 91. David Herbert Donald, *Lincoln* (New York: Simon & Schuster, 1995), 331–33.

6. Donald, *Lincoln*, 331–33 and 342–48.

border states at $400 each would cost no more than the expense of fighting the war for only eighty-seven days.[7]

Before making his proposal to Congress, Lincoln had quietly cultivated the support of some abolitionists. Recognizing that the vast majority of unionist sentiment was strongly against granting equal social and political rights to free blacks, Lincoln also sought to gain support for colonizing newly emancipated blacks in another country where they would have the opportunity to prosper economically and politically. Remarkably, Lincoln's plan for voluntary, gradual emancipation gained the commendation of a majority of the Northern public and of Congress.[8]

Unfortunately for Lincoln's proposals, the border state congressmen, including those from Missouri, were overwhelmingly opposed to the plan. Their attitudes reflected the values of their constituents, most of whom were not yet ready to yield their right to slavery. One Missouri congressman argued that agitation of the slavery question had caused the war and he could not see how its reintroduction into the public debate could be useful. A second Missouri congressman objected to Lincoln's proposal, noting the number of Missourians who had flocked to the army of Confederate General Sterling Price after the promulgation of Fremont's proclamation. Yet another member of the House denied that slavery was the cause of the rebellion, but rather its real cause was "the belief that [slavery] will be destroyed." This was his way of blaming the North for the South's decision to secede. Moreover, it was observed that different members of Congress had already proposed measures to provide help for the new freedmen and freedwomen with little success. This legislation had not passed after the impracticability of the plans became evident. Missouri's congressmen also noted the unwillingness of Northerners to invite former slaves to their states and communities, most of which had stringent, discriminatory laws that either reduced blacks to a status with few civil and political rights or prohibited free blacks from residing there completely. However, despite

7. Message to Congress, 6 March 1862; Abraham Lincoln to Henry J. Raymond, 9 March 1862; and Abraham Lincoln to Horace Greeley, 24 March 1862, in Michael P. Johnson, ed., *Abraham Lincoln, Slavery, and the Civil War: Selected Writings and Speeches,* the Bedford Series in History and Culture (Boston: Bedford/St. Martin's , 2001), 186–89. James G. Randall, *Constitutional Problems Under Lincoln* (Urbana: University of Illinois Press, 1951), 365–67.

8. Donald, *Lincoln,* 345–47. Randall, *Constitutional Problems,* 365–67.

their own reservations, some of Missouri's congressmen indicated that they were willing to submit Lincoln's proposal to their constituents, while one of their number, Frank Blair Jr., the brother of Postmaster General Montgomery Blair, unreservedly supported Lincoln's proposal and offered an amendment to colonize the former slaves.[9]

After passing a resolution promising compensation to the loyal slave states accepting gradual emancipation, the particulars of the matter, as Lincoln had envisioned, were to be settled by the border states themselves. In Missouri this led to a policy debate concerning the wisdom and practicability of emancipation. Most conservatives believed emancipation to be a mistake for a variety of reasons. One of the first objections to Lincoln's proposal concerned provisions in the state constitution prohibiting the legislature from emancipating slaves "without the consent of their owners, or without paying them" in full before the slaves' emancipation. Slaveowners were also responsible for ensuring that their former slaves did "not become a public charge." Moreover, the constitution prohibited any restrictions against immigrants bringing slaves to Missouri. Many agreed with their representatives in Washington who feared that the policy would create a larger and more determined foe. Some demagogic opponents warned that emancipation would mean black equality, that former slaves would be armed and led by Kansas Jayhawkers, and that whites would lose the benefit of black labor. More responsible opponents to emancipation believed sincerely that the institution was too completely "interwoven into the fabric of society" for anyone to make Missouri a free state. These critics also argued that slavery benefited blacks as much as

9. John B. Henderson, *Speech of Hon. J. B. Henderson of Missouri on the Abolition of Slavery delivered in the Senate of the United States, March 27, 1862* (Washington, D.C.: L. Towers, 1862), 1–15. Frank P. Blair Jr., *Speech of Hon. F. P. Blair Jr. of Missouri on the Policy of the President for the Restoration of the Union and Establishment of Peace delivered in the House of Representatives, April 11, 1862* (New York: Baker & Godwin, 1862), 3–8. E. H. Norton, *Speech of Hon. E. H. Norton of Missouri on Confiscation and Emancipation delivered in the House of Representatives, April 24, 1862* (Washington, D.C.: n.p., 1862), 2–8. John S. Phelps, *Confiscation of property and Emancipation of Slaves: Speech of Hon. John S. Phelps of Missouri in the House of Representatives, May 22, 1862* (Washington, D.C.: n.p., 1862), 1–8. Frank P. Blair Jr., *Confiscation, Emancipation, and Colonization "Indemnity for the Past and Security for the Future": Speech of Hon. F. P. Blair Jr. of Missouri in the House of Representatives, May 23, 1862* (n.p., 1862), 1–7.

whites and rejected the radical assertion that anyone against emancipation was disloyal.[10]

The supporters of the president's policy in Missouri were found mostly among German immigrants in St. Louis. These immigrants brought to Missouri a foreign culture and an animosity for slavery and conservative politicians. However, it would be a mistake to presume that no disagreement existed among them. While the vast majority of Germans voted for Lincoln in 1860, and general agreement remained in their desire to end slavery, nevertheless, disagreement was evident concerning how best to achieve this goal. Two German newspapers in St. Louis, the *Anzeiger des Westons* and the *Westliche Post*, reflected these different views. The *Post*, the more conservative of the two, supported amending the state constitution and thereby removing that obstacle. The *Anzeiger*, however, basing its position on natural rights theory, argued that the proslavery sections of the constitution were already void.[11]

Before passing a resolution promising compensation for any state adopting gradual emancipation, Congress, reflecting the nation's hardened attitude toward anyone supporting the rebellion, passed a bill prohibiting the military from slave catching. In July 1862, Congress next prohibited the return of slaves of disloyal masters for any reason, after these slaves had reached the lines of the Union army.[12]

When he convened the state convention and gave his opening address, Gamble, perhaps believing the issue to be too volatile for consideration at the time, omitted mention of the congressional offer of compensation to slaveowners who were willing to free their slaves. The convention, however, soon deliberated on Lincoln's proposition when on June 6 Samuel M. Breckinridge, a conservative from St. Louis, offered "an ordinance to pro-

---

10. St. Louis *Missouri Republican*, 26 March, 1 and 18 May, 1, 5, 7, 10, and 22 June, and 15 July 1862.

11. Translated excerpts from local German newspapers, the *Anzeiger des Westons* and the *Westliche Post*, in the St. Louis *Missouri Republican*, 1, 2, 13 May and 6 and 9 June 1862. For a full discussion of the impact German immigrants had on the war see Virgil C. Blum, "The Political and Military Activities of the German Element in St. Louis, 1859–1861," *Missouri Historical Review* 42 (January 1948): 103–29.

12. Randall, *Constitutional Problems*, 356–57.

vide for submitting to a vote of the people of Missouri certain amendments to the constitution, and a scheme for the gradual emancipation of slaves." Arguing that the war would soon extinguish slavery as a viable institution in Missouri, Breckinridge wanted to make the transition to free labor as smooth as possible. Moreover, he was impressed with the fairness of Lincoln's proposition to which, he argued, the convention owed a respectful answer. Furthermore, Breckinridge believed that an important opportunity was being lost, for the adoption of an emancipation plan would end the attempt of the South to bring Missouri into their confederation and would go far toward ending the conflict in the state. Breckinridge, however, made clear that newly emancipated slaves must leave Missouri, for he considered free blacks "a pest upon her bosom—a class necessarily inferior and depraved."[13]

U.S. Senator John B. Henderson—also a member of the state convention—supported Breckinridge's ordinance. Having voted in favor of Lincoln's proposal in the Senate, he argued that the war's continuance, even for a brief duration, made emancipation inevitable. A majority of soldiers were now convinced that slavery was the cause of the war. Moreover, Lincoln as commander-in-chief, with whom Henderson had consulted on this subject, believed he had the power to emancipate the slaves as a war measure. Henderson agreed with Lincoln that without slavery Missouri would never become a member of the Confederacy.[14]

Opposition to Breckinridge's ordinance was led by former Missouri Supreme Court justice James H. Birch. Born in Virginia, Birch strongly supported slavery and threatened to side with the South if the convention accepted Lincoln's proposal. He also claimed that emancipation would cost too much and asserted that as a constitutional right slavery could not be abolished. Another member stated that emancipation would convert the Southern states into a waste controlled "by brutal negroes alone." Apparently, the majority of the convention agreed, or more probably believed that emancipation was still then unnecessary, for Breckinridge's recommendation was quickly laid aside by a vote of 52 to 19.[15]

13. *Proceedings, June 1862*, 72–77.
14. Ibid., 98–100.
15. Ibid., 82–84, 89–94, 103, and 136–37.

Having monitored the convention's deliberations, Governor Gamble intervened to encourage the delegates at least to make a respectful reply to Lincoln's proposal. Such courtesy seemed proper and expedient, Gamble believed, for Lincoln had provided funds, arms, and federal troops to defend Missouri. Other members, however, disagreed, revealing a strong animus against Lincoln and emancipation. However, after debating the issue for some time, the delegates voted 37 to 23 to thank Lincoln for "the liberality" of his proposition.[16]

RADICAL VERSUS CONSERVATIVE

Hoping to gain political advantage from Gamble's failure to address the issue of emancipation in his opening address to the state convention, Missouri's abolitionists decided to hold their own assembly. Meeting shortly after the adjournment of the state convention, the main goal of the abolitionists was to urge the passage of legislation presenting the issue of emancipation to the people in 1864. By this measure Missouri could benefit from federal aid offered by Lincoln and supported by the resolution of Congress. The abolitionists wanted to free all slaves born after the adoption of the law. To enable them to take care of themselves, slaves would not be freed until they were twenty-five years of age. Such *post-nati* laws—legislation affecting only those slaves born after the bill's passage—had been adopted by many of the Northern states during and after the American Revolution.[17]

After convening in Jefferson City, the abolition convention elected Federal District Court Judge Robert W. Wells to preside over its proceedings. Wells seemed a strange choice as president of the convention, for he was a slaveholder who had ruled against Dred Scott in his appeal from the Missouri Supreme Court. In fact, his former career as a lawyer had demonstrated little if any sensitivity for the plight of slaves. However, Wells was convinced that slavery was the cause of the war and that compensated emancipation and colonization of the freed slaves would improve the economy. He also believed that without slavery the immigration

16. Ibid., 227 and 239–41. Parrish, *Turbulent Partnership*, 130–33.
17. St. Louis *Missouri Republican*, 5 June 1862. Parrish, *Turbulent Partnership*, 133.

of industrious free persons would increase dramatically. For these reasons Wells supported gradual emancipation.[18]

Wells's conservative views, however, represented only a minority of the convention, for a more radical element led by B. Gratz Brown soon dominated the proceedings. Brown quickly pushed through resolutions accusing the state convention of disloyalty and equating proslavery ideology with rebellion. In this way Brown criticized Governor Gamble and a majority of the delegates to the state convention. Much of the criticism stemmed from the radicals' frustration that harsher methods had not been employed against those supporting the rebellion in Missouri.[19]

During the emancipation convention, radicals also demonstrated hostility toward Governor Gamble's handling of other issues. Pointing to some of his administration's more moderate measures, the radicals accused Gamble of disloyalty. While this position was probably not then shared even by a majority of radicals, one of the German papers called for Lincoln to oust Gamble and for the appointment of a military governor. Under Brown's leadership, the radicals passed a resolution condemning Governor Gamble for his criticism that troops from other states were "hostile to our people and to our institutions." The resolution accused Gamble of having defamed all federal troops from other states. Some of the members of the convention defended Gamble, one remarking that he was a loyal man who had been misunderstood. Wells, relinquishing the chair, also defended Gamble, noting that more than one interpretation of his statement was possible. Nevertheless, Brown and a majority of the abolitionist convention were unmoved and the resolution criticizing

18. Robert W. Wells, *Letter from Judge Wells, Jefferson City, June 6th 1862* (St. Louis: George Knapp, 1862), 3–8. St. Louis *Missouri Republican*, 9 and 20 June 1862. Lawrence O. Christensen et al., eds., *Dictionary of Missouri Biography* (Columbia: University of Missouri Press, 1999), s.v. "Wells, Robert William (1795–1864)" by Lawrence H. Larsen. Years before the war, in a freedom suit in which he was one of the attorneys for the slaveholder, Wells sought to arrange the case before the Missouri Supreme Court when the return for slaves was highest. Apparently, the slaveholder had indicated that he intended to sell the slaves "down South." Such an arrangement would ensure more money for Wells and his fellow lawyer Abiel Leonard, for their fees were a percentage of the slaves' value. See Dennis K. Boman, *Abiel Leonard, Yankee Slaveholder, Eminent Jurist, and Passionate Unionist*, Studies in American History, vol. 38 (New York: Edwin Mellen, 2002), 133–35.

19. St. Louis *Missouri Republican*, 10 and 18–21 June 1862.

Gamble and his administration was adopted. For his part, Gamble wrote a brief defense of his statement by noting that he had in mind only Kansans who had crossed the border to commit violence against Missourians.[20]

Although unable to pass resolutions more critical of Gamble, radical leaders soon began to work secretly to undermine his authority. Just days after the emancipation convention, Brown wrote to Montgomery Blair accusing Gamble of conspiring against the federal government and seeking to create hostility between the state militia and federal troops in Missouri. Moreover, Brown believed that Gamble had no intention of supporting emancipation. Brown's letter was forwarded to Lincoln. Soon Lincoln received a flurry of letters from Missouri, some seeking Gamble's removal while others were written in his support. The radicals soon leveled a criticism, repeated over and over again in private correspondence and in many newspapers throughout Missouri, premised on the assertion that anyone supporting slavery was disloyal. Many proslavery unionists were accused of conspiring against the federal government, or at the very least, of being sham patriots. These accusations became favorites leveled against Gamble. Conservative unionists countered correctly, as it turned out, that the "Black Republicans" were conspiring to overthrow, or at least to undermine the authority of, the provisional government. These events led to a greater fragmentation of unionist efforts in Missouri.[21]

By the end of the congressional session nothing had come of Lincoln's proposal to provide compensation to the border states for the emancipation of their slaves. Perhaps frustrated by the failure of Missouri and the other border states to act, Lincoln asked the border state congressmen to meet with him at the White House on July 12. In the meeting he urged them upon their return home to press the leaders and people of their states to adopt his plan. The reply of the majority was disappointing. They complained that too little time was available for them to consult their constituents, that the funding of compensation was unconstitutional and would create a huge debt, and that agitation of the slavery question would

20. St. Louis *Missouri Republican*, 6 and 19–21 June 1862.

21. B. Gratz Brown to Montgomery Blair, 24 June 1862; Samuel T. Glover to Montgomery Blair, 6 and 20 August 1862; Frank P. Blair Jr. to Montgomery Blair, 8 August 1862; Montgomery Blair to Lincoln, 10 August 1862; Henry Blow to Lincoln, 12 August 1862, Lincoln papers. St. Louis *Missouri Republican*, 21 and 22 June and 7 July 1862.

undermine support for the Union in their states. Furthermore, while a minority of border state congressmen agreed with Lincoln that the South would be weakened by striking at slavery, it was doubtful the congressmen's support could persuade the majority in their states to agree even to gradual emancipation.[22]

In part, because of the rejection of his compensated emancipation plan, Lincoln edged toward using his powers as commander-in-chief to end slavery in the rebellious states as a war measure. This conclusion led to Lincoln's decision in September 1862, after a great deal of deliberation, to issue the preliminary emancipation proclamation. In it he declared that on January 1, 1863, all slaves held in rebellious states would be free. He believed this measure would shore up his support in the North, where many had lost their enthusiasm for a war that did not resolve the slavery issue. Moreover, Lincoln hoped to deny to the South the labor of slaves who were employed to do much of its menial labor on both the war and home fronts.[23]

As many critics of Lincoln's emancipation policy have noted, the measure freed no slaves immediately. Another deficiency, according to critics, was that it did not free slaves in the loyal border states, leading to the oft-repeated criticism that the Emancipation Proclamation declared slaves free where it had no authority while accomplishing nothing for those where it could. Lincoln disagreed with his critics; although desperately wanting the border states to accept his offer of compensation, he still believed that his constitutional authority to end slavery as a war measure extended only to those states that had seceded. For this reason, the issue of slavery was far from decided in Missouri and became a very important matter during the fall 1862 election.[24]

RENEWED CONFEDERATE OPERATIONS

In June 1862, while the state and abolition conventions were being held, both regular and irregular Confederate forces renewed military opera-

22. Donald, *Lincoln*, 362. Majority Border State Response, 14 July 1862; and Minority Border State Response, 15 July 1862, Lincoln papers.

23. Donald, *Lincoln*, 362–76.

24. Ibid., 375. Parrish, *Turbulent Partnership*, 135–36.

tions in Missouri. While these forces were not strong enough to retake the state, they were able to create a good deal of turmoil and trouble for Gamble and General John M. Schofield. Confederate forces were emboldened by the withdrawal of most unionist federal forces and their replacement with Missouri State Militia troops. These included fourteen regiments of cavalry, a regiment of infantry, and a battery of artillery. Schofield then commanded approximately 17,000 troops over three-quarters of the state. Of these forces the vast majority were militia and many had been ordered to Missouri's southern border to support General Curtis's command, which was then before Little Rock, Arkansas. These dispositions left much of Missouri exposed to attack, especially once Curtis's command moved south to Helena.[25]

To meet the emergency presented by the general uprising then occurring, Schofield first asked for reinforcements and for Curtis to coordinate his operations to provide some support. However, little help was provided and Schofield then sought Gamble's aid in organizing and calling into service Missouri's entire militia force, which he hoped would enable him to destroy the various guerrilla bands and restore peace to the state. The desperate condition of affairs is most evident in the extraordinary measures taken to secure the state. When at the end of the recruitment of the Missouri State Militia it was learned that 3,000 more troops had been raised than authorized by Congress, Schofield requested that Gamble ask the surplus regiments to consent to enter the service of the United States. Apparently wishing to avoid the possibility of being ordered out of Missouri, most of the extra recruits were unwilling to serve in federal regiments. Upon receiving this answer, Schofield next requested that the governor send a telegram "to the War Department informing the authorities of his intention to disband the surplus, and also the reasons urged by General Schofield that it should not be done." General Halleck replied that the secretary of war had agreed to accept the surplus militia temporarily. Still in want of troops, under his authority as governor Gamble created a new force that came to be called the Enrolled Missouri Militia. On July 22 all men "capable of bearing arms and subject to military duty" were or-

25. "Report of Brigadier General John M. Schofield, U.S. Army of Operations in Missouri and Northwestern Arkansas, April 10–November 20, 1862," *Official Records*, series 1, vol. 13, 7–21.

dered to organize themselves into military units, to bring and seize what weapons were readily available, to elect their officers, and to report to the nearest military post in preparation for military service. In response to Gamble's and Schofield's call for troops, within seven days 20,000 enrolled militia were formed into units for active service. Some of the enrolled militia served in the field, but many others relieved regular militia forces from duty guarding important strategic points such as railroads and forts. Learning that Schofield had failed to gain reinforcements from Halleck, Gamble also wrote to Attorney General Bates requesting that four regiments of volunteer infantry be sent to Missouri.[26]

In meeting the immediate emergency with enrolled militia, new problems arose, some of which were created by deficiencies in Schofield's policies, while others resulted from the reaction of disloyal elements and Governor Gamble's political enemies. In part to help pay for the subsistence of the enrolled militia and to allow disloyal persons a means to avoid military service, Schofield permitted anyone not wishing to serve to pay $10 for a release from duty. This order was quickly rescinded after many loyal persons complained that it was unfair that they bear the burden of keeping the peace while those responsible for the emergency often were allowed to escape military service after paying the small fee. Shortly after the order establishing the enrolled militia was issued, reports from commanders in different parts of the state indicated that large numbers of disloyal men, many of whom had remained at home until then, joined guerrilla bands and other Confederate units to avoid being enrolled in the militia. Most discouraging of all, however, was the reaction of many persons in St. Louis, where little danger existed from guerrilla bands and where the radicals claimed that Gamble, with his willing accomplice Schofield, were enrolling the militia to set up a military dictatorship in Missouri. Others

26. Ibid. Edwin M. Stanton to Hannibal Hamlin, 16 February 1863; General Orders, Nos. 19 and 20, 22 and 24 July 1862; Gamble to Edward Bates, 27 August 1862; and William Woods to Thomas M. Vincent, 6 February 1863, *Official Records*, series 1, vol. 13, 506, 508–9, and 515; and series 3, vol. 3, 52–54. Despite Gamble's and Schofield's efforts to enlist militia into the federal service, radicals later accused them of secretly discouraging such enlistments. See *Report of the Committee of the House of Representatives of the Twenty-second General Assembly of the State of Missouri Appointed to Investigate the Conduct and Management of the Militia: Majority and Minority Reports with the Evidence* (Jefferson City, Mo.: W. A. Curry, Public Printers, 1864), 252–59.

in Illinois, some of whom had close ties to the president, complained of the turmoil in northeastern Missouri and blamed it on Gamble's "inefficiency and bad management." However, by the end of September the crisis was over and Schofield had the enrolled militia withdrawn from service and ordered commanders not to activate them for more than thirty days without his consent. Moreover, he reminded his commanders that the enrolled militia were to be activated primarily "for the protection of their homes and that they are to be kept from their ordinary business as little as possible." Certainly, these were not the actions of a partner to a military coup as the radicals claimed.[27]

During the crisis, a meeting was held in St. Louis to rally support for the war effort. In a speech, which was made before a capacity crowd in the Mercantile Library Hall, Gamble explained his policies as governor and expressed his support for the president. Noting his own differences of political opinion from those of Lincoln and his party, Gamble nevertheless expressed his firm belief that the president wished to restore peace to the country and had proven himself an earnest friend of Missouri. In this way Gamble reminded his own critics that despite their disagreements with him, they owed support to him and his administration during this time of danger. In answer to those who complained that he had mismanaged the war, Gamble noted the efforts he had made and the cooperation he had received from Lincoln for his offer to pardon returning Confederate soldiers and for Gamble's plan to form the Missouri State Militia, which if its size had not been substantially reduced by Congress, soon would have returned the state to a condition similar to "a sleeping child." The war in Missouri continued, according to Gamble, because of Congress's inadequate action and the treachery of many Missourians who persisted in their disloyalty to the federal government.[28]

27. General Orders, No. 21, 24 July 1862; General Orders, No. 22, 27 July 1862; General Orders, No. 23, 28 July 1862; James Totten to C. W. Marsh, 30 July 1862; General Orders, No. 24, 4 August 1862; O. H. Browning to Lincoln, 4 August 1862; and General Orders, No. 12, 24 September 1862, *Official Records*, series 1, vol. 13, 509, 516, 518–19, 522–23, 533–35, and 664–65. St. Louis *Missouri Republican*, 27 July and 4 and 6 September 1862. For the radical case arguing that Gamble was seeking to establish a military dictatorship see Charles D. Drake, "Autobiography," 812–21, Western Historical Manuscripts Collection, State Historical Society of Missouri, Columbia, Missouri. Drake's case is unconvincing.

28. St. Louis *Missouri Republican*, 22 August 1862.

In October, to celebrate the enrolled militia's role in the war and to demonstrate his own commitment to the war effort, Gamble reviewed the First Division in St. Louis. Commanded by Brigadier General John B. Gray, the division numbered 13,000 men and in parade line stretched for 2 miles along streets decked out with American flags of all sizes and others carried by the crowd. The review was held on a beautiful Saturday and business was suspended, giving the day the feel of a holiday. Gamble was accompanied by his staff, which included his son and namesake and seven other officers. General Curtis, General Davidson, and General Gray and their staffs were also present and the group was accompanied by a body guard. The entire party was on horseback. In one newspaper account the spectacle was described in this way:

> It was a beautiful sight, and one not soon to be forgotten. The Governor rode with his head uncovered, and as they passed along the commanding officers saluted the party, while a portion of Col. Almstedt's artillery thundered forth a salute. The accompanying staff and body guard formed a splendid cavalcade and together with the long column stretching away out of sight made it a most imposing scene. The people of a mighty city joined together for the protection of their homes were assembled there to show how willing and able they would be to battle should occasion require. . . . Passing along the whole line up Washington avenue to Fourteenth street, then south to Clark avenue, and down it and Myrtle to Fourth, the reviewing party stopped in front of the Court House.

The review ended with the troops then forming to march past Gamble and the rest of the reviewing party accompanied by a band playing.[29]

By the early fall of 1862 when the military review was held, Gamble could point to real accomplishments of the state militia and felt justified in celebrating Missouri's participation in securing its own peace. The organization of both the Missouri State Militia and the Enrolled Missouri Militia were accomplishments not important to Missouri alone, but to the entire war effort, for the militia's ability to put down the insurrection had enabled forces to press home their hard-won advantages after the victories under General Grant's leadership. A disaster in Missouri would have

29. St. Louis *Missouri Republican*, 13 October 1862.

forced Lincoln to send federal troops back to Missouri and most probably would have delayed Grant's attempt to take Vicksburg and keep the pressure on the Confederacy.[30]

Despite these benefits to the overall war effort, Gamble encountered unexpected resistance from the Lincoln administration to his request for funding to pay the Enrolled Missouri Militia. Already, Gamble and Schofield had arranged to subsist the enrolled militia through seizures and assessments against disloyal persons. For some time, however, the enrolled militia served without pay, causing a good deal of hardship among Missourians who had patriotically answered the call to meet the emergency. Apparently the matter of pay and another controversy concerning Gamble's power to dismiss and appoint militia officers was part of the fallout from a larger dispute that had emerged concerning the authority of governors from other states over their volunteer troops.[31]

The larger dispute stemmed from the dissatisfaction of some Northern governors who had consistently criticized Lincoln's war policies, his reluctance to use the war to emancipate the slaves, and his choice of army commanders. These governors, some of whom were Radical Republicans, faulted Lincoln for being indecisive, by which they meant that he had refused to emancipate the slaves and use blacks as soldiers. These governors, faced with the difficult challenge of filling large troop quotas, had hoped to enlist blacks as soldiers. Moreover, in September 1862, when Gamble and Schofield were struggling to prevent a general uprising in Missouri, these radical governors were pushing the president to sack General George B. McClellan and replace him with John C. Fremont or some other general with abolitionist credentials. Wishing better to coordinate their efforts

30. Report of Thomas B. Biggers, 8 August 1862; "Report of Brigadier General John M. Schofield, U.S. Army of Operations in Missouri and Northwestern Arkansas, April 10–November 20, 1862"; Benjamin Loan to Schofield, 1 August 1862; Lewis Merrill to commanding officer at Mexico, 5 August 1862; Schofield to James Totten, 8 August 1862; Special Orders, No. 7, 12 August 1862; Schofield to Hallack, 28 August 1862; and Samuel R. Curtis to Halleck, 12 October 1862, *Official Records*, series 1, vol. 13, 12–13, 190–91, 527, 539, 546–47, 564, 601, and 729.

31. "Report of Brigadier General John M. Schofield, U.S. Army of Operations in Missouri and Northwestern Arkansas, April 10–November 20, 1862"; Lewis Merrill to John Henderson, 2 September 1862; Special Orders, No. 3, 29 September 1862; and Special Orders, No. 37, 17 November 1862, *Official Records*, series 1, vol. 13, 12, 612–13, 691, and 800. A detailed report of how the enrolled militia was subsisted is in *Report of the Committee*, 19–29.

and arrive at a consensus, the radicals called for a governors' conference to gather at Altoona, Pennsylvania, where a dozen governors, both radical and conservative, assembled together to discuss war policy. First on the radicals' agenda was emancipation and the replacement of McClellan with Fremont. However, the conservative governors, Governor David Tod of Ohio in particular, were against McClellan's removal, especially because he had just won an important victory and had driven General Robert E. Lee out of Maryland. Lincoln's preliminary Emancipation Proclamation left the radical governors with little else of their agenda for which to push in the pronouncement they were preparing. This problem and the governors' inability to agree on many issues produced a confused address in which the governors congratulated Lincoln for his proclamation and argued for the establishment of a reserve army to meet any future emergencies.[32]

Even if Gamble had been inclined to attend and no emergency in Missouri had then existed, Attorney General Bates had warned him not to attend the governors' meeting, explaining that "the end is revolutionary." Upon Massachusetts Governor John A. Andrew's letter, with which had been enclosed a copy of the governors' address, Gamble noted that he had refused to endorse the governors' appeal to Lincoln. Gamble, unlike some of the other governors, was uninterested in using the war to gain fame for Missouri and political advantage for himself. Moreover, he had never insisted on concessions from the federal government in return for his cooperation in raising volunteer troops for the service of the United States. Unfortunately, the War Department's difficulties in gaining cooperation from many of the governors soon caused a misunderstanding between Gamble and Halleck, who had just recently been appointed to the overall command of U.S. forces.[33]

In writing to General Halleck, it is obvious that Gamble expected support from him concerning the extent of Gamble's authority over the militia in Missouri. Anticipating the possibility of a confrontation with

32. William B. Hesseltine, *Lincoln and the War Governors* (New York: Alfred A. Knopf, 1948), 249–72.

33. Edward Bates to Gamble, 19 and 21 September 1862, Bates papers. John A. Andrew to Gamble, 29 September 1862, Gamble papers. Gamble to Edwin M. Stanton, 27 August 1862, *Official Records*, series 3, vol. 2, 474–75.

Brigadier General Davidson, federal commander of the St. Louis District, Gamble sought to end the controversy before it began by gaining an authoritative statement from Halleck supporting his position. As was his custom, Gamble immediately established the issue on which the entire question turned: Were the Missouri State Militia and the Enrolled Missouri Militia state or U.S. forces? The issue was particularly important, for Davidson believed he had authority to command the enrolled militia and to call them into service. While it is unclear what the consequences of such action might have been, many who had served in the enrolled militia had already suffered a good deal of financial loss and had families to support. To demonstrate his assertion that Davidson had no authority over the militia, Gamble cited "the document filed in the War Department" detailing the arrangement made between him and the president in November 1861 designating the Missouri State Militia a state force. One can only imagine Gamble's astonishment upon receiving Halleck's reply. In it, Halleck answered Gamble's query from the premise that the Missouri State Militia was in the service of the United States. The tone of the reply was surprising also, for Halleck wrote as if the letter was addressed to a subordinate or student to whom instruction must be imparted. What Gamble did not know at the time was that other governors had sought to extend their authority over nine-month militia from their states in the service of the United States. This circumstance had prompted Secretary of War Stanton to order Halleck to use his reply to Gamble to answer the other governors as well. It is unclear why Halleck did not inform Stanton that the issues regarding Gamble's question were very different from those relating to the other governors.[34]

In his letter, Halleck first established the constitutional authority by which militia were brought into the service of the United States and the consequences of this. Apparently, some of the governors had insisted that only officers appointed by themselves could command their militia. Halleck correctly noted that such a system could never work, for state militia would then operate independently from the rest of the military. Furthermore, without flexibility in their use the militia's value to the U.S. military

34. Gamble to Halleck, 22 September 1862; and Halleck to Gamble, 27 September and 30 October 1862, *Official Records*, series 3, vol. 2, 579, 591–93, and 703–4.

was greatly reduced. However, his reply to Gamble did not address the special circumstances of the militia in Missouri. Perhaps because of the necessity to gain resources from the federal government to pay the enrolled militia, Gamble did not immediately reply to Halleck's letter, which had been published in the newspapers throughout the country.[35]

Apparently, in an attempt to assert his authority in the matter of command over militia regiments, Secretary of War Stanton moved to overturn Gamble's decision to remove from command Colonel Albert Jackson of the Twelfth Regiment of Cavalry, Missouri State Militia. In a letter explaining the department's decision, Halleck noted that Jackson had requested Stanton's intervention in his case. Again, proceeding on the premise that the Missouri State Militia was in the service of the United States, Halleck asserted that Gamble had no authority over Missouri's militia, for it was now under the authority of Congress and was subject to the regulations of the U.S. military. Under these rules, while a governor may fill an officer's vacancy in militia units from his state, he cannot create a vacancy by the dismissal of an officer. Unwilling to allow such a misreading of his arrangement with the president to stand, Gamble responded to Halleck on October 10. First, he noted his agreement with Halleck that "great inconveniences, if not absurdities" would be created if militia in the service of the United States were not placed under the firm authority of the U.S. military. Next, turning to the main issues of the controversy Gamble wrote:

> The surprise produced by your reply, general, was not on account of the novelty of your positions, but on account of their utter irrelevancy to the question which I had submitted to your consideration. I never doubted the authority of U.S. generals to command regiments of militia called into the service of the United States as regiments. My question concerned a special corps of militia raised under a special agreement with the President, in relation to which I sought no other advantage than that the expense should be borne by the United States, because the State could not meet it. It was but natural that I should expect that my question—whether this corps raised under the agreement is a U.S. force or a State force—should be answered by an examination and construction of the written agreement.

35. Ibid. Gamble to Salmon Chase, 17 September 1862; and Charles Gibson to Gamble, 3 October 1862, Gamble papers.

Then noting the terms of the understanding he had with the president, Gamble demonstrated the absurdity of its many stipulations if one premised that it was a U.S. force. For instance, why stipulate that the force was to be governed by the U.S. Army regulations and the Articles of War if it was already in the service of the United States? Why mention that the Missouri State Militia would be "armed, equipped, clothed, subsisted, transported, and paid by the United States"? Finally, why insist that the commander of the department also command the militia if it was already a U.S. force? Would not the militia automatically be under the departmental commander's authority if it was already in the service of the United States?[36]

After establishing his position on the nature of the Missouri State Militia, Gamble finally took up the matter of Colonel Jackson's dismissal, which he noted was the first instance when the question of the nature of the militia's status as a state or national force had "any practical importance." Pointing to the muster rolls of the Missouri State Militia then filed in the office of the adjutant-general in Washington, Gamble noted that the rolls themselves demonstrated that Jackson and his regiment—and all the other regiments as well—"were mustered into the service of the State, and not into the service of the United States." Therefore, "Colonel Jackson was in the service of the State, and was properly dismissed by me upon the report of his incompetency by an examining board."[37]

In November 1862 Gamble traveled to Washington to consult with the administration regarding his authority and the character of the militia. In a letter to Lincoln, Gamble explained why these matters were important both to him and to Missouri. Operating on the assumption that the Missouri State Militia was a state force, he had removed and accepted the resignation of officers and filled their vacancies. Gamble, in pushing for a resolution of the issue, reminded Lincoln that he had never sought to exercise any "doubtful power over Missouri volunteers." Such an accusation, or even the suspicion, that Gamble was grasping for power was particularly troubling to him. In fact, one of the reasons he had pursued the controversy as vigorously as he had was that Gamble did not want it

36. Halleck to Gamble, 3 October 1862; and Gamble to Halleck, 10 October 1862, *Official Records*, series 3, vol. 2, 646–47 and 658–62.

37. Ibid.

thought he had "been exercising for a year past powers which [he] did not possess and that confusion shall not now be introduced into the organization by a decision which would change the character of the force." In Lincoln, however, Gamble did not find a sympathetic ear, for other governors had already unnecessarily imposed on the president's patience in their struggle to gain "power" and "patronage" in their disputes with him. Apparently, not wishing to take sides in the dispute between the interpretations of the agreement between Gamble and the War Department, Lincoln complained that the entire controversy was unimportant. Nevertheless, he did not believe the militia was "strictly either 'State troops' or 'United States troops,'" and he perceived no advantage in deciding the matter one way or the other. He preferred, therefore, to settle only the issue of whether or not Gamble had the right to sack militia officers and proposed "to let Governor Gamble make vacancies, and he (the Secretary [of War]) to ratify the making of them." This compromise solution he hoped would be satisfactory to both parties. While Gamble was probably disappointed that his motivations may have been misunderstood, his authority to remove officers was upheld (both past and future), including presumably his action to oust Jackson.[38]

THE FALL 1862 ELECTION

As already noted, during its June 1862 session, the delegates of the Missouri state convention debated the propriety of holding wartime elections. The consensus among the delegates—a majority of whom were conservatives—was that it would be unwise to hold elections for the state executive offices, for Governor Gamble and Lieutenant Governor Willard P. Hall had proven themselves to be very effective leaders and had developed good relationships with Lincoln and his cabinet. Nevertheless, the absence of a state legislature to deliberate on fiscal and internal matters had proven to be a handicap and it was decided that elections for legislators should

38. Gamble to Halleck, 4 November 1862; Lincoln to Edward Bates, 29 November 1862; and Special Orders, No. 417, 28 December 1862, *Official Records*, series 3, vol. 2, 735–36, 882–83, and 955.

be conducted in the fall. Besides, if Missouri was to have representatives in Congress, an election must be held. However, to ensure that members of the legislature supported the Union, the state convention required all candidates and voters to take a strict loyalty oath and delayed the election until November to enable out-of-state Missouri regiments to vote.[39]

The fall campaign also marked the organization of an opposition to Gamble's administration. The radicals, as they sometimes referred to themselves, made gradual emancipation a major plank of their party and criticized many of the provisional government's policies. In particular, they faulted Gamble for not having urged the state convention to pass an emancipation bill in his opening message to its June 1862 proceedings. In August 1862 a committee of radicals traveled to Washington, D.C., to convince Lincoln that Gamble had failed as governor and that Samuel R. Curtis should replace him, acting in the capacity of a military governor. This effort proved fruitless, in part because of the Lincoln administration's fear that the radicalization of the state government would cause the loss of conservative support for the war effort. However, perhaps in an effort to mollify the radicals, Lincoln decided to appoint Curtis to the command of the District of Missouri. Unfortunately, the radical attempt to replace Gamble with Curtis also led both men to distrust the other. This distrust festered over the next few months and made it very difficult for Lincoln to gain cooperation between them.[40]

Having failed in their attempt to remove Governor Gamble and to install a radical military commander over Missouri, the opposition soon concentrated on electing members to Congress and to Missouri's General Assembly who would support emancipation and the use of more severe measures in the prosecution of the war. The opposition came to be known as the Charcoals, the radical wing of the Republican Party. In turn, the radicals referred to moderate members of their own party as Claybanks.

39. *Proceedings, June 1862*, 43–71, 95–97, 105–7, 109–113, 119, 130–31, 146, 172, 174–76, 178–79, 200–201, 205–11, 216–18, and 222. St. Louis *Missouri Republican*, 22 October 1862. Parrish, *Turbulent Partnership*, 136.

40. Parrish, *Turbulent Partnership*, 90–98. Frank P. Blair to Montgomery Blair, 8 August 1862, Lincoln papers. John M. Schofield, *Forty-Six Years in the Army*, foreword by William M. Ferraro (New York: Century, 1897; Norman: University of Oklahoma Press, 1998), 56–61.

Remarkably, the election, although marred by some minor irregularities, was conducted successfully, largely due to the efforts of the state militia forces to prevent violence and interference in the campaign.[41]

The majority of candidates elected to Congress and the legislature favored Lincoln's plan for emancipation and all were unionists. This result demonstrated the wisdom of the state convention's measures to prevent the disloyal from voting and holding office. In the end, five Republicans, one Democrat in favor of emancipation, two unconditional unionists, and two proslavery Democrats were elected to Congress. Moreover, the majorities elected to both houses of Missouri's General Assembly could be expected to elect members to the U.S. Senate with similar views. Nevertheless, as Gamble was to learn, working with a radical majority in the legislature would be difficult, leading to heightened tensions between Gamble and the Charcoal leadership.[42]

41. St. Louis *Missouri Republican*, 9 and 14 October and 17, 18, and 25 November 1862; James H. Birch to Gamble, 7 September 1862, Gamble papers. Samuel T. Curtis to Henry W. Halleck, 24 November 1862, *Official Records*, series 1, vol. 22, part 1, 788–89. Parrish, *Turbulent Partnership*, 135–36.

42. St. Louis *Missouri Republican*, 9 November and 13 December 1862. Frank P. Blair Jr. to Abraham Lincoln, 14 November 1862, Lincoln papers.

Chapter Nine

The Command of Samuel R. Curtis

Even after the fall election of 1862, the radical attacks on Hamilton R. Gamble and his administration continued unabated through speeches and newspaper editorials. Alternately, the radicals portrayed Gamble as a fool incapable of doing anything right, or as a Machiavellian operator whose schemes purposely undermined the Union war effort. By this time, Gamble must have realized that the spirit and nature of the opposition to him had changed significantly from earlier in the war and that his every decision would be subjected to the closest possible scrutiny. According to the radicals Gamble's war policies were always inadequate, at best half measures. They asserted that winning the war required the implementation of more ruthless policies, ones that would crush the opposition into submission. Gamble, who unlike most of his critics dealt with the daily realities of the war in Missouri and understood the relative strengths and weaknesses of both sides, believed that many of the radical recommendations, if implemented, would lead to disaster and were unjust. In a letter to President Abraham Lincoln, Gamble explained why he had rejected the radicals' war policies:

> When I took office the Union men were oppressed and outraged all over the State, now they are organized and feel that the strength is with them. In these circumstances there has arisen a desire for vengeance, which however natural it may be, is utterly hostile to good government and would desolate the State. It would be easy to go with this current but duty requires that endeavor to moderate and restrain the vindictiveness which would ruin a

class (many of whom are no doubt criminal) without benefitting any other class permanently.[1]

Because of dangers present during time of war, especially a civil war, some liberties enjoyed in peacetime are restricted to provide greater security to the government. In the exercise of these powers Gamble had taken bold action at the war's beginning in recommending the ouster of the administration of Governor Claiborne F. Jackson when it became evident that he was seeking to bring Missouri out of the Union. Recognizing the inadequacy of half measures, Gamble had then argued that the state convention as an extraconstitutional institution had authority from the people to assume whatever powers were needed to defend the state militarily. However, by late 1862 General Ulysses S. Grant's victories had removed the major struggle in the West from Missouri to the Confederate stronghold of Vicksburg situated on the bluffs commanding the Mississippi River. These circumstances led Gamble to move tentatively toward the restoration of civil rights and the reestablishment of civilian rule in Missouri.[2]

For this reason, Gamble intervened when efforts were undertaken to punish ministers of the gospel whose loyalties were considered suspect by some unionists. During the secession crisis and the first months of the war in Missouri, the preponderate sentiment expressed from the pulpits was secessionist, but over time this changed as some of these ministers were silenced by provost-marshals, ousted by their congregations, or decided voluntarily to go South. Nevertheless, some ministers, who had discretely refused to side with either faction—either believing that their first duty was to the spiritual well-being of their congregation, or believing that their secessionist sentiments were too dangerous to express—refused every effort by some to draw them into worldly controversies.[3]

1. Hamilton R. Gamble to Abraham Lincoln, 4 February 1863, Lincoln papers.

2. Henry W. Halleck to Samuel R. Curtis, 17 February 1863, *The War of the Rebellion: A Compilation of the Official Records of the Union and Confederate Armies*, 128 vols. (Washington, D.C.: U.S. Government Printing Office, 1880–1902), series 1, vol. 22, part 2, 113.

3. Galusha Anderson, *The Story of a Border City During the Civil War* (Boston: Little, Brown, 1908), 142 and 191–95. Benjamin G. Farrar to the commanding officer at Glasgow, Missouri, 25 March 1862, series 2, vol. 1, 175–76.

In September 1862, General Samuel R. Curtis took command of the Department of the Missouri. Curtis was a former Republican congressman from Iowa and sympathetic to radical policies, so his appointment was not a welcome choice to Gamble. After taking command, Curtis issued an order delineating his policy toward different disloyal elements remaining in Missouri. Of particular concern to him was the existence "of pretended loyal men" who sought to undermine the efforts of the federal government to maintain its authority. Included among these were disloyal preachers. Curtis warned that he would expel from the state any minister who encouraged others to join the rebellion. Apparently, Curtis decided to make an example of Reverend Samuel B. McPheeters, minister of the Pine Street Presbyterian Church in St. Louis, who had not explicitly stated his support for the Union. This refusal had caused radical leaders to suspect his loyalties and had led Curtis to banish him from Missouri. As he later explained, Curtis believed it preferable to deal harshly with McPheeters, whom he considered to be a prominent case, rather than "ousting two or three others." Curtis justified his action by asserting that "rebel priests are dangerous and diabolical in society."[4]

Evident from the ensuing correspondence and newspaper articles written concerning McPheeters's case, the controversy began as a dispute between three radical members of his congregation over McPheeters's baptism of a rebel couple's son, who was christened Sterling Price after the Confederate general and former Missouri governor. This incident, McPheeters's Southern birth, and his wife's open and firm pro-Southern support had outraged the radicals, who, as a consequence, sought McPheeters's removal. After failing to gain a majority vote among the Pine Street Church congregation to oust him, the radicals then turned to the military authorities to intervene. On December 19, without providing McPheeters an opportunity to answer the charges of disloyalty against him, Curtis ordered him to stop preaching immediately, to surrender to his accusers the records of the Pine Street Church, and to leave Missouri

---

4. Lawrence O. Christensen et al., eds., *Dictionary of Missouri Biography* (Columbia: University of Missouri Press, 1999), s.v. "Samuel Ryan Curtis," by John F. Bradbury Jr. General Orders, No. 35, 24 December 1862, *Official Records*, series 1, vol. 22, part 1, 869. Samuel R. Curtis to Lincoln, 28 December 1862, Lincoln papers.

within ten days for the free states where he and his wife were to reside for the remainder of the war.[5]

To explain his course of action, McPheeters published a letter and wrote privately to Attorney General Edward Bates, who along with Gamble was a member of the Presbyterian denomination. In his public letter McPheeters explained that he had not known the name of the child to be baptized until in the very act of the sacrament. Moreover, McPheeters expounded the principles on which he had refused to make a declaration of his loyalty before his congregation. His refusal was in conformity with "the Constitution of the Presbyterian Church," which forbade its ministers from involving themselves "with civil affairs which concern the commonwealth." However, McPheeters also maintained publicly that all Christians were bound by duty "to obey law, to submit to the authorities, to pray for them — to render them the honour due their several stations & to promote peace and quietness." It was in the interest of peace and submission that he had taken the oath of allegiance to the governments of the United States and Missouri and was willing to submit to Curtis's decision to banish him and his family.[6]

Believing Curtis's action unjust, McPheeters went to Gamble to learn the address of Attorney General Edward Bates through whom he hoped to gain a meeting with the president. Taking interest in his fellow sectarian's plight, Gamble wrote a letter to the president for McPheeters recommending him as a loyal man and asking for his release. Upon reflection, McPheeters determined not to use the letter, for he worried that he would gain the repeal of the military order at the forfeiture of "the principles for which I have been contending, and the maintaining of which has been the occasion of my pulpit being taken from me." He therefore returned Gamble's letter to him and explained that he hoped, for the sake of the Church, that he could convince Lincoln not to allow the military to have authority over ministers and churches. Although sympathetic with his mission, Gamble was skeptical that McPheeters could convince Lincoln to side with him. McPheeters conceded that his expectations were not

5. Published letter of Samuel B. McPheeters, 19 December 1862; Archibald Gamble to Edward Bates, 22 December 1862; Samuel B. McPheeters to Edward Bates, 23 December 1862; and Special Orders, No. 152, 19 December 1862, Lincoln papers.

6. Published letter of Samuel B. McPheeters, 19 December 1862. Samuel B. McPheeters to Edward Bates, 23 December 1862, Lincoln papers.

high but that he must try. Upon their parting, Gamble gave his blessing, telling the minister to "go, and God be with you."[7]

After traveling to Washington, D.C., McPheeters and Bates met with Lincoln, requesting him to overturn the banishment order and to stop the military's further interference in ecclesiastical matters. According to McPheeters, Lincoln struggled with the question, in part, because of its complexity and ramifications, and in part, because of his reluctance to overturn the orders of his military commanders. Deciding that the matter merited further consideration, on the day of their meeting (December 27) Lincoln suspended the banishment order. In the days following, Curtis and others supporting his order attempted to convince Lincoln of the need to deal harshly with McPheeters and other disloyal elements in Missouri, who they claimed were influential in persuading many to rebel against the government. After considering the matter carefully, Lincoln explained his conclusions about McPheeters's and Curtis's handling of the controversy:

> The Dr. [McPheeters] . . . showed me the copy of an oath which he said he had taken, which is, indeed, very strong, and specific. He also verbally assured me that he had constantly prayed in church for the President and Government, as he had always done before the present war. In looking over the recitals in your order, I do not see that this matter of the prayer, as he states it, is negative; nor that any violation of his oath is charged; nor, in fact, that any thing specific is alledged [sic] against him. The charges are all general—that he has a rebel wife & rebel relations, that he sympathizes with rebels, and that he exercises rebel influence. Now, after talking with him, I tell you frankly, I believe he does sympathize with the rebels; but the question remains whether such a man of unquestioned good moral character, who has taken such an oath as he has, and can not even be charged of violating it, and who can be charged with no other specific act or omission, can, with safety to the government be exiled upon the suspicion of his secret sympathies.

However, despite these conclusions, Lincoln did not order Curtis to restore McPheeters to his ministerial office, maintaining his policy not to

7. Rev. John S. Grasty, *Memoir of Rev. Samuel B. McPheeters, D.D.*, with an introduction by Rev. Stuart Robinson (St. Louis: Southwestern, 1871), 159–61.

interfere with commanders "on the spot" who are better able to determine what is best for "the public good." Nevertheless, having restored his authority in McPheeters's case, Lincoln warned Curtis not to "undertake to run the churches." Unless an individual proved to be dangerous to the public welfare, especially if he was a minister, he should be let alone. Lincoln concluded his policy by adding that "it will not do for the U.S. to appoint Trustees, Supervisors, or other agents for the churches."[8]

Despite Lincoln's warning, Curtis did not allow McPheeters to resume his ministry and control of the Pine Street Church was handed over to its radical members. In March 1863, McPheeters's supporters again petitioned Curtis to reconsider his decision. Both men, however, stubbornly held to their former views, Curtis requiring, and McPheeters politely declining to provide, answers that would settle the issue of McPheeters's loyalty once and for all. Curtis also refused to allow McPheeters the opportunity to defend himself at the St. Louis Presbytery and later at the Missouri Synod in October 1863. There the matter stood until the end of the year, when Lincoln discovered to his dismay that the controversy, like so many others in Missouri, had not been concluded and that he was asked to reconsider the entire controversy.[9]

In November and December 1863, Lincoln received letters requesting that McPheeters once again be allowed to preach. Given his instructions to Curtis not to interfere in the affairs of any churches, Lincoln was surprised at the request and was somewhat incredulous that the reports were true. In part, he disbelieved them because the different accounts presented an inconsistent picture of McPheeters's circumstances. Furthermore, it is apparent that Lincoln had not read, or at least had forgotten, the letter and correspondence that Curtis had sent him in April explaining his order not to allow McPheeters to resume preaching. The entire matter put Lincoln out of temper somewhat, for he was unsure of the exact facts and was

8. Lincoln to Samuel R. Curtis, 27 December 1862; Curtis to Lincoln, 27 December 1862, *Official Records*, series 1, vol. 22, part 1, 877–78. Apolline A. Blair to Montgomery Blair, 29 December 1862; Curtis to Lincoln, 29 and 30 December 1862; St. Louis Citizens to Lincoln, 30 December 1862; and Lincoln to Curtis, 2 January 1862, Lincoln papers. Grasty, *Memoir*, 183–86.

9. Curtis to Samuel B. McPheeters, 28 March 1863; McPheeters to Curtis, 31 March 1863; and Curtis to Lincoln, 3 April 1863, Lincoln papers. Grasty, *Memoir*, 186–95.

sensitive to the charge that he had interfered inappropriately in a religious controversy. In reply to the petitioners seeking McPheeters's reinstatement, Lincoln demanded proof that Curtis had disobeyed his order not to interfere with the churches. Here the matter stood until Gamble wrote to Bates, enclosing a letter from McPheeters. Apparently these letters removed all confusion concerning the McPheeters case, for Bates wrote on December 31 that the president had directed McPheeters to be restored to his full "ecclesiastical rights," advising that he resume them "quietly . . . as if no interruption had occurred."[10]

Another civil liberties issue over which Gamble disputed with the radicals was the military assessment controversy. In late 1861, to provide funds for unionist refugees driven from their homes, General Henry W. Halleck had ordered the confiscation of property from wealthy disloyal persons to pay for the refugees' subsistence and had forced wealthy rebels to give up or share their homes with them. In June 1862, after many federal troops had been sent to Arkansas and Tennessee, a serious increase in guerrilla activity occurred, leaving very few troops available to protect much of Missouri. To meet this emergency the enrolled militia was organized and put into the field and Schofield, who was then in command, instituted a system of assessments to provide subsistence for them. With Gamble's agreement, Schofield ordered commanders of each division of the District of Missouri to establish boards of assessment to raise $5,000 for each soldier or civilian killed and from $1,000 to $5,000 for anyone wounded. Moreover, the value of all property stolen or destroyed would be replaced. The property of persons who did not pay the assessments made against them within "a reasonable time" would be seized and sold to provide the necessary funds. Anyone resisting these proceedings was liable to arrest and possible trial before a military court. In determining the amount for which a person was responsible, a board was directed to "be

10. John Whitehill and others to Lincoln, November 1863; Oliver D. Filley to Lincoln, 9 November 1863; Nathan Ranney to Edward Bates, 9 November 1863; John D. Coalter to Edward Bates, 13 December 1863; and Lincoln to Oliver D. Filley, 22 December 1863, Lincoln papers. Grasty, *Memoir*, 196–99. Later, before the Synod held in Newark, New Jersey, the St. Louis Presbyter again sought McPheeters's removal. The decision went against McPheeters and he eventually removed to Mulberry, Kentucky, where he had received a call to preach. Grasty, *Memoir*, 331.

governed by the wealth of an individual and his known activity in aiding the rebellion."[11]

After Schofield ordered assessments for $500,000 be made in St. Louis County, Gamble requested from the banks in St. Louis a loan of $150,000. This sum, he suggested, should be divided between them in proportion to their capital holdings and paid back when the assessments against disloyal persons had been collected. However, in early December 1862 Gamble received numerous complaints about the assessments, causing him to investigate the method of their collection. From his investigation he learned that the St. Louis County assessment board relied upon "hearsay evidence, rumors, and 'general impressions,'" and that the witnesses did not testify under oath. These procedural problems coupled with the "general impression of inequality in the rule of assessment and its application," Gamble believed, justified the suspension of assessments, especially since the original emergency that had required them was no longer present. For these reasons, Gamble requested that the banks agree to accept a promise from the state to repay the loans, clearing the way for a suspension of the assessments in St. Louis County.[12]

Those persons against whom the assessments were made also appealed to General Curtis, who was uncertain about what he should do. As he related in a letter to President Lincoln, Curtis considered the board's actions to be irregular at best and unconstitutional at worst. However, when Gamble and others asked him to stop the assessments, instead of taking the responsibility himself, or allowing Gamble to do so, Curtis decided to write his commanding officer Halleck to resolve the matter. In doing this, Curtis may have wished to avoid angering the radicals in St. Louis, who were strongly in favor of the assessments. Believing that the assessments were unjust and unwise as public policy, Gamble and others also wrote to

11. Report of John M. Schofield, 10 April to 20 November 1862; and Special Orders, No. 91, 28 August 1862, *Official Records*, series 1, vol. 13, 12; and series 1, vol. 22, part 1, 826. *Report of the Committee of the House of Representatives of the Twenty-second General Assembly of the State of Missouri appointed to Investigate the Conduct and Management of the Militia: Majority and Minority Reports with the Evidence* (Jefferson City, Mo.: W. A. Curry, Public Printers, 1864), 350–51.

12. *Report of the Committee*, 353–55. John M. Schofield to James S. Thomas, 5 December 1862; and William G. Eliot, 1 December 1862, *Official Records*, series 1, vol. 22, part 1, 801–2 and 810–12. Gamble to Lincoln, 5 December 1862, Lincoln papers.

Lincoln encouraging him to stop the work of the assessment board. When Lincoln ordered him to suspend the assessments until notified to do otherwise, Curtis requested that Lincoln not take the further step of ending assessments altogether, for the threat of the assessment board resuming its work would warn "Southern sympathizers" not to support efforts to disrupt Union rule in Missouri. Moreover, he thought it a matter of fairness to allow those against whom the board had acted to bring evidence to exonerate themselves.[13]

While some sought a reform of the assessment regime, Gamble and other influential persons, including all but one of Missouri's congressional delegation, wrote to Lincoln arguing that no military emergency then existed requiring the continuance of assessments under martial law. In late December 1862, Gamble ordered the enrolled militia, over which he had complete authority as a state force, not to obey any orders from U.S. commanders or officers to establish assessment boards. As he explained, "the enrolled Militia are under the *exclusive* command of their own officers, except when they are by express orders placed under the command of United States officers, *and they will be governed only by such orders as may be issued from these Headquarters.*" Gamble then wrote to Lincoln telling him of his action and urging him to suspend the activities of the assessment boards operating under the authority of federal officers outside of St. Louis County. A short time later Lincoln ordered the end of assessments in Missouri.[14]

While the McPheeters and assessment controversies continued, Governor Gamble, in preparation for the legislative session of the Twenty-second General Assembly, consulted with friends concerning policy issues

13. Richard C. Shackelford and T. J. Thompson to Lincoln, 5 December 1862; Gamble to Lincoln, 5 December 1862; Samuel T. Glover to Montgomery Blair, 7 December 1862; Lincoln to Samuel R. Curtis, 10 December 1862; Curtis to Lincoln, 10 and 12 December 1862; and James S. Thomas to Curtis, 16 December 1862, Lincoln papers. John M. Schofield to Thomas, 5 December 1862; Curtis to Gamble, 10 December 1862; and William G. Eliot to Henry W. Halleck, 13 December 1862, *Official Records*, series 1, vol. 22, part 1, 810–12, 827, and 830.

14. *Report of the Committee*, 352. Gamble to Lincoln, 31 December 1862; Missouri congressional delegation to Lincoln, January 1863; and William A. Hall to Lincoln, 7 January 1863, Lincoln papers. Lincoln to Samuel R. Curtis, 5 January 1863; Edwin Stanton to Samuel R. Curtis; and General Lewis Merrill to assessment commission, 20 January 1863, *Official Records*, series 1, vol. 22, part 2, 64.

and began to draft a message to the legislature. Gamble's primary goal was to end the strife between radical and conservative unionists. In an attempt to reconcile at least a portion of the German and radical opposition to himself, Gamble sent trusted operatives such as his nephew Charles Gibson to St. Louis to find, if possible, some common ground on which cooperation could be fostered. To achieve this, Gamble developed a plan for emancipation similar to that pending before the U.S. Congress and supported by the president. When Missouri's General Assembly convened in early 1863, Governor Gamble presented to the legislature a message in which he urged its members to pass emancipation legislation. Gamble proposed providing for the emancipation of slave children born after the plan's passage. Their owners would raise them until they reached maturity and could take care of themselves. This plan, although not freeing slaves then living before the bill's passage, had the advantage of reducing the cost of compensating slaveowners significantly and circumventing the need to gain their consent, both requirements of the state constitution. Gamble believed that gradual, compensated emancipation would ensure a smooth transition from a slave to a free labor system, which was already occurring because of the war, would encourage free immigration into Missouri, and would secure the state for the Union.[15]

However, despite a majority of the General Assembly's members favoring emancipation, the inexperience and partisanship of these legislators proved to be a major obstacle preventing the passage of legislation. Moreover, a significant minority of ideologues on both sides of the slavery issue were unwilling to compromise.[16] From the start of the legislative session, the Radical Republicans (Charcoals) took charge of the legislature's operations through the election of radical officers to the House and Senate, most of whom were novice legislators. The radicals insisted that only im-

15. Charles Gibson to Edward Bates, 9 December 1862, Lincoln papers. Charles Gibson to Hamilton R. Gamble, 6 January 1863, Gamble papers. Virgil C. Blum, "The Political and Military Activities of the German Element in St. Louis, 1859–1861," *Missouri Historical Review* 42 (January 1948): 107–8. Earl J. Nelson, "Missouri Slavery, 1861–1865," *Missouri Historical Review* 28 (July 1934): 267–69. William E. Parrish, *Turbulent Partnership: Missouri and the Union, 1861–1865* (Columbia: University of Missouri Press, 1963), 136–37. St. Louis *Missouri Republican*, 9, 12, and 18 November 1862.

16. William G. Eliot to Abraham Lincoln, 18 December 1862, Lincoln papers.

mediate emancipation was acceptable and that B. Gratz Brown should become Missouri's next U.S. senator. By holding these positions radical legislators represented well the views of their constituents, especially those in St. Louis. The moderate Republican members (Claybanks) found themselves increasingly alienated from their more radical counterparts. For this reason the business of the General Assembly bogged down and debate often degenerated into personal vituperations. Additionally, time was consumed by investigations into alleged election irregularities and challenges to the legality of the election of some to the legislature. Well into the legislative session, the radicals, recognizing that they could not force an immediate emancipation bill through the legislature, instead sought to establish a new state convention. By this means the radicals hoped to supersede the old convention and to elect enough radicals to ensure the passage of an emancipation bill meeting their specifications.[17]

The emancipation issue was not the only controversial matter before the General Assembly. The radicals objected to Gamble's military appointments, accusing him of nominating only conservatives and seeking to exercise dictatorial control over the militia. Moreover, some senators complained that Gamble was tardy in providing Missouri's Senate with his nominations. Gamble explained that the delay was necessary and unavoidable. Apparently this explanation was considered unsatisfactory by many senators, and it is probable that Gamble had delayed the announcement of his nominees to gain some tactical advantage in the ratification process. If he anticipated difficulty in gaining ratification for some of his appointees, Gamble's political instincts were confirmed when some of his nominees for brigadier generalships were rejected. However, Gamble's important staff positions were filled, although he wisely refrained from nominating his personal aide Colonel William D. Wood for the position of adjutant-general. Critics accused Wood of being disloyal because he had been captured and paroled at Camp Jackson in May 1861. In the immediate aftermath of the incident, however, Gamble had explained to Lincoln that a majority of the captured militia were not disloyal, for they had only obeyed the orders of their superior officers in assembling there.

17. St. Louis *Missouri Republican*, 16 December 1862, 17, 22, 23 January, 2, 6, and 19 February, and 9, 10, and 13 March 1863.

Evidently, Gamble was satisfied that Wood was loyal—and Wood's subsequent behavior proved him correct—but also understood that the radicals would use this incident to defeat his nomination. For this reason Gamble did not nominate Wood, but instead retained him as his personal aide, a position for which Senate approval was unnecessary.[18]

During the session, Gamble exercised his prerogative in signing and occasionally vetoing bills passed by the legislature. Sometimes Gamble's objection to legislation was not strong enough for him to veto it, such as in the circumstance of a bill to fund the enrolled militia. Gamble believed that the provision allowing soldiers to pay an exemption fee of $10 would enable too many men to avoid service. He recommended that this part of the bill be repealed or modified to ensure that enough soldiers would be available to protect the state. Soon it became apparent that the exemption law made it altogether too easy for persons of military age to avoid military service. In another instance, however, Gamble vetoed a bill "to regulate [contract] executions." In his message to the House, he argued that the legislation was unconstitutional, for both the U.S. Supreme Court and Missouri's constitution prohibited the passage of any act that would "impair the obligation of contracts." Because this was a settled matter of law, Gamble considered his veto part of his "obligation to support the Constitution of the United States, and the Constitution of this State."[19]

These and other differences often surfaced in opposition newspapers and on the floor of the House and Senate. Eventually, the radicals passed resolutions criticizing Gamble and demanding that the federal government deal more harshly with disloyal persons in Missouri. In this environment, perhaps it was inevitable that some members in caucus sought support to oust Gamble from the governorship. In constructing their case against Gamble, the Charcoals pointed to a number of measures that to them indicated his complicity in weakening the effort to defend Missouri. Of these measures, the most compelling evidence (on the face of it) re-

18. St. Louis *Missouri Republican*, 11 and 12 March 1863. Hamilton R. Gamble and James E. Yeatman, 15 May 1861, Lincoln papers.

19. Buel Leopard and Floyd C. Shoemaker, eds., *The Messages and Proclamations of the Governors of the State of Missouri* (Columbia: The State Historical Society of Missouri, 1922), 476–77 and 490–91. *Annual Report of the Adjutant General of the State of Missouri for the Year 1863* (St. Louis: n.p., 1864), 66–67.

garded Gamble's attempt to persuade Lincoln to remove all federal troops from the region north of the Missouri River. In December 1862, Gamble had consulted with Lincoln concerning this and other matters relating to Missouri. Unknown to the public and Gamble's political opposition, Lincoln had first proposed the removal of federal troops from Missouri. As the Union effort in the West appeared to have bogged down, Lincoln asked General Curtis if "the civil authority [could] be introduced into Missouri in lieu of the military to any extent with advantage and safety?" Curtis, whom Gamble correctly suspected of wishing to pursue radical policies, replied that he feared the withdrawal of federal forces would endanger the property and lives of many loyal Missourians. Gamble, whose original military plan for Missouri had envisioned establishing a large militia force to take over control of the state once peace was restored, was confident that the enrolled militia could maintain security north of the Missouri River. All that was required was the federal government to provide proper "subsistence, clothing, and pay for time they may be in actual service." In substituting militia for federal troops in Missouri, Gamble hoped to reduce tensions between Missourians and the military.[20]

Realizing that Lincoln was seriously considering withdrawing federal troops from Missouri, Curtis enlisted Provost-Marshal General Franklin A. Dick to convince Lincoln that rebellion had only been driven underground and that at the first opportunity disloyal elements would renew guerrilla operations. Moreover, Curtis drafted a letter in which he argued that persons favoring slavery believed that they could "hold their negroes better under the Enrolled Militia, many of whom are commanded by proslavery officers." Curtis also warned that Gamble desired "sole control of the Enrolled Militia, and partial control of the 10,000 Missouri State Militia." However, after unburdening himself to Lincoln about his concerns, Curtis apparently sensed that his position was weak and understood that Lincoln expected him to cooperate with Gamble, for he soon ordered his subordinates not to interfere with Gamble's determinations in a num-

20. St. Louis *Missouri Republican*, 31 January, 9 and 27 February, 2 March, and 22 April 1863; and Gamble to Lincoln, 4 February 1863; William R. Strachan to Lincoln, 10 March 1863; and Henry T. Blow to Lincoln, 22 March 1863, Lincoln papers. Lincoln to Samuel R. Curtis, 17 December 1862; Curtis to Lincoln, 17 December 1862; Lincoln to Gamble, 18 December 1862; and Gamble to Lincoln, 18 December 1862, *Official Records*, series 1, vol. 22, part 1, 839–40.

ber of matters, including the enforcement of state slave law. Conceding that Gamble had an obligation to enforce the law, even law protecting slavery, Curtis ordered his command not to interfere with the governor's activities so long as they had no adverse affect on the military. However, Curtis made it clear that state slave law did not override congressional legislation freeing the slaves of disloyal citizens. Later, Governor Gamble proposed that Lincoln send federal cavalry to General Ulysses S. Grant, whose command was stretched thin holding strategic parts of Kentucky, Tennessee, and Mississippi. Grant, never one to rest on his laurels or provide the enemy with time to recover, had set in motion his Vicksburg campaign. For these reasons, Gamble's suggestion to send troops to Grant was tempting, although in the end Lincoln was unwilling to order the cavalry out of Missouri without Curtis's agreement. To effect this, Lincoln replied that it would be best for Gamble and Curtis to discuss the matter with one another. "Confer with him, and I shall be glad to act when you and he agree."[21]

As Lincoln had suggested, Gamble and Curtis met in early January 1863 to discuss these and other military matters and work out a plan of action. Before the meeting Curtis wrote to Gamble that he had found it necessary to send most of the remaining federal troops south of the Missouri River, leaving the enrolled militia to act "as sentinels in each neighborhood." In their meeting, Gamble proposed reorganizing a part of the enrolled militia into provisional regiments from "companies of known loyalty and efficiency" and to appoint over these regiments "field officers of approved capacity and faithfulness." The provisional regiments, Gamble argued, were needed to provide protection no longer available from the Missouri State Militia, all of which was then south of the Missouri River. Most of the federal troops were then serving in Arkansas to hold territory then under federal control and to advance on Little Rock. Curtis believed that this movement would fix enemy troops in Arkansas, prevent-

---

21. Samuel R. Curtis to Lincoln, 20 December 1862; Franklin A. Dick to Lincoln, 19 December 1862; and Curtis to J. T. K. Hayward, 26 December 1862; Gamble to Lincoln, 27 December 1862; Lincoln to Gamble, 27 December 1862; Curtis to Gamble, 4 January 1863; and Lincoln to Curtis, 5 January 1863, *Official Records*, series 1, vol. 22, part 1, 853–54, 875–76, and 878; series 1, vol. 22, part 2, 16–18; and series 2, vol. 5, 99–100. Ulysses S. Grant, *Personal Memoirs of U. S. Grant* (New York: Library of America, 1990), 283.

ing their transfer to those forces defending Vicksburg. Curtis objected to Gamble's plan because of its cost, although he offered no alternative strategy for eradicating guerrillas in Missouri. Gamble, believing that continued guerrilla activity in Missouri justified him in moving forward without Curtis's agreement, implemented his plan, establishing several provisional regiments under his own authority. As commander of the District of Missouri, Curtis was placed in a potentially difficult situation, for these provisional regiments, like the enrolled militia from which they were composed, were not under Curtis's direction, although Gamble was careful to coordinate the provisional regiments' movements with U.S. forces.[22]

Nevertheless, after slowing during the winter, increased guerrilla activity was renewed in the spring. Mostly in small bands, guerrilla leaders such as Charles Quantrill, William Jackman, Cole Younger, and others specialized in hit-and-run terror tactics. Because these guerrilla bands often received help from local Confederate sympathizers, it was difficult to stop the attacks, which occurred in all parts of the state. Fortunately, many of the leaders of these irregular troops did not like one another and rarely coordinated their efforts. Missouri State Militia and Enrolled Missouri Militia regiments sent out patrols, which sometimes managed to kill a few members of a group, although often the guerrillas were alerted beforehand and escaped. For these reasons, efforts to eradicate the guerrillas in Missouri were unsuccessful to the end of the war.[23]

The radicals, who by then were openly questioning Gamble's military policies, asserted that the enrolled militia units were composed of many disloyal officers and men. From his correspondence and published orders

22. Samuel R. Curtis to Gamble, 4 January 1863; William D. Wood to T. J. Bartholow, 3 February 1863; Report of Major General John M. Schofield, U.S. Army, commanding Department of the Missouri, of operations 24 May–December 10, 1863; and General Orders, No. 24, 26 September 1863, *Official Records*, series 1, vol. 22, part 1, 12–13; series 1, vol. 22, part 2, 12–13, 16–17, 95–96, and 577–78. *Report of the Adjutant General*, 27–28 and 50. Gamble to Lincoln, 4 February 1863, Lincoln papers. Gerald R. Duffus, "A Study of the Military Career of Samuel R. Curtis: 1861–1865" (Master's thesis, Drake University, 1966), 60.

23. See the numerous reports of various actions against guerrillas in *Official Records*, series 1, vol. 22, part 1, 219–22, 225–27, 229, 233–36, 313–14, 319–20, 332–33, 343, and 375–76. Jay Monaghan, *Civil War on the Western Border, 1854–1865* (Lincoln: University of Nebraska Press, 1955), 274–89. Michael Fellman, *Inside War: The Guerrilla Conflict in Missouri During the American Civil War* (New York: Oxford University Press, 1989), 80–131.

issued at the time, it is clear that Gamble aggressively moved to find and to eradicate any disloyal persons from the militia. To accomplish this, Gamble ordered commanders of enrolled militia to report to the adjutant-general any persons or companies of troops known to be disloyal. More-over, Gamble investigated accusations made by private persons against militia units; doing his best to determine the truth of the information, he moved quickly to remove those persons who could not be trusted. As with any matter requiring the exercise of independent judgment, Gamble's de-cisions, which were based on information he could gain from commanders and others he trusted, were often questioned and criticized by the friends of those removed. Later, Gamble's political opponents accused him of removing radical officers from the militia and replacing them with con-servative or disloyal persons. However, by this time the rift between the governor and his opposition had broadened to the point that some went so far as to question Gamble's loyalty. These accusations, he learned from Attorney General Bates, had even reached Washington and had briefly un-dermined the confidence of some, including Secretary of War Edwin M. Stanton and General-in-Chief Halleck, in his leadership. According to Bates, they had believed the accusations of some Missourians and con-sidered Gamble a "suspected person," thereby weakening his ability to govern "by belittling & degrading him before his own people." Such be-havior, Bates warned, "could only lead to anarchy in Mo [sic] & calamity & shame to the nation." After "some pretty hard quarreling," however, Bates believed that their attitudes had changed. Whatever was then the circum-stance, more important was that President Lincoln still had no doubts about Gamble's loyalty. In the midst of these troubles, noting the policy disagreements between Gamble and others, Lincoln, who then as later in vain would seek cooperation between unionists in Missouri, observed to General Curtis that

> as usual in such cases, each questions the other's motives. On the one hand, it is insisted that Governor Gamble's Unionism, at most, is not better than a secondary spring of action; that hunkerism and a wish for political influence stand before Unionism with him. On the other hand, it is urged that arrests, banishments, and assessments are made more for private malice, revenge, and pecuniary interest than for the public good. . . . Now, my belief is that

Governor Gamble is an honest and true man, not less so than yourself, that you and he could confer together on this and other Missouri questions, with great advantage to the public; that each knows something which the other does not, and that acting together you could about double your stock of pertinent information.[24]

Soon after Lincoln's decision in the fall of 1862 to replace Schofield with General Curtis as commander in Missouri, Gamble and other conservatives expressed their concern that he was ill-suited for the position. Because he had filled various military posts in Missouri, Gamble had observed Curtis from the beginning of the war and concluded that he was too closely aligned with the Radical Republicans. For these reasons, Gamble and Curtis distrusted each other and disagreed on issues such as the expediency of banishing the disloyal, slavery policy, and control over the enrolled militia and provisional regiments. Another difference concerned whether it was necessary to maintain martial law throughout Missouri. Moreover, Gamble doubted Curtis's military abilities and his honesty, believing the stories then circulating about his involvement in cotton speculations.[25]

In early December 1862, Curtis published General Order No. 35, expanding the provost-marshal system in Missouri. In each district a provost-marshal and an assistant were to gather information on disloyal civilians and to interrogate and submit reports on prisoners of war. Provost-marshals were to arrest anyone behaving in a disloyal manner, providing supplies or money to the rebels, and anyone involved in guerrilla

24. Samuel R. Curtis to Lincoln, 19 and 20 December 1862; and J. T. K. Hayward to Lincoln, 27 January 1863, Lincoln papers. Hayward to Gamble, 5 January 1863; and Barton Bates to Gamble, 21 January 1863, Gamble papers. Curtis to Lincoln, 30 December 1862; Lincoln to Curtis, 5 January 1863; General Orders, No. 7, 19 February 1863; Chester Harding Jr. to H. Z. Curtis, 25 March 1863; Samuel R. Curtis to Gamble, 28 March 1863, *Official Records*, series 1, vol. 13, 534–35; series 1, vol. 22, part 1, 853–54 and 884; and series 1, vol. 22, part 2, 17–18, 119, and 179–80. John Thome to Gamble, 23 February 1863, Alvord Collection, Western Historical Manuscripts Collection, State Historical Society of Missouri, Columbia, Missouri. Kersey Coates to Gamble, 5 March 1863, Missouri Militia Records, Duke University Library, Durham, North Carolina.

25. Gamble to Montgomery Blair, 24 September 1862; and Gamble to Lincoln, 13 July 1863, Lincoln papers. Charles Gibson to Lincoln, 23 February 1863, Gamble papers.

activities. Provost-marshals were also ordered to disarm disloyal persons and arrest those hindering the recruitment of troops or otherwise impairing the effectiveness of the military. Persons guilty of disloyal activities and crimes were to face charges before a military commission, even if the civil courts were operating in the region. Curtis also ordered that runaway slaves owned by disloyal persons were free when they came into Union military lines and were not to be surrendered to their masters. Moreover, he ordered that slaves of disloyal persons then incarcerated without criminal indictment were to be freed. Provost-marshals were to investigate and report immediately upon all such cases to the provost-marshal general. Those slaves owned by loyal persons, however, were not to be freed and the provost-marshal was not to interfere with them.[26]

At a time when Missouri was relatively peaceful, many conservatives and moderate Republicans considered the expansion of the provost-marshal organization unnecessary. These concerns reached Lincoln, who asked Curtis if civil authority could not be reestablished in many parts of Missouri. In his answer, Curtis argued that only military power ensured that peace was maintained in Missouri and warned that rebels would gain an upper hand in some parts of the state and would "ruin the Union men who have joined the military power to put down the rebellion." Despite his objections, on January 14, 1863, Curtis was ordered to suspend General Order No. 35 and any other orders in which the discipline of federal troops was not involved. The next day Curtis was directed to allow no provost-marshal to exercise his authority outside of a military post and then only when it related "to military offenses." Curtis, who was obviously surprised that his measures were being overturned, argued that the provost-marshals were his only sources of intelligence in some parts of the state and that their expanded roles had secured peace to many regions. For these reasons, he asked that he be given time to explain his policies before being made to suspend his provost-marshal orders. This request was granted, although Curtis was warned to avoid "arbitrary" measures.[27]

26. General Orders, No. 23, 1 December 1862; and General Orders, No. 35, 24 December 1862, *Official Records*, series 1, vol. 22, part 1, 803–4 and 868–71.
27. Lincoln to Samuel R. Curtis, 17 December 1862; Curtis to Lincoln, 17 December 1862; Edwin M. Stanton to Curtis, 14 and 17 January 1863; Henry W. Halleck to Curtis, 15 and 22 January 1863; and Curtis to Stanton, 15 January 1863, *Official Records*, series 1, vol. 22, part 1, 839; and series 1, vol. 22, part 2, 41–45, and 50. *Report of the Committee*, 270–81.

For his part, Gamble considered the provost-marshal system a temporary expedient to be used only when the civil authority could not function. In this opinion Gamble was supported by the policy of the United States and the published opinion and orders of General-in-Chief Halleck before and during the war. Wherever civilian control could be reestablished, it was unwarranted for the military to supersede the authority of Missouri's courts, especially "in parts of the State where there was no military force nor any necessity for one." Concerning this, Gamble later argued that Lincoln should have removed Curtis from command when he employed the provost-marshals improperly, delegating to them, instead of to the courts, the authority to determine the status of slaves as ordered by Congress. Moreover, Curtis had erred badly when he allowed the provost-marshals to hold onto the loyalty bonds, once again usurping the authority of the courts. In this way, Gamble believed that Curtis tried to maintain military control over parts of Missouri unnecessarily.[28]

In early February 1863, with tensions rising between conservatives and radicals in the legislature and the press, an editorialist in the St. Louis *Neue Zeit* accused Gamble of being disloyal and called for the overthrow of the state government. Gamble, who to this point had largely ignored his critics, perhaps overreacted when he demanded that Curtis suppress the *Neue Zeit*, arguing that any paper seeking the overthrow of the government during time of war should be suppressed. Apparently, Curtis disagreed with Gamble's assessment of the situation, for he refused to suppress the paper. Certainly, he could honestly point to War Department instructions that prohibited him from interfering in civilian matters except as a last resort. Gamble, having observed Curtis's active support of the radicals, undoubtedly concluded that he was part of the political opposition and was someone with whom he could no longer work. These considerations probably were the impetus to Gamble's efforts by the end of February to devise a strategy to apply pressure on Lincoln to remove Curtis. Soon Attorney General Bates, U.S. Senator John B. Henderson, Congressman James S. Rollins, and others visited Lincoln to urge Curtis's removal. Both Secretary of War Stanton and General-in-Chief Halleck

28. Henry W. Halleck to Samuel R. Curtis, 22 January 1863, *Official Records*, series 1, vol. 22, part 2, 66–67. Gamble to Lincoln, 13 July 1863, Gamble papers. *Report of the Committee*, 270.

had sought to prevent this, but, in the end, on March 10 Lincoln ordered General Edwin V. Sumner to take command of the District of Missouri. Unfortunately, Sumner died before he could fill his new post, which led to a new round of letters and visits to Lincoln from both conservatives and radicals. In the meantime, Curtis was left in command serving as a sort of lame duck until the end of May, when General John M. Schofield was reappointed to the command in Missouri.[29]

Although Schofield was unenthusiastic about his new command, having observed from the war's beginning the internal disputes in Missouri, Gamble and most moderates and conservatives welcomed his return as a commander whose views were more in accord with their own. The immediate result of this expectation was Gamble's decision to place the enrolled militia and provisional regiments under Schofield's direct command. In turn, Schofield requested and gained authorization to issue clothing and camp equipment to the enrolled militia and provisional regiments, something that Curtis had refused to do. This type of cooperation was important for the Union cause in Missouri, for it allowed Gamble to turn his attention from military matters to the most pressing political issue of the day.[30]

29. Gamble to Samuel R. Curtis, 9 February 1863; Hamilton R. Gamble Jr. to Gamble, 6 March 1863; John B. Henderson to Gamble, 30 March 1863; and Gamble to Lincoln, 2 May 1863, Gamble papers. St. Louis *Missouri Republican*, 9 and 27 February 1863. Howard K. Beale, ed., *The Diary of Edward Bates, 1859–1866* (Washington, D.C.: U.S. Government Printing Office, 1933), 278–79, 292, and 294. Edward Bates to E. V. Sumner, 7 and 14 March 1863; and Edward Bates to Gamble, 19 March and 23 April 1863, Bates papers. Missouri legislature to Lincoln, 2 March 1863; Henry T. Blow et al. to Lincoln, 21 March 1863; Gamble to Lincoln, 30 March 1863; and Henderson to Lincoln, 30 March 1863, Lincoln papers. Curtis to Charles H. Howland, 22 February 1863; Henry W. Halleck to Curtis, 16 March 1863; and Curtis to Halleck, 24 March 1863, *Official Records*, series 1, vol. 22, part 2, 120–21, 156–57, and 176–77.

30. John M. Schofield to Gamble, 26 May 1863, Gamble papers. General Orders, No. 17, 29 May 1863; and Henry W. Halleck to Schofield, 3 June 1863, *Official Records*, series 1, vol. 22, part 2, 296 and 307–8.

Chapter Ten

Loss of the Lighthouse

ith the appointment of General John M. Schofield as commander of the District of Missouri, Hamilton R. Gamble probably hoped that many of the difficulties associated with federal troops stationed in Missouri would soon end. He trusted Schofield as a man of sound judgment and one knowledgeable of the circumstances of the state. Nevertheless, for peace to be restored to Missouri, Gamble believed that the issue of slavery must be resolved. Although in his inaugural speech as governor, Gamble had promised the people of Missouri to preserve the institution of slavery, as the war progressed he concluded that some solution to the problem must be found. Unfortunately, the radicals, in seeking to gain power, believed their political interests were better served, not through the behavior of a loyal opposition, but rather through the discrediting of Gamble and his administration of the state government. Over the summer and early fall of 1863, the radicals stepped up their attacks against Gamble until it was clear no hope for reconciliation between him and his critics remained.

After the lackluster performance of General Samuel R. Curtis as commander of the District of Missouri, General Schofield's superiors in Washington, D.C., offered advice to help him avoid his predecessor's military and political mistakes. In a friendly and supportive letter, General-in-Chief Henry W. Halleck urged Schofield not to invade Arkansas from the northwestern region of the state as General Curtis had done. Moreover, Halleck believed that Curtis had erred seriously in refusing to send the

majority of his troops from the interior of Missouri, who were then without much to do, down the Mississippi River to join General Ulysses S.
Grant's command, or to report to General William S. Rosecrans in Tennessee. Halleck and the administration were confident that Schofield's best
line of operations was along the Mississippi River once it was opened to
the Arkansas River. This action would make it impossible for Confederate
General Sterling Price to invade Missouri again with a large force. Another advantage of this policy was that it would remove reasons for complaint against some federal troops in Missouri who disliked and distrusted
many of the civilians where they were stationed. This circumstance was
prevalent especially wherever troops with strong abolitionist beliefs were
posted among a proslavery community, or wherever a good deal of guerrilla activity prevailed. Unimpressed with loyalty oaths, troops usually
considered suspect, and sometimes harassed, former soldiers of Price's
army. Heeding the advice of Halleck, in early June 1863 Schofield sent
Major General Francis J. Herron with eight infantry regiments and three
artillery batteries to join General Grant and other commanders. Later,
he sent three infantry regiments, making a final total of roughly 8,000
men out of his command. By the end of the summer, Schofield dispatched
3,700 more troops to other commands, thereby reducing the number of
troops in Missouri "to the lowest possible defensive limit." However, as he
explained later, Schofield could never have provided troops for other sec-
tors of the war if Gamble had not made available to him large numbers of
enrolled militia and provisional regiments. With these troops, and by re-
arranging those remaining federal troops along the Kansas-Missouri border, Schofield hoped he could prevent any further troubles in the region.[1]

Schofield also received advice from President Abraham Lincoln, so
much of whose time had been taken up in resolving disputes between Missouri unionists. In a confidential letter, he warned Schofield against taking
sides in the "pestilent factional quarrel" between the radicals and conserva-

1. Henry W. Halleck to John M. Schofield, 22 May 1863; Schofield, 10 December 1863,
The War of the Rebellion: A Compilation of the Official Records of the Union and Confederate Armies,
128 vols. (Washington, D.C.: U.S. Government Printing Office, 1880–1902), series 1, vol. 22,
part 1, 12–17; and series 1, vol. 22, part 2, 290–92. John M. Schofield, *Forty-Six Years in the Army*,
foreword by William M. Ferraro (New York: Century, 1897; Norman: University of Oklahoma
Press, 1998), 69–71.

tives. In his analysis of the dispute, Lincoln identified Curtis as the head of
the radical faction and Gamble as the leader of the conservatives. Lincoln
then added that he had been unable to resolve the controversy, and not
having the power to "remove Governor Gamble, I had to remove General
Curtis." In his reply, Schofield promised to remain neutral in his administration of the department and expressed his hope that with the resolution
of the slavery issue in Missouri, much of the reason for factionalism would
disappear. Many years later in writing about these events Schofield concluded that "it soon became evident that nothing would satisfy the radical
leaders short of the overthrow of the existing State government; that a
reconciliation of the quarrel between the 'pestilent factions' in Missouri,
so much desired by Mr. Lincoln, was exactly what the radicals did not
want and would not have." The radicals, somehow gaining possession of
Lincoln's letter to Schofield, later published it in the newspapers, creating
a good deal of controversy and making Gamble angry with Lincoln.[2]

   After the failure of Missouri's legislature and Congress to pass an emancipation law of some kind, Governor Gamble, convinced that slavery in
Missouri was doomed, sent out a proclamation to reconvene the state convention to consider "some scheme of Emancipation" to be adopted. By
doing this, Gamble hoped to remove the contentious issue of slavery from
Missouri's Civil War politics. Radical politicians, however, were unwilling
to settle for anything less than full and immediate emancipation. Some
radicals, believing that whites and blacks had the natural right to freedom
and equality, sought immediate emancipation regardless of its impact on
the war effort. Other radicals argued that the destruction of slavery would
precipitate the war's end. Moreover, opposition to gradual emancipation
appealed to the radical leaders' supporters and kept the slavery issue alive,
providing them with much political advantage and preserving a useful
issue with which to oppose Gamble's administration. On the other hand,
moderates, although often morally opposed to slavery, welcomed gradual
emancipation as an expedient less disruptive to the social and economic
order. Leading up to the state convention, the prevalent views on slavery might be summarized thus: conservatives and moderates regarded

2. Schofield, *Forty-Six Years in the Army*, 68–72. Schofield to Lincoln, 1 June 1863, *Official
Records*, series 1, vol. 22, part 2, 301.

emancipation as a means to winning the war; radicals considered it an all-important end but with an important residual benefit of ultimate victory.[3]

Prior to the commencement of the final session of the state convention in June 1863, radical elements in St. Louis continued their attacks on Gamble, which had been almost unrelenting in the German newspapers since the fall of 1862. The radicals argued that Gamble had only called the convention together to preempt their plan to establish a new convention whose members would emancipate the slaves immediately. The radicals, especially the German element, distrusted Gamble, for they still considered him to be proslavery in sentiment and suspected that his calls for emancipation were nothing less than a ploy to extend slavery as an institution far into the future. Their frustration and feelings of powerlessness had been exacerbated recently when Lincoln had categorically and firmly rejected resolutions passed at a radical meeting in St. Louis calling for the removal of his two Missouri cabinet members, Montgomery Blair and Edward Bates, and the sack of Halleck. Moreover, most devastating was Lincoln's statement that he preferred gradual to immediate emancipation.[4]

On June 15, 1863, the state convention convened in Jefferson City. In a message to the delegates Gamble explained why he had called them together. State constitutional constraints had prevented the legislature from passing an emancipation ordinance; therefore, only through amendment or the action of an extraconstitutional body, such as the state convention, could the issue of slavery be resolved conclusively. Gamble also explained that although he never held a "prejudice against the institution," he had thought for some time that a free system of labor would benefit the economy of Missouri. Recognizing that some conservatives would object to his call for the end of slavery, he stated that "the necessity for action at this time grows out of the present condition of the country. A great rebellion

3. *Journal of the Missouri State Convention, Held in Jefferson City, June 1863* (St. Louis: George Knapp, 1863), 3. St. Louis *Missouri Republican*, 6 February 1863.

4. Virgil C. Blum, "The Political and Military Activities of the German Element in St. Louis, 1859–1861," *Missouri Historical Review* 42 (January 1948): 107–8. The St. Louis *Missouri Republican* ran a series entitled the "Spirit of the German Press," in which were provided translations of editorial columns critical of Gamble's administration primarily from the St. Louis *Neue Zeit* and the *Westliche Post*. For attacks on Gamble leading into the convention and Lincoln's reply to the radical meeting's resolutions see St. Louis *Missouri Republican*, 23 May, and 3, 5, 6, 9, 11, and 12 June 1863.

against our Government exists, and its primary object is to inaugurate a government in which slavery shall be fostered as the controlling interest. If the leaders of this rebellion do really desire to have our State within their pretended confederacy, there can be no more effectual mode of extinguishing that desire than by showing our purpose to clear the State ultimately of the institution which forms the bond of cement among the rebellious States." Noting the controversial nature of the issue, he urged the delegates to work together to find a reasonable compromise. However, in devising a workable plan, Gamble urged the delegates to enter into the debate over emancipation with open minds, in a spirit of compromise, and to take care not to deprive citizens of their rights "farther than is necessary to make the public benefit certain and sure."[5]

Gamble also answered his radical critics who had claimed that the establishment of the enrolled militia was a cover to gain the removal of federal troops. Moreover, some of his political opponents asserted that most of the militia were disloyal and might be used to remove Missouri from the Union. While conceding that a few members of the enrolled militia were disloyal, Gamble thought that no one could honestly hold that a majority were rebels when one considered "the alacrity with which they take the field, endure hardships, and engage in battle." Such behavior was hardly that of persons uncommitted to preserving the peace and maintaining the Union. With the help of the few remaining federal troops, Gamble was certain the Missouri State Militia and the enrolled militia under Schofield's command could handle any emergency, for the danger of "any formidable invasion from the South" into Missouri had passed. Likewise, the end of slavery would diminish the incentive to violence and resistance for those in their midst who secretly harbored some hope that Missouri could still become part of the Southern Confederacy.[6]

If in his opening remarks Gamble hoped he could establish a spirit of compromise and conciliation, he was sorely disappointed, for both conservatives and radicals attacked his proposal. His conservative critics, such as James H. Birch, a former Missouri Supreme Court justice, argued that Gamble had betrayed their trust, for when the convention had made him

5. St. Louis *Missouri Republican*, 17 June 1863. *Journal, June 1863*, 3–6.
6. *Journal, June 1863*, 6–9.

provisional governor it was on the assumption—confirmed at the time
by Gamble's own words—that he would do nothing to end slavery. On
the other hand, radical leader Charles D. Drake, a newly elected delegate
from St. Louis, argued that Gamble, in calling the convention together,
hoped to pass an emancipation ordinance "so feeble and inert as to pro-
long Slavery in this State, with a continuance of the wretchedness it has
brought upon us, until some distant day." Drake thought it better to allow
the next legislature to establish a new convention that would better reflect
the views of the people then.[7]

Despite the criticism of some, the convention established a committee on emancipation and appointed Gamble as chair. A majority being
composed of conservatives, it was not surprising that the committee soon
presented to the convention a plan for gradual, rather than immediate,
emancipation. The plan repealed those sections of the state constitution
requiring the consent and compensation of owners in an emancipation
bill. According to this plan, slavery would end on July 4, 1876, a century
after the traditional date of the signing of the Declaration of Independence. The committee also stipulated that all slaves brought into the state
owned by nonresidents would be free. One member of the committee
objected to the plan, instead wanting an earlier date for emancipation and
a prohibition on slave sales. Another member argued that blacks benefited
from slavery and that emancipation would harm many white families.[8]

Early in the debate some of the delegates, whether as a real concern
or as an argument to forestall action, expressed some doubt that Lincoln
would respect the convention's action. This question came to Lincoln's
attention when General Schofield, whom some delegates had apparently
consulted in the matter, sent a telegram requesting Lincoln to direct him
how to answer these queries. Lincoln, who to this point had not interfered in the convention's deliberations, responded that he would support
the convention's action so long as military necessity did not dictate otherwise. However, he stated his preference for gradual emancipation, believing that such a policy was beneficial "for both black and white." For

7. *Proceedings of the Missouri State Convention Held in Jefferson City, June 1863* (St. Louis: George Knapp, 1863), 11, 15, and 34–35.

8. *Journal, June 1863*, 24. *Proceedings, June 1863*, 135–36, 144–45, and 229.

this reason he perceived little possibility that the military would interfere with slavery in Missouri, especially if the temporary transitional period to emancipation was brief.[9]

As the delegates debated the committee's emancipation plan, amendments were presented and voted on. These amendments addressed a number of concerns and objections to the committee's plan and represented the wide range of opinion among the delegates. Representing the radicals' position, early in the deliberations Drake presented a plan to emancipate the slaves on January 1, 1864, and to establish a period of apprenticeship to provide slaves and masters with a transition from slavery to freedom. This moderate plan was shelved until the committee on emancipation had presented its work to the convention. As the debate unfolded Drake, whom Gamble had mentored as a young lawyer and influenced to join the Presbyterian Church, accused Gamble of having called the convention together to pass a "feeble" emancipation ordinance. Later, Drake offered an amendment to establish January 1, 1866, for emancipation and challenged Gamble to vote for it. Perhaps to demonstrate that he was not conspiring to save slavery, Gamble voted for Drake's amendment. However, probably hoping to curry favor with his radical constituents, Drake soon changed course again, advocating absolute and immediate emancipation. U.S. Senator John B. Henderson, who was also a delegate to the state convention, noted the inconsistency of Drake's positions on slavery, inferring that Drake and his radical supporters were more interested in preserving slavery as a political issue than they were in solving it conclusively. Interestingly, radical delegates joined with proslavery delegates in supporting a motion to require a statewide vote on any emancipation measure passed by the convention. Gamble on the floor of the convention noted this agreement of members on opposite poles of the slavery issue, suggesting that the measure was meant to kill emancipation.[10]

9. James S. Rollins to Lincoln, 12 June 1863, John M. Schofield to Lincoln, 21 June 1863, and Lincoln to John M. Schofield, 22 June 1863, Lincoln papers. Michael Burlingame and John R. Turner Ettlinger, eds., *Inside Lincoln's White House: The Complete Civil War Diary of John Hay* (Carbondale: Southern Illinois University Press, 1997), 88–89. James L. McDonough, *Schofield: Union General in the Civil War and Reconstruction* (Tallahassee: Florida State University Press, 1972), 44–47.

10. *Journal, June 1863*, 12 and 27. *Proceedings, June 1863*, 34–35, 285–86, 290, and 315–17.

After debate had continued for some time and the delegates had been unable to arrive at any agreement, Gamble suggested that the issue be tabled until a new convention could be elected to revisit the matter. This suggestion may have been calculated to spur the delegates to action, especially because he had already made it clear that he would not continue as governor without the passage of an emancipation order. If so, the maneuver worked, for the majority passed a final compromise meeting the criteria of both Gamble and Lincoln in their messages to the convention. First, the measure repealed the state's constitutional prohibitions to emancipation. According to the plan, which ended up being very similar to Gamble's emancipation proposal, slavery was to cease on July 4, 1870. However, the plan established an intermediate condition for slaves as "servants" to their former masters, allowing a transition for both slave and master and preventing an interruption in the supply of laborers in Missouri. Exhibiting the same prejudice prevalent among most whites of his generation, Gamble noted that "the interest of the master is to be considered as well as that of the slave. We must have no such Utopian notions as that by breaking of his shackles the slave becomes an angel—becomes at once an intelligent man, capable of sustaining himself under all the trials of life. Do not fall into such a notion as that. Everybody who has ever seen five negroes together knows better than that. Act upon the subject as you know it to be; so that it may promote the greatest amount of benefit to all concerned." These paternalistic notions, premised on a belief in black inferiority, were addressed in the ordinance by stipulating that those slaves over forty years of age on July 4, 1870, would remain servants for life. Those under twelve years would remain servants until they reached the age of twenty-three, while the remainder would be released from their temporary servitude on July 4, 1876. The convention also prohibited the sale of slaves and their removal from the state after July 4, 1870. This measure anticipated the possibility that the South might win its independence and have a ready market for slaves after the war.[11]

At the end of his opening message to the state convention, Gamble resigned as governor. In explaining his decision, after surveying his career

11. *Proceedings, June 1863*, 280–85, 297, 344, and 367.

as governor to that point, Gamble noted that Missouri was no longer in danger of becoming part of the Southern Confederacy and that peace throughout most of the state had been restored. Therefore, Gamble believed the time had then come that he

> could conscientiously say that [he] had performed all you asked me to undertake. When I was chosen to the office, the only question which engaged our attention was, whether the *status* of Missouri as a State in the Union could be preserved; whether our rights as citizens of the United States could be protected against those who sought to bind us to the Confederacy of the revolted States. I regard such questions as settled. . . . I feel, then, that the service you required of me has been rendered, and that there is no further demand upon me to continue the sacrifice of my own tastes and interests.[12]

The reaction to Gamble's announcement was mixed. Within the hall where the governor's message was read, one observer noted that an intense and pervasive "stillness" fell over the delegates. Soon thereafter, however, editorialists in radical newspapers welcomed his departure or greeted it with skepticism, suspecting that his resignation was some sort of ploy. For their part, Gamble's supporters, most of whom were moderates and conservatives, were initially surprised and unsure what to do. James H. Birch, strongly proslavery and notoriously ambitious for political office, opportunistically made a motion to accept Governor Gamble's resignation, thereby clearing the way for an election of executive officers in the fall. This motion was rejected. The prospect of an undesirable person becoming governor prompted the passage of a motion to learn if they could persuade Gamble to reconsider.[13]

Gamble's reluctance to accept the challenges and responsibilities of the state's highest executive office was well known. Having released himself from this heavy burden, delegates commissioned to urge Gamble not

12. *Journal, June 1863*, 10.

13. St. Louis *Missouri Republican*, 17, 18, 23, and 26 June 1863. *Journal, June 1863*, 10, 22, 25, 45–46, and 48–49. *In Memoriam: Hamilton Rowan Gamble, Governor of Missouri* (St. Louis: George Knapp, 1864), 88–89.

to resign found him very uncooperative. They reported that he had told them "that if it were God's will, he would rather die." As different persons expressed their disappointment and concerns about his departure, Gamble gradually softened his refusals and soon conceded that it might be best if he remained. However, it is apparent that he sought more latitude in some areas in return for his remaining as governor. In a letter to General Schofield, who had also urged him not to resign, Gamble sought his promise to suppress any "unlawful" actions against the provisional government, to punish any military personnel resisting civil and criminal court proceedings, to prohibit the recruitment of blacks in Missouri without written permission from Gamble, and to stop the military's seizure of property and slaves. Furthermore, Gamble promised to support Schofield fully so long as he implemented these measures. According to Schofield he declined to make this promise, although, as will be seen later, his policies mirrored these proposals very closely. In the end, Gamble agreed to retract his resignation in spite of the troubles he anticipated. From his statement to the convention it is clear that Gamble had discussed the same issues with the delegates as he had proposed to Schofield and that he had received the assurances he had requested. Years later, a member of the convention remembered vividly that when Gamble came before the convention he appeared haggard with a "palid face, furrowed with the ravages of care and disease, his hair like burnished silver, his eyes aglow with the fire of martyrdom." His statement demonstrated, however, his undiminished commitment to sacrificing his own interests for the public good.

> The request contained in your resolution involves the idea that I am to undertake a new labor—that labor can be nothing less than that I shall endeavor to restore order and the supremacy of civil government over the discordant elements at work within the State. . . . The discord of a family must cease when their dwelling is on fire, until they have extinguished the fire. When the State is restored to internal quiet, we may resume our party disputes about men and measures. The work of restoring order within the State is one which will subject me to even more vile and unmeasured calumnies, which have been continually heaped upon me ever since the people lost their fear of being overcome by the rebels. . . . I have taken part in your deliberation and action upon this great question, and during its progress I made the declaration in your presence, that, if some scheme

was not adopted, I could not consent to hold office; thereby giving a kind of assurance that I would continue to act if you would adopt a scheme of emancipation.[14]

STRAINED RELATIONS WITH LINCOLN

During this last session of the convention, Lincoln's letter to Schofield advising him not to side with any faction was leaked to the press. At the time, because of a constant stream of letters and delegations from Missouri to him, members of his cabinet, and congressmen, Lincoln's equanimity and patience had been tested for several months. Having tired of the many controversies into which he had been repeatedly dragged, Lincoln began to make notations upon letters from Missouri that they represented "one side" or "the other side" of these "quarrels." Moreover, he began to protest to those bringing their disputes to him that "it is very painful to me that you in Missouri can not, or will not, settle your factional quarrel among yourselves. I have been tormented beyond endurance for months by both sides. Neither side pays the least respect to my appeals to your reason." It was in this context that Lincoln referred to Gamble as the leader of a "faction."[15]

The president's characterization of Gamble in the letter upset him very much and led to a decided chilling in their relations. In his speech agreeing to continue as governor of Missouri until January 1865, Gamble did not disguise his anger when he said: "I therefore withdraw my resignation, and will again involve myself in the cares and perplexities of office; not to be, as the *sagacious* President of the United States regards me, the head of a faction, but an officer of the State, above all party influences, and careless of everything but the interest of the State." On July 13, 1863, two weeks after the publication of Lincoln's letter in newspapers throughout Mis-

14. Schofield, *Forty-Six Years*, 71–74. *Proceedings, June 1863*, 148–57 and 368. John Philips, "Hamilton Rowan Gamble and the Provisional Government of Missouri," *Missouri Historical Review* 5 (October 1910): 13.

15. Lincoln to Schofield, 27 May 1863, *Official Records*, series 1, vol. 22, part 2, 293. Samuel T. Glover to Edward Bates, 13 April 1863; St. Louis Citizens to Lincoln, 1 May 1863; Henry T. Blow to Lincoln, 5 May 1863; Glover to Bates, 15 May 1863; Lincoln to Henry T. Blow and others, 15 May 1863, Lincoln papers.

souri, Gamble wrote what Lincoln later referred to as "a very 'cross'" letter. Gamble considered Lincoln's description of him as the leader of a faction "a most wanton and unmerited insult." He denied that he had acted as a political partisan since accepting the office of provisional governor and on numerous occasions had defended Lincoln himself from criticism. Moreover, until then Gamble asserted that although he had disapproved of some measures instituted by Lincoln "I have carefully abstained from denouncing you, or those concerned with you in conducting the government, and this because I thought I might damage the cause of my country by weakening public confidence in you. . . . I will not address this to you through the newspapers as I would be justified in doing at once, after the publication of your letter but will leave its publication for future consideration." After declining to read Gamble's letter, Lincoln claimed that he had never intended to offend Gamble, and that he "was totally unconscious of any malice or disrespect towards you." Soon after this, perhaps recognizing that he had some reason to be angry, Lincoln proposed that Gamble come to the White House where they could work out their differences.[16]

Passage of the emancipation ordinance did not end the controversy between unionists in Missouri. Instead, the radicals intensified their attacks on Gamble, General Schofield, and many of the officers of state militia forces whom he had appointed. Viewing the war through their abolitionist prism, the radicals suspected anyone who did not do everything possible to eradicate slavery immediately. Perhaps the spirit and attitudes of Gamble's critics were best exemplified in the Twenty-second General Assembly's passage of resolutions in January 1863 to establish an investigatory committee to consider if the militia had been used properly. Dominated by a majority of radical and zealous legislators determined to prove Gamble's maladministration of the militia, committee members sent out questionnaires and took depositions from those claiming that members of the Missouri State Militia, the enrolled militia, and the provisional regiments were disloyal. The majority report of the committee was divided into several sections ranging over several hundred pages, consisting of

16. Gamble to Lincoln, 13 July 1863; Lincoln to Gamble, 23 July 1863; and Edward Bates to Gamble, 3 August 1863, Lincoln papers.

depositions taken under oath and letters from persons—mostly fellow radicals—claiming that proslavery and disloyal officers were undermining the peace and were secretly in league with the rebels to take Missouri out of the Union.[17]

Often the evidence presented in the committee's report showed irregularities and abuses that might be expected in military units hastily organized and officered by civilians elected by enlisted men. As already noted, the same problems arose earlier in the war among U.S. volunteer troops, who also elected their lower-ranking officers. From the start, such circumstances of command impaired an officer's ability to instill discipline and promoted a strong inclination among enlisted men toward independence of action. Of course, much depended on the quality of the commanding officers who were appointed. Without good leadership, militia units could misuse their authority to loot their neighbors or to take revenge against personal enemies. These sorts of action were justified easily as necessary for the restoration of peace. In the instances when radical officers were relieved from duty because of such activities, although they were not the only officers cashiered for improper conduct, radicals on the committee accused Gamble of an unfair purge to make room for proslavery and disloyal officers appointed by him. For his part, Gamble believed that the militia should not have the authority summarily to punish anyone, excepting guerrillas captured with arms in the field. Having investigated these incidents carefully, Gamble concluded that too often militia troops, who were usually operating in their own neighborhoods, were settling old scores. Moreover, zeal or frustration led some troops to punish persons who were innocent, or at least against whom little evidence existed that they were disloyal. These types of incidents disturbed him, for often persons' homes were destroyed and men were killed based solely on a rumor or a suspicion that an individual was disloyal, or perhaps, was only sympathetic to the rebels. To prevent a continuance of these atrocities, Gamble recommended to the state convention the establishment of a judicial tribunal to try persons accused of belonging to or aiding guerrilla bands. The existence of such a court, Gamble asserted, would end the

17. *Report of the Committee*, 62–63, 68–69, 89–113, 244–45, 248–51. *Journal, June 1863*, 6–7.

need for soldiers taking the law into their own hands, excepting only instances when soldiers captured armed guerrillas.[18]

Another issue illustrating the differences between Gamble and his radical critics concerned the enlistment of black soldiers from Missouri. It is clear from criticism of both Gamble and Schofield that nothing short of unrestricted recruitment would satisfy the radicals. While he never publicly expressed an opinion concerning the efficacy of using black soldiers, Gamble was not opposed to their recruitment in Missouri. However, he did ask Schofield first to gain his permission before a recruiter came into the state, to restrict enlistments to free blacks, and to ensure that no state laws were violated. Because these were reasonable requests and did not violate War Department policy, Schofield made certain that Gamble's concerns were carefully followed. Nevertheless, Schofield declined making any promises to Gamble on this controversial subject and wrote to Secretary of War Stanton to ascertain how best to determine the status of blacks in Missouri. The military's policy was dictated by congressional acts and Lincoln's and his subordinates' orders implementing the legislation. On August 6, 1861, Congress passed the first of several acts to establish procedures for the manumission of slaves employed to support the Confederacy. In it, Congress prohibited the military from intervening in these matters. Instead, slaves were to sue their masters in court for their freedom. Passed on July 17, 1862, a second act protected slaves from being enslaved again who were owned by persons in military service against the United States, or in some other way helping the rebellion. In this instance the military was ordered to prevent masters of these slaves from retrieving them. To slaves freed under this legislation, the military issued certificates attesting to their free status. Presumably, all free blacks were available for recruitment.[19]

Like so many other policy questions, Schofield soon discovered that the circumstances in Missouri created special problems not encountered elsewhere. Having gained permission from Gamble to begin their work, during the summer of 1863 recruiters entered Missouri seeking to enlist

18. Dennis K. Boman, "Conduct and Revolt in the Twenty-fifth Ohio Battery: An Insider's Account," *Ohio History* 104 (Summer–Autumn 1995): 163–83. *Journal, June 1863*, 10.

19. John M. Schofield to Lorenzo Thomas, 10 June 1863; and Joseph Holt to Edwin M. Stanton, 17 August 1863, *Official Records*, series 3, vol. 3, 328–29; and series 2, vol. 6, 209–11.

free blacks to serve in segregated regiments under white officers. However, after one regiment was formed, recruiters discovered that very few free blacks remained in Missouri. Apparently, free blacks of military age, as with many runaways, had left the state, many of these removing to Kansas. Schofield detailed these problems in letters to the War Department. Of particular concern was the tendency of some recruiters to enlist blacks who were owned by loyal masters, or at least persons against whom no disloyal act could be proven since the passage of the confiscation act. These recruiting officers soon came into conflict with district commanders of the state militia—at least two recruiters were arrested—leading to radical criticism of Gamble and Schofield. Believing that most unionists would not resist a change in policy, so long as it was carried out lawfully, Schofield suggested that the U.S. government enlist all blacks, whether slave or free, whether owned by a loyal or disloyal person. He suggested that loyal owners be compensated and that some regular method be established to determine to whom compensation should be provided. Soon after this, Schofield's suggestions were adopted in General Order No. 329. This order authorized recruiters to enlist slaves whose masters allowed them to go. If an insufficient number of blacks were enlisted, recruiters were given the authority to enlist slaves without their masters' permission. Owners of enlisted slaves received certificates entitling them to compensation of up to $300. However, these owners were required to file a deed of manumission and prove their title to the slave. All slaves serving in the U.S. military were to gain their freedom. In the end, these recruitment efforts had little effect on the war effort for by February 1864 a total of only 3,700 blacks were enlisted in Missouri.[20]

One reason very few free blacks and slaves were available for recruitment, especially in western and northern Missouri, was that blacks had

20. John M. Schofield to Lorenzo Thomas, 26 September 1863; Schofield to E. D. Townsend, 29 September 1863; Lincoln to Schofield, 1 October 1863; General Orders, No. 329, 3 October 1863; and Schofield to Edwin M. Stanton, 12 November 1863, *Official Records*, series 3, vol. 3, 847–49, 860–61, and 1021–22; and series 1, vol. 22, part 2, 585–86. William G. Eliot to John M. Forbes, 30 October 1863, Lincoln papers. Schofield, *Forty-Six Years in the Army*, 99–100. *Report of the Committee*, 127 and 259–62. Earl J. Nelson, "Missouri Slavery, 1861–1865," *Missouri Historical Review* 28 (July 1934): 262–64. *Annual Report of the Adjutant General of the State of Missouri, for the Year 1863* (St. Louis: n.p., 1864), 61–64.

enlisted in Iowa and Kansas regiments. Moreover, U.S. volunteers and other armed bands from Kansas had crossed the border and stolen Missouri's slaves and other property. These activities were a continuation of the hostilities that had begun in the mid-1850s over the question of whether Kansas would become slave or free. During the war most of the aggression came from Kansas and other out-of-state regiments ordered into Missouri to help defeat General Sterling Price's army. Soldiers of these regiments often disregarded orders from their commanders not to interfere with slaves, while others, such as James Lane and Charles Jennison, encouraged their troops to steal slaves from both unionists and secessionists. These activities were significantly curtailed under General Halleck, especially after most out-of-state forces had been removed from Missouri. However, cross-border incursions still occurred occasionally. Curtis, Gamble, and Schofield all attempted to end this war within a war with varied success. Radicals criticized these measures as efforts to protect slavery and disloyal persons in western Missouri.[21]

After the surrender of the garrison at Vicksburg to General Grant on July 4, 1863, defeated Confederate soldiers from Missouri began to return home. Wishing to prevent an outbreak of violence with their return, Schofield published an order offering to the returning Confederate soldiers the opportunity to take the oath of allegiance and live peacefully where they were directed by the local provost-marshal. To those wishing to join or aid guerrilla fighters, Schofield promised swift retribution, especially those committing robbery or murder. As the summer progressed, it became increasingly clear that more protection was needed for loyal persons along the border, especially after guerrilla forces formed themselves into "Border Guards." On August 21, Charles Quantrill's infamous raid on Lawrence, Kansas, provoked Schofield and General Thomas Ewing, commander of the District of the Border, to issue orders addressing the

21. Edward M. Samuel et al., 8 September 1862; and Samuel statement, 8 September 1863; James McFerran report, 29 November 1862; court-martial proceedings against Charles Adams and J. E. Hayes; and N. P. Chipman to James Blunt, 15 January 1863, *Official Records*, series 1, vol. 13, 618–19; series 1, vol. 22, part 1, 39–41; series 1, vol. 22, part 2, 46–47 and 821–26. *Report of the Committee*, 180–81. The best accounts of the border conflicts are found in Jay Monaghan, *Civil War on the Western Border, 1854–1865* (Lincoln: University of Nebraska Press, 1955). Michael Fellman, *Inside War: The Guerrilla Conflict in Missouri During the American Civil War* (New York: Oxford University Press, 1989).

emergency. Schofield ordered commanders to allow "loyal and peaceable citizens in Missouri" to possess weapons to protect themselves. Moreover, he sent to Ewing the draft of what later became famous as General Order No. 11. Schofield's intention was for Ewing to consider how best to implement this policy and to make preparations necessary to prevent the violence the order's implementation might provoke. However, probably because he was blamed for the massacre at Lawrence and great pressure was upon him to act, Ewing decided to issue General Order No. 11 immediately. In it Ewing ordered everyone—excepting persons near certain towns—in Jackson, Cass, and Bates counties in northwestern Missouri to move out of the area within fifteen days. Those persons who could prove their loyalty to the commander of a post nearest their place of residence would be permitted to live near there. This measure demonstrated the frustration of the authorities with the majority of residents in northwestern Missouri who had aided and harbored guerrilla bands led by Quantrill and others. The precipitous nature of the order ensured that both loyal and disloyal persons experienced a great deal of hardship. The order had the desired effect of removing support from the guerrillas and forcing them to operate in different regions. Only loyal persons with written permission were allowed to return home briefly in October. In November, unionists were allowed again to reside in their homes. Men of military age were then organized into militia units to protect their neighborhoods. Furthermore, in the aftermath of the Lawrence massacre, Kansans led by U.S. Senator James Lane and other radicals organized an irregular armed band to enter Missouri ostensibly to punish those responsible and to recover the property stolen from them. Missourians feared the Kansans would instead plunder, steal slaves, and murder indiscriminately. Working with Ewing, Schofield took measures to prevent Lane's invasion.[22]

During this period of turmoil, Governor Gamble happened to be in

22. Richard C. Vaughan to John M. Schofield, 31 July 1863; General Orders, No. 10, 18 August 1863; Schofield to Thomas Ewing, 25 and 26 August 1863; Ewing to Schofield, 25 August 1863; General Orders, No. 11 and 86, 25 August 1863; Schofield to Lincoln, 28 August 1863; General Orders, No. 16, 2 October 1863; and General Orders, No. 20, 20 November 1863, *Official Records*, series 1, vol. 22, part 2, 413, 460–61, 471–76, 482–84, 594–95, and 713–14. Charles R. Mink, "General Orders, No. 11: The Forced Evacuation of Civilians During the Civil War," *Military Affairs* 34 (December 1970): 132–37. Albert Castel, "Order No. 11 and the Civil War on the Border," *Missouri Historical Review* 57 (July 1963): 357–68. McDonough, *Schofield*, 55–60.

Pennsylvania with his wife and children. On July 21 Gamble and his wife Caroline left Missouri by train for Philadelphia to consult with a doctor to determine if surgery might improve the eyesight of his wife, whose vision was partially impaired and feared to be progressively worsening. After returning to their home in Norristown and presumably consulting with physicians, Gamble traveled to Washington to meet with Lincoln. Their disagreement concerned a letter Lincoln had written to Schofield when he had taken command in Missouri in May 1863. In it Lincoln had referred to Gamble as the leader of a faction in Missouri and presented the actions of both sides as morally equivalent. This characterization angered Gamble very much, for he had never sought the position of governor and had tried to cooperate with all unionists, regardless of their political viewpoints, abolitionist or otherwise. Many years after the war in his memoirs, Schofield wrote that the radicals had used the issue of slavery for political advantage and that it was impossible for Gamble or anyone else to please them. Because the letter was meant to remain private, Lincoln probably had not used the care he might have otherwise in stating the circumstances in Missouri. Instead of going into all the particulars, most of which Schofield already knew, Lincoln had referred to both the conservatives and radicals as factions, using the term as a shorthand for the ongoing dispute. In this way he could avoid writing a much longer letter explaining a number of the issues about which he had long ago tired. After Gamble protested the publication of this letter, Lincoln had invited him to Washington to discuss the matter.

Unfortunately, the meeting did not go well. Gamble, who had expected to have a private meeting with the president in which they could fully discuss their differences, was disappointed to have met only briefly with him. As he explained to Attorney General Bates, Gamble only had enough time to refer to "the personal insult that was contained in his letter," when William Dennison, former governor of Ohio, interrupted their meeting. Gamble believed that Lincoln had invited him to Washington only to prevent publication of the letter, which he had sent privately to Lincoln in reply to his "Schofield letter." Moreover, Gamble thought that Lincoln had arranged Dennison's interruption to escape discussing the matter fully. Angry and distraught over his damaged reputation, Gamble stated that he no longer believed Lincoln to be "an honest man," and declared him "a mere intriguing, pettifogging, piddling politician." Despite his strong feelings of animosity, for the good of Missouri and the country Gamble continued to work with the president.[23]

While Gamble was sitting in the train on his return to Philadelphia with his right arm protruding out the window his arm struck a bridge and was seriously broken above the right elbow. For the next few weeks Gamble remained with his family and consulted with doctors. Although then sixty-five years of age and worn down by the strenuous nature of his gubernatorial duties, within a few days Gamble reported that his arm was "making fair progress" and began to answer correspondence through his son David, who was then eighteen or nineteen years of age. Much of the business was routine, having to do with enlistments, the signing of vouchers, and the payment of troops among other miscellaneous details connected with maintaining troops in the field. Most of these matters were handled by Lieutenant Governor Willard P. Hall. However, Hall decided to consult with Gamble concerning Schofield's order to the enrolled militia not to help civil authorities "in the arrest or return of fugitive slaves." Having placed the enrolled militia under Schofield's command, Gamble probably felt betrayed, for he had always insisted that as a state force the enrolled militia would enforce Missouri law, including statutes providing for the capture of runaway slaves. Moreover, Gamble had met resistance from radical officers and had personally ordered them to provide help and security to civil officers performing their duties. Hall and Adjutant-General John B. Gray both believed that Schofield was pandering to the radicals and that his command of the enrolled militia should be revoked. Gamble, believing that he was too far removed from Missouri to determine the matter himself, left this decision to Hall, who eventually decided against relieving Schofield of the command.[24]

23. Gamble to Lincoln, 13 July 1863; Lincoln to Gamble, 23 July 1863; and Edward Bates to Gamble, 3 August 1863, Lincoln papers. Gamble to Bates, 10 August 1863, Bates papers. Schofield, *Forty-Six Years in the Army*, 68–72. Schofield to Lincoln, 1 June 1863, *Official Records*, series 1, vol. 22, part 2, 301.

24. As early as 1838, Caroline Gamble had problems with her eyesight. See Wilbert Henry Rosin, "Hamilton Rowan Gamble: Missouri's Civil War Governor" (Ph.D. diss., University of Missouri, 1960), 26. D. K. Pitman to Gamble, 14 July 1863; Gamble to J. B. Rogers, 17 July 1863; John B. Gray to Gamble, 1, 7, 10, 15, 29 August and 9 September 1863; General Orders, No. 75,

A Radical Delegation Demands a Military Government

Having recuperated enough to return to Missouri by September 19, Gamble resumed his duties as governor on a part-time basis. While still in Pennsylvania, Gamble had received reports from various persons concerning the attacks against him and his administration. Back in Missouri, Gamble learned firsthand about the activities of the Radical Republicans, who were then preparing to send a large delegation to Washington to undermine the authority of both Gamble and Schofield. These reports described the radicals as "revolutionists" and "Jacobins," who sought to overthrow Gamble's conservative government. Despite the cacophony of complaint from his enemies, much to the consternation of his supporters, Gamble refrained from defending his administration. However, after receiving letters from his older brother Archibald and trusted friends warning that the situation was fast becoming a crisis, Gamble decided that he must defend himself and appeal to Lincoln for support. Ill and in pain, Gamble unburdened himself in a letter to Lincoln, complaining that his "patience is entirely exhausted by the constant repetition of accusations of disloyalty which designing, unprincipled, and desperate men have piled up before you." From the beginning of his administration, Gamble noted, the radicals had accused him of being a rebel sympathizer, among other things, and that they then hoped to overthrow his administration. In particular, Gamble had in mind the recent mutiny of some radical members of the Eleventh Provisional Regiment and the attempt of the radical officers and men of the Twenty-third Missouri Volunteers to remove Lieutenant Colonel Quinn Morton. Finally, Gamble recalled his administration's efforts to support the federal government and reminded Lincoln of his constitutional obligation to prevent the overthrow of Missouri's provisional government. Perhaps still smarting from Lincoln's characterization of him as the leader of a faction, Gamble concluded his letter by stating that

29 July 1863; Edward Bates to Gamble, 3 August 1863; Willard Hall to Gamble, 10, 19, and 31 August 1863; Gamble to Hall, 15 August 1863, Gamble papers. St. Louis *Missouri Republican*, 22 July, 11 August, and 20 September 1863. General Orders, No. 89, 27 August 1863, *Official Records*, series 1, vol. 22, part 2, 481.

"as to the success of political parties I care but little about any of them, so that the state can be kept at peace and be restored to prosperity."[25]

Caught in the middle of Missouri's political warfare without any prospect of satisfying either faction, Lincoln, having heard many misrepresentations, or at least very one-sided accounts from both conservatives and radicals, was skeptical about the veracity of what he was told. When he had placed Schofield in command, Lincoln had hoped to have a neutral to sort out the truth and work as an intermediary between both factions. Nevertheless, after a short time Schofield ran afoul of the radicals when he arrested the editor of the St. Louis *Missouri Democrat* for publishing without permission Lincoln's May 27 letter to him. Radicals instantly wrote to Lincoln asserting that the arrest of William McKee was politically motivated. Fearing that his instructions had been ignored, Lincoln expressed his regret that the arrest might have lost for Schofield "the middle position" in the factional contest. Having already allowed McKee to return home on his own recognizance, Schofield proposed to let the matter drop, thereby defusing the controversy. Lincoln gratefully accepted this solution. However, during the summer the radicals became increasingly critical of both Gamble and Schofield for their military and political policies. By this time, Schofield had come to the same conclusion as Gamble—that the radicals were conspiring to overthrow the state government by violence. To prevent this, Schofield published an order instituting martial law against anyone encouraging insurrection among the troops and the people. In particular, he warned editors of newspapers not to publish misrepresentations intended to undermine his authority. This action, which Lincoln approved, provoked the radicals to organize a delegation of sev-

25. Hamilton R. Gamble Jr. to Gamble, 26 August and 6 September 1863; John B. Gray to Gamble, 9 September 1863; Samuel T. Glover to Gamble, 28 September 1863; Lieutenant Colonel Mote to Gamble, 28 September 1863; Quinn Morton to Gamble, 28 September 1863; Archibald Gamble to Gamble, 29 September 1863; and Gamble to Lincoln, 30 September 1863, Gamble papers. Special Orders, No. 144, 7 September 1863; Special Orders, No. 146, 9 September 1863; General Orders, No. 96, 17 September 1863; Special Orders, No. 255, 18 September 1863; and Schofield to Henry W. Halleck, 20 September 1863, *Official Records*, series 1, vol. 22, 542–47; and series 1, vol. 34, part 4, 86–87. To better understand the distrust that existed even among regiments see series 1, vol. 22, part 1, 707–21.

enty men to proceed to Washington and try to persuade Lincoln to replace both Schofield and Gamble with a military governor.[26]

Heading the delegation was Charles D. Drake, one of the harshest critics of both Lincoln and Gamble since the convention. Lincoln's private
secretary John Hay recorded a conversation he had with Lincoln before
the meeting in his diary. According to his account, Hay had warned Lincoln that without the radicals' help he could not carry Missouri in the up-
coming presidential election. Lincoln did not disagree with Hay's analysis
or his assertion that on the whole the radicals' principles were more in
agreement with them than were the conservatives in Missouri. However,
Lincoln was under no illusion about the radicals' attitude toward him.
Referring to a letter he had just received from Hay's uncle, who lived near
St. Louis, he noted that at a recent radical meeting Drake had "denounced
him for a tyrannical interference with the convention through his agent
Schofield." Of course, Drake had in mind Lincoln's letter to Schofield
authorizing him to communicate his support for gradual emancipation.
Acknowledging the political danger of his position, Lincoln, nevertheless,
reaffirmed his determination not to compromise his principles despite the
possible consequences.[27]

On September 30, 1863, the delegation of seventy men met with Lincoln for two hours in the White House. Drake read his prepared address
in which he presented a rather lengthy account of the issues and circumstances in Missouri. He first asserted the premise on which all radical
policy rested: slavery was the cause of the war; therefore, the only effective
way to win the war was through the complete and immediate eradication of the institution. The conservatives, Drake claimed, were composed
mostly of disloyal men, former rebels, sympathizers with the rebellion,
and those opposed to the Emancipation Proclamation and the abolition of

26. Henry T. Blow to Lincoln, 13 July 1863; Lincoln to Schofield, 13 and 20 July 1863;
Schofield to Lincoln, 14 July 1863; Henry T. Blow to Edwin M. Stanton, 13 July 1863; James O.
Broadhead, 14 July 1863; Schofield to Henry W. Halleck, 20 September 1863; General Orders,
No. 96, 17 September 1863; and enclosure of radical articles from Missouri, *Official Records*, series
1, vol. 22, part 2, 366, 373–75, 383, 546–65; and series 2, vol. 6, 110 and 115. Schofield, *Forty-Six
Years in the Army*, 84–88. McDonough, *Schofield*, 47–49.

27. Michael Burlingame and John R. Turner Ettlinger, eds., *Inside Lincoln's White House: The
Complete Civil War Diary of John Hay* (Carbondale: Southern Illinois University Press, 1997),
88–89. Joseph A. Hay to Abraham Lincoln, 11 September 1863, Lincoln papers.

slavery. This characterization was ingenious and misleading, for it did not distinguish conservatives who favored secession from those who did not. The vast majority of conservative delegates at the state convention, although against immediate emancipation, had supported Lincoln from the beginning of the war at considerable risk to themselves when it seemed probable that Missouri would become part of the Southern Confederacy. Many of the radical delegates, including Drake himself, had not shared in these dangers, nor had many of them served in the military.[28]

Next, Drake repeated the charge that Governor Gamble had called together the state convention to prevent the election of a new convention and the passage of a real plan for emancipation. In reference to the gradual emancipation plan adopted by Gamble and the conservatives, Drake asserted that it was "adverse to true loyalty, and to the vital interests of our State. . . . The policy of our State Executive represses and chills the loyal heart of Missouri, as a pro-Slavery policy represses and chills loyal hearts everywhere." Moreover, Drake accused Gamble of coddling rebels. All of these measures, according to Drake, had the darker purpose of secretly helping the rebellion in Missouri.[29]

As Lincoln had anticipated, Drake sought to persuade him to remove Schofield and replace him with General Benjamin Butler as commander of the Department of Missouri. According to Drake, Schofield was in league with Gamble and the conservatives, was seeking to suppress freedom of speech and the press, had illegally suspended the writ of *habeas corpus* in ordering the conscription of Missourians into the militia, had supported Gamble's desire to remove federal troops from Missouri, and had ordered the arrest of an officer commissioned to recruit blacks into the military. In conclusion Drake asserted that during Schofield's tenure as commander conditions in Missouri had worsened progressively. He also demanded that the civil and military government sustain the election laws.[30]

Lincoln's response to the delegation demonstrated his determination to pursue his own policies. Hay, who was present, strongly disliked Drake,

28. Charles D. Drake, "Autobiography," 918–22, Western Historical Manuscripts Collection, State Historical Society of Missouri, Columbia, Missouri. Charles Gibson and James S. Rollins to Abraham Lincoln, 11 October 1863, Lincoln papers.

29. Drake, "Autobiography," 918–22.

30. Ibid., 923. Burlingame and Ettlinger, eds., *Diary of John Hay*, 88.

whom he described as having read his speech "pompously as if it were full of matter instead of wind." In contrast, Hay described the president's handling of Drake and the rest of the radical delegation as demonstrating Lincoln's superior logic and strength of character. At the end of their personal conference Lincoln promised the delegation to make a written reply after considering their demands.[31]

During this period of deliberation, Lincoln also received communications from Schofield, Gamble, and others replying to many of the issues and accusations raised by the radical press and the Drake delegation. Schofield provided Missouri Congressman James S. Rollins with a memorandum answering the charges that conditions in Missouri had only worsened under his command and that he was in league with Gamble. Moreover, Schofield noted his efforts to aid the passage of the emancipation ordinance at the state convention. Rollins incorporated these arguments and others in a letter sent to Lincoln, who also employed them to advantage in his reply to the radical delegation.[32]

Gamble also defended himself against radical charges. These primarily consisted of assertions that he was secretly disloyal. Gamble made the countercharge that the radicals were then conspiring to overthrow the state government and demanded that Lincoln take a strong stand against the radicals. Attorney General Bates and Charles Gibson, a federal judge who had made frequent visits to Washington as Gamble's emissary, both pressed Lincoln to provide support to the provisional government against a radical conspiracy to overthrow it. Bates reminded Lincoln that the federal government was constitutionally obligated to protect state governments from rebellion. Lincoln did not disagree with Bates's interpretation of his constitutional responsibilities. Gibson, believing that Lincoln was seeking to straddle the issues once again, leaked to the *New York Times* Gamble's demand for Lincoln's intervention against the radicals. In the end, Lincoln declined to take the precipitous action of intervening before a real danger presented itself. Furthermore, he disagreed with Gamble's

31. Burlingame and Ettlinger, eds., *Diary of John Hay*, 88–89.

32. Schofield, *Forty-Six Years in the Army*, 89–99. Charles Gibson and James S. Rollins to Lincoln, 11 October 1863, Lincoln papers. John M. Schofield to Henry W. Halleck, 30 September 1863; Lincoln to John M. Schofield, 1 and 4 October 1863; and John M. Schofield to Lincoln, 3 October 1863, *Official Records*, series 1, vol. 22, part 2, 581–82, 585–86, 595, and 601.

analysis of the situation, and judging from the resolutions passed at the radicals' latest convention, he believed that only a few of the radicals were advocating violence. Lincoln promised, however, that if necessary he would not hesitate to use federal power to put down an insurrection.[33]

On October 5 Lincoln drafted his reply to the radical delegation, although he waited until the fourteenth to release it. In it he provided the radicals with his own analysis of the circumstances in Missouri and the motives of the actors involved. The radicals, Lincoln noted, had demanded that Butler replace Schofield, that national forces replace the state militia, and that the election laws be enforced, especially the measure prohibiting the disloyal from voting. Lincoln observed that Drake and the committee had cited many instances of unionists' suffering as proof that Schofield and the state government were responsible for the prolonged warfare in Missouri. Lincoln, however, came to a different conclusion, stating that "the whole can be explained on a more charitable and, as I think, a more rational hypothesis. We are in civil war."[34]

To emphasize this point Lincoln next enumerated the different beliefs of unionists in Missouri to demonstrate how these led to unnecessary disagreements and disunity. Of these there were

those who are for the Union with, but not without, slavery; those for it without, but not with; those for it with or without, but prefer it with; and those for it with or without, but prefer it without. Among these, again, is a subdivision of those who are for gradual, but not for immediate, and those who are for immediate, but not for gradual, extinction of slavery. It is easy to conceive that all these shades of opinion, and even more, may be sincerely entertained by honest and truthful men, yet all being for the Union, by reason of these differences each will prefer a different way of sustaining the Union. At once sincerity is questioned and motives are assailed. Actual war coming, blood grows hot and blood is spilled; thought is forced from

---

33. Gamble to Lincoln, 30 September 1863, Lincoln papers. Gamble to Lincoln, 30 September 1863; Charles Gibson to Gamble, 12 and 13 October 1863; and Lincoln to Gamble, 19 October 1863, Gamble papers. Howard K. Beale, ed., *The Diary of Edward Bates, 1859–1866* (Washington, D.C.: U.S. Government Printing Office, 1933), 16 October 1863, 308.

34. Lincoln to Charles D. Drake, 5 October 1863, *Official Records*, series 1, vol. 22, part 2, 604–7.

old channels into confusion; deception breeds and thrives, confidence dies, and universal suspicion reigns.[35]

This condition of affairs having continued from the beginning of the war until then, Lincoln disagreed with the radicals' assertion that Gamble and Schofield were culpable and declined to replace them with a military governor. In answer to the demand for federal troops to replace militia forces in Missouri, Lincoln asked from where the radicals proposed he remove federal forces. Moreover, he emphasized the important role regiments formerly in Missouri had played during the summer when Grant's command had been threatened by Confederate General Joseph Johnston's attempt to reinforce the garrison at Vicksburg. In the end, Lincoln agreed to meet only one of the radicals' demands in ordering Schofield to ensure that Missouri's election laws be enforced.[36]

On October 12, 1863, while Missourians awaited Lincoln's answer to the Drake delegation's demands, Gamble published a proclamation warning the public that a revolutionary faction was then conspiring to overthrow the state government. Although not naming radical leaders, it was obvious he had them in mind in his warning. Gamble, who in the tradition of the conservatism of his day often had refused even to notice the attacks of his adversaries, for the first time extensively answered some of the charges leveled against him. In part, his proclamation was written to refute the false charges that tended to undercut his authority and to reassure his supporters, one going so far as to warn Gamble that "unless something is done these men [radicals] will soon have their ropes round our necks." Because the radical attacks were premised on misrepresentations of his career as governor and accusations of disloyalty, Gamble felt justified in defending his record before the public. Regarding the charge of disloyalty, he gave a summary of the dangers he and other unionists faced when the convention elected him provisional governor and, to demonstrate his

35. Ibid.

36. Ibid., and General Orders, No. 101, 28 September 1863, *Official Records*, series 1, vol. 22, part 2, 577. No doubt, a reason for Lincoln's apparent exasperation with the radicals was their demand that he appoint a military governor, something for which he had previously been criticized. See William C. Harris, *With Charity for All: Lincoln and the Restoration of the Union* (Lexington: University Press of Kentucky, 1997), 65–66.

loyalty, he cited his organization of the Missouri State Militia and the En-rolled Missouri Militia. Gamble also defended his decision to convene the state convention to pass an emancipation ordinance instead of adopting the plan of radical legislators who wanted to establish a new convention for that purpose. Moreover, Gamble accused the radicals—again not by name—of making a number of false accusations to prejudice the public against him. These false charges portrayed Gamble as disloyal, against emancipation, and conspiring to bring Missouri out of the Union, or at least to help the guerrilla forces harm loyal interests in Missouri. Finally, Gamble reminded Missourians that every government has the right "to protect itself against violence" and that state law provided penalties of long imprisonment and even death for those convicted of treason.[37]

Soon after Gamble's proclamation was published, Lincoln's response to the radical delegation ended whatever momentum existed supporting "revolution," or even the appointment of a military governor in Missouri. The radical delegation returned to Missouri demoralized, having finally come to the realization that Lincoln would not side with them in political and military matters. Of course, this was not the end of the radical move-ment in Missouri, although some radical leaders quickly adjusted their political opposition to meet the circumstances. Even Drake recognized the futility of further agitation, for soon after his return to St. Louis he re-quested from Schofield a modification of an order he had issued to ensure a peaceful and democratic election. Moreover, Lincoln wrote to Gamble declining to interfere in Missouri's affairs except when imminent danger necessitated it. In particular, Lincoln focused on Gamble's proclamation of October 12 in which he had stated that removal of the executive must be accomplished by the people's will, rather than by violence. Lincoln believed that this statement, if properly applied, demonstrated why he should not then intervene against the radicals in Missouri as Gamble had requested.

> In the absence of such violence, or imminent danger thereof, it is not proper for the national Executive to interfere; and I am unwilling, by any formal action, to show an appearance of belief that there is such imminent danger,

37. St. Louis *Missouri Republican*, 13 October 1863. For a representative selection of the op-position press of the time see *Official Records*, series 1, vol. 22, part 2, 547–65.

before I really believe there is. I might thereby to some extent, bear false witness. You tell me "a party has sprung up in Missouri, which openly and loudly proclaims the purpose to overturn the provisional government by violence." Does the party so proclaim? If I mistake not, the party alluded to recently held a State Convention, and adopted resolutions. Did they therein, declare violence against the provisional State government? No party can be justly held responsible for what individual members of it may say or do.

Apparently, either perceiving the correctness of Lincoln's analysis or concluding that the president was determined not to intervene in Missouri except when absolutely necessary, Gamble and his representatives let the matter drop.[38]

Still recovering from the injury to his right arm, Gamble was forced to dictate his written communications and may have shifted a good bit of the daily burdens of his office to Lieutenant Governor Hall. Nevertheless, Gamble oversaw policy and continued to issue orders to commanders in the field. As winter approached, enemy activity in Missouri was limited to guerrilla actions, most of which were inconsequential from a military point of view, but often were devastating from the perspective of the communities affected. The forced evacuation of most of the inhabitants in northwest Missouri did not prevent all enemy activity there, although the number of guerrillas was reduced considerably. Anxious to pacify the region once and for all, Gamble ordered Lieutenant Colonel Bazel F. Lazear to capture "a band of thieves and robbers" operating in Johnson County. Gamble believed that imprisonment in the state penitentiary would serve as a greater deterrent to others than would killing them. In addition to this, despite orders forbidding it, Kansas troops were still entering Missouri, where they ransacked homes, stealing property abandoned after the evacuation order. These incidents were investigated and measures were taken to prevent their repetition. Nevertheless, given the overall peaceful condition of the state, Gamble, after coordinating with General Schofield

38. Charles Gibson to Gamble, 12 and 13 October 1863; Odon Guitar to Gamble, 13 October 1863; and Lincoln to Gamble, 19 October 1863, Gamble papers. Lincoln to Schofield, 1 October 1863, *Official Records*, series 1, vol. 22, part 2, 585–86. Schofield, *Forty-Six Years in the Army*, 99–101.

and the War Department, encouraged members of the Missouri State Militia to "re-enlist as Veterans into the United States service."[39]

After a peaceful election in which the Radical Republicans gained large majorities in the legislature, Gamble prepared for the impending session of the General Assembly. Before the Twenty-third General Assembly met, however, in November Gamble addressed the Twenty-second General Assembly, which had taken the unusual step of holding a continued session after adjourning the previous spring. In his message, Gamble reported triumphantly that "no military organization hostile to the Government of the United States" was operating in Missouri since state troops alone, both state and enrolled militia, had driven out the invading force of General Joseph O. Shelby. These operations were expensive, but given their importance to the overall war effort, Gamble believed that eventually the federal government would reimburse the state. In the meantime, he proposed issuing $1.5 million in war bonds. With victory in the West, Gamble expected peace to prevail in Missouri for the remainder of the war. Moreover, as he planned for a peaceful future, Gamble looked beyond the war and sought ways to promote economic development. Recognizing that without slavery new laborers would be needed, he commissioned Frederick Roerer as Missouri's European agent to encourage immigration. Using his connections to the Lincoln administration, Gamble obtained for Roerer a special recommendation from the state department. From the legislature he also requested $2,500 a year to cover Roerer's salary and expenses.[40]

During the continued session, the legislature presented bills unacceptable to Gamble. As a former judge, he was particularly sensitive to any

39. Gamble to Bazel F. Lazear, 24 November 1863, Gamble papers. George H. Hall to Oliver D. Greene, 28 November 1863; Lazear to James H. Steger, 9 December 1863; report of John M. Schofield, 10 December 1863; and Lazear to James McFerran, 30 January 1864, *Official Records*, series 1, vol. 22, part 1, 12–17; series 1, vol. 22, part 2, 722 and 734; and series 1, vol. 34, part 2, 214. *Report of the Adjutant General*, 51–52 and 61.

40. Buel Leopard and Floyd C. Shoemaker, eds., *The Messages and Proclamations of the Governors of the State of Missouri* (Columbia: The State Historical Society of Missouri, 1922), 465–72. Papers regarding commission of Frederick Roerer, 5 and 6 October 1863, Gamble papers. Beale, *Diary of Edward Bates*, 314.

encroachment by the legislature on the prerogatives and powers of the judiciary. In his veto message of an act concerning the St. Louis Police Board, he regarded it a "dangerous tendency" for the legislature to order the judges of the circuit court, the court of common pleas, and the criminal court to meet together to elect four commissioners to the police board. Seemingly, the matter was of small significance, for the act ordered the sheriff of Platte County to execute a court judgment, but it was a clear violation of a provision of the state constitution prohibiting the intrusion of one branch of the government into the functions of the other. In a final veto, Gamble protected his gubernatorial power to appoint colonels, lieutenant colonels, and majors in the Missouri State Militia, military offices that the legislature had sought to make elective among the officers and men of their regiments. Not only did this affect gubernatorial powers, but Gamble believed the legislation would undermine the proper maintenance of discipline in the militia. In his message he explained that "in times of profound peace, such a mode of selecting officers might not produce any bad results, but in times of war and commotion, when strict discipline is necessary to the success of military operations it is not in my judgment safe, to have the field officers of a regiment in a condition in which they shall feel that they are indebted to the men under them for their positions."[41]

In the midst of the session, Gamble was seriously injured when on December 16 he fell on the icy steps of the Governor's Mansion and broke his arm again. Because he was sixty-five years of age and already weakened by a prolonged convalescence, Gamble's aides and friends grew alarmed when a physician expressed doubts about his recovery. Because he was confined to his bed and incapacitated, most of Gamble's gubernatorial responsibilities were transferred to Lieutenant Governor Hall. Nevertheless, Gamble was able to dictate a final message to the legislature in which he supported the adjutant-general's report and recommendations. In this message, Gamble apologized for not "giving the report that careful examination which it would otherwise have received from my hands." Apparently, some hope of recovery existed until he developed pneumonia. Without the strength to sustain the fight any longer, while the church

41. Leopard and Shoemaker, eds., *Messages*, 477–79.

bells rang Hamilton R. Gamble died on Sunday, January 31, 1864, at
11:45 a.m. Just a few short hours before his death, Gamble, having been
awakened to greet a friend, spoke his last words, which to his admirers at
least, summed up the principles upon which he had lived his life. "I shall
try to do what is right and proper to do, and shall prevent anything from
being done which it is wrong to do."[42]

The ensuing days brought preparations for the funeral and eulogies for
the deceased. Over the state capitol the flag was flown at half-mast and, in
a sign of mourning, civil officers and military personnel wore black arm-
bands. To enable members of the General Assembly to attend Gamble's
funeral, the Missouri Pacific Railroad provided a special train from Jefferson City to St. Louis and back. Presiding over the funeral was Reverend
Brooks, who provided a brief account of Gamble's private, religious, and
public life. He spoke of Gamble's upbringing in the Presbyterian Church,
his struggle to overcome alcoholism, and his return to the Christian faith.
Reverend Brooks spoke of Gamble's generosity in giving both of his time
and money after he had become wealthy through his successful law practice. After the service, seventy-five carriages followed the hearse drawn
by four horses in which the mahogany casket bearing Gamble's remains
was placed for its journey to Bellefontaine Cemetery. As a sign of respect,
General William S. Rosecrans, who had only recently assumed command of the Department of the Missouri, ordered an artillery battery to
fire a salute every ten minutes while the procession made its way to the
cemetery.[43]

The most notable and eloquent summation of Gamble's life was provided by his brother-in-law, law partner, and longtime friend and supporter Edward Bates. In it he expressed his sorrow and surprise that he
had until then not fully appreciated the talents and character of his colleague of over forty years. "He stood, like a lighthouse on a rock in the
edge of a stormy sea, not only to give warning of the danger, but to resist

42. St. Louis *Missouri Republican*, 15 January and 1 and 5 February 1864. St. Louis *Missouri
Democrat*, 1, 2, and 4 February 1864. Leopard and Shoemaker, eds., *Messages*, 511.

43. St. Louis *Missouri Democrat*, 4 February 1864. St. Louis *Missouri Republican*, 5 February 1864. *In Memoriam*, 70–72, 78–79, and 88–91. A little more than a year later the
same hearse would carry Lincoln's body through the streets of Springfield to his final resting
place.

its violence. And to me, his loss is a sore grievance—far greater than I had supposed—We have been friends for Forty years, and yet I did not know how highly I prized him, nor what a blank his death would make in both my heart and mind." While recognizing how easily Gamble could be misunderstood by the public, Bates believed his strength of character had ensured that the state government under his leadership was stable and just.

> His tone was stern—not to say harsh—and he had little about him to wooe [*sic*] those tender emotions commonly called *fondness*. But his great characteristics—strong will, uprightness, courage, devotion to truth and principle—these, guided by his superior talents, gave him a title, long ago, to my unwavering confidence and unqualified respect. In fact, I learn only by his loss, how much I admired and loved him. . . . The services he has done the state, in patiently and successfully resisting the revolutionary violence of headlong jacobins, are now seen and appreciated; and purity of this personal character now shines all the brighter, because of the clouds of wicked calumny with which his and the State's enemies have so long labored to obscure him.[44]

SOME FINAL THOUGHTS

Hamilton R. Gamble's character was shaped by his strict upbringing according to the principles of the Presbyterian Church, his education, the practice of law, and his devotion to family and friends. While a young man still in his twenties and living independently for the first time, Gamble developed a drinking problem that almost ended his promising career and life. Gamble's return to the Christian faith, encouraged by his brother and wife, provided him with a new sense of purpose. Through his activities as an elder in his church, as a lawyer, and more reluctantly as a politician, Gamble worked in a low-key way to have a positive influence on his community. Uninterested in fame or political office, he preferred to demonstrate through example the proper conduct of a Christian gentleman in his professional and private life. Drawn by his prestige as a successful lawyer, young men sought Gamble's advice in matters of law. Recognizing him as a man of God, his friends found in him the unusual and welcome

---

44. Beale, *Diary of Edward Bates*, 328–29.

example of a Christian who put his faith into practice. A contemporary who observed Gamble's conduct of the governorship during the crisis of the Civil War described him as "one of the purest minded, most unselfish and wisest of men, a sincere patriot and Christian gentleman."[45]

Gamble's contributions to his community and state were important and multifaceted. Although conservative in temperament, he embraced non-radical reform movements including temperance and the emancipation and colonization of slaves in West Africa. Gamble also favored developing the American economy through the building of railroads and other internal improvement projects that would tie the country together better. On the other hand, he was suspicious of persons who were impatient for change and willing to disrupt and even destroy society in order to impose their vision on others and the country. Gamble believed that republican government was necessary for reforms to take hold and prosper, otherwise the benefits of change would soon be swallowed up in the resulting chaos that was certain to follow. Even slaves were better off in bondage, if, having gained their freedom, they were without even the minimal protections and rights they had been accorded as slaves.

These attitudes explain Gamble's resistance as judge to the decision of the majority in *Scott v. Emerson*. The Constitution and precedent vouchsafed law and the rights of the individual, including those of a slave. Temporary disputes, if allowed to override these principles, could lead to a further erosion of the rights of others, especially of those persons or groups unpopular with the majority. Once such a path was taken, no one could know to where it would ultimately lead. For this reason, Gamble resisted the almost inexorable movement toward war in 1861. Of all types of war internecine conflict presented the greatest danger to life, freedom, and good government. With the passions of men wrought up, no one could predict the lasting impact of civil war on society and the extent of turmoil and chaos that would be unleashed.

Fortunately, the war had two important lasting and redeeming results. The first was to settle the question of secession and the supremacy of the national government over that of individual states. The second result was the abolition of slavery. Gamble as governor of Missouri contributed to

45. Philips, "Gamble," 13.

both of these results, although he did not live to see the end of the war. By resisting the temptation of surrendering to the desire for vengeance, he demonstrated to Confederate soldiers and their leadership that it was possible to return home and live peacefully. This policy, however, was balanced and complemented by a determination to ensure a vigorous prosecution of the war. The securing of Missouri for the Union in this way contributed significantly to Northern victory, a contribution without which it is difficult to conceive of a similar result. Finally, Gamble proved himself a good practical politician and statesman in moving the state toward emancipation. Unafraid to lead public opinion, he demonstrated courage as a leader willing to take prudent and necessary risks. Nevertheless, such courage, unaccompanied by ample amounts of political acumen and savvy, could have eroded his contemporaries' confidence in him and possibly led to his replacement by another without the requisite skills to navigate the ship of state through the stormy seas of civil war.

Bibliography

PRIMARY SOURCES

Alvord Collection. Western Historical Manuscripts Collection, State Historical Society of Missouri, Columbia, Missouri.

Bates, Edward. Unpublished diary. Bates family papers, Missouri Historical Society, St. Louis, Missouri.

Broadhead, James O. Papers. Missouri Historical Society, St. Louis, Missouri.

Columbia *Missouri Statesman*, 7 April 1848.

Drake, Charles D. "Autobiography." Western Historical Manuscripts Collection, State Historical Society of Missouri, Columbia, Missouri.

Dred Scott v. Emerson documents. Missouri State Archives, Jefferson City, Missouri.

Fayette *Missouri Intelligencer*, 7 March 1828.

Franklin *Missouri Intelligencer*, 15 November 1819; 1 April and 2 September 1820; 16 April 1821; 13 August, 24 September, 10 and 15 October 1822; 13 February, 17 and 24 June, 1 and 8 July, 18 November 1823; 27 November 1824.

Gamble, Archibald. "Family Record by Archibald Gamble," 15 January 1858 and 15 January 1863, Hamilton R. Gamble papers, Missouri Historical Society, St. Louis, Missouri.

Gamble, Hamilton Rowan. Papers. Missouri Historical Society, St. Louis, Missouri.

Howard Circuit Court Records, Fayette, Missouri.

Jefferson City *Jefferson Inquirer*, 14 and 21 November, and 19 and 26 December 1844; 4 January and 8 February 1845; 22 and 29 December 1846; 12 June 1858.

Leonard, Abiel. Papers. Western Historical Manuscript Collection, State Historical Society of Missouri, Columbia, Missouri.

Liberty *Tribune*, 19 May 1848; 12 February 1858.

Lincoln, Abraham. Papers. Library of Congress, Washington, D.C.

Missouri Militia Records. Duke University Library, Durham, North Carolina.

Napton, William B. Papers. Missouri Historical Society, St. Louis, Missouri.

Pennsylvania Census. 1860.

St. Louis Census. 1830, 1840, 1850.

St. Louis County Circuit Court. *Maria Whiten v. Garland Rucker*, November 1829 term, case number 14; *Cary, a man of color v. Benjamin Wilder*, March 1831 term, case number 53; *Thenia v. Green Crowder*, March 1832 term, case number 9; *Harriet, an infant v. Samuel T. McKinney and James Walker*, July 1833 term, case number 17; *Abraham Dutton, a free boy of color v. John Paca*, July 1834 term, case number 115; and *Delph, a mulatress v. Stephen Dorris*, March 1836 term, case number 4.

St. Louis *Farmers' and Mechanics' Advocate*, 20 March 1834.

St. Louis *Free Press*, 7 and 21 February 1833.

St. Louis *Mill Boy*, 10 February, 9 March, and 10 August 1844.

St. Louis *Missouri Argus*, 5 July 1831; 19 June 1835; 11 and 18 March 1836; 2 and 9 December 1837; 23 February and 21 June 1838; 11 June and 10 October 1840; 20 June 1844.

St. Louis *Missouri Democrat*, 4 February 1864.

St. Louis *Missouri Republican*, 26 January and 31 August 1826; 27 December 1827; 29 January, 5, 12, and 19 February 1833; 22 August and 31 October 1834; 2 and 6 December 1844; 10 February, 26 March, and 3 April 1845; 3 and 18 February, 4 April, 1 and 8 May, and 1 July 1850; 12 and 18 April, and 19 August 1851; 28 December 1855; 18 January, 10, 11, 16 April, 12 and 14 June, 7, 24, and 30 July, 1, 2, 5, 9, 15, 21, and 26 August, 10, 11, and 15 September 1861; 10 January, 26 March, 1, 2, 13, and 18 May, 1, 2, 3, 5, 6, 7, 9, 10, 18–22 June, 7, 15, 27 July, 22 August, 4 and 6 September, 13 October, 9, 12, 18 November, 13 and 16 December 1862; 17, 22, 23, 31 January, 2, 6, 9, 19, and 27 February, and 2, 6, 9, 10, 11, 12, and 13 March, 22 April, 23 May, 3, 5, 6, 9, 11, 12, 17, 18, 23, 26 June, 13 October 1863; 15 January, 1 and 5 February 1864.

St. Louis Probate Records. Number 6711.

SECONDARY WORKS
Books, Dissertations, Pamphlets, and Government Documents

Anderson, Galusha. *The Story of a Border City During the Civil War*. Boston: Little, Brown, 1908.

Annual Report of the Adjutant General of the State of Missouri for the Year 1863. St. Louis: n.p., 1864.

Bailyn, Bernard. *The Ideological Origins of the American Revolution.* Cambridge, Mass.: Harvard University Press, 1992.

Bay, William V. N. *Reminiscences of the Bench and Bar of Missouri, with an Appendix, containing Biographical Sketches of Nearly All of the Judges and Lawyers who have Passed Away, Together with many Interesting and Valuable Letters Never Before Published of Washington, Jefferson, Burr, Granger Clinton, and Others, Some of Which Throw Additional Light Upon the Famous Burr Conspiracy.* St. Louis: F. H. Thomas, 1878.

Beale, Howard K., ed., *The Diary of Edward Bates, 1859–1866.* Washington, D.C.: U.S. Government Printing Office, 1933.

Benson, Lee. *The Concept of Jacksonian Democracy: New York as a Test Case.* Princeton: Princeton University Press, 1961.

Blair, Frank P., Jr. *Confiscation, Emancipation, and Colonization "Indemnity for the Past and Security for the Future": Speech of Hon. F. P. Blair Jr. of Missouri in the House of Representatives, May 23, 1862.* n.p., 1862.

———. *Speech of Hon. F. P. Blair Jr. of Missouri on the Policy of the President for the Restoration of the Union and Establishment of Peace delivered in the House of Representatives, April 11, 1862.* New York: Baker & Godwin, 1862.

Boman, Dennis K. *Abiel Leonard, Yankee Slaveholder, Eminent Jurist, and Passionate Unionist.* Studies in American History, vol. 38. Lewiston: Edwin Mellen, 2002.

Boorstin, Daniel J. *The Mysterious Science of the Law: An Essay on Blackstone's* Commentaries *Showing How Blackstone, Employing Eighteenth-Century Ideas of Science, Religion, History, Aesthetics, and Philosophy, Made of the Law at once a Conservative and a Mysterious Science.* Chicago: University of Chicago Press, 1941; reprint, 1996.

Bradshaw, Herbert Clarence. *History of Hampden-Sydney College: From the Beginnings to the Year 1856.* Vol. 1. Privately printed, 1976.

Brinkley, John Luster. *On this Hill: A Narrative History of Hampden-Sydney College, 1774–1994.* Hampden-Sydney, Va.: Camdus, 1994.

Burlingame, Michael, and John R. Turner Ettlinger, eds. *Inside Lincoln's White House: The Complete Civil War Diary of John Hay.* Carbondale: Southern Illinois University Press, 1997.

Castel, Albert. *General Sterling Price and the Civil War in the West.* Baton Rouge: Louisiana State University Press, 1968.

Chafee, Zechariah, Jr. *Free Speech in the United States.* Cambridge, Mass.: Harvard University Press, 1942.

Chambers, William Nisbet. *Old Bullion Benton: Senator from the New West, Thomas Hart Benton, 1782–1858.* Boston: Little, Brown, 1956.

Christensen, Lawrence O., et al., eds. *Dictionary of Missouri Biography.* Columbia:

University of Missouri Press, 1999, s.v. "Wells, Robert William (1795–1864)" by Lawrence H. Larsen.

Darby, John F. *Personal Recollections of Many Prominent People Whom I have known, and of Events—especially of those relating to the History of St. Louis—During the First Half of the Present Century.* St. Louis: George Knapp, 1880.

Donald, David Herbert. *Lincoln.* New York: Simon & Schuster, 1995.

Duffus, Gerald R. "A Study of the Military Career of Samuel R. Curtis: 1861–1865." Master's thesis, Drake University, 1966.

English, William Francis. "The Pioneer Lawyer and Jurist in Missouri." Ph.D. diss., University of Missouri-Columbia, 1943.

Fehrenbacher, Don E. *The Dred Scott Case: Its Significance in American Law and Politics.* Oxford: Oxford University Press, 1979.

———. *Slavery, Law, and Politics: The Dred Scott Case in Historical Perspective.* Oxford: Oxford University Press, 1981.

Fellman, Michael. *Inside War: The Guerrilla Conflict in Missouri During the American Civil War.* New York: Oxford University Press, 1989.

Finkelman, Paul. *An Imperfect Union: Slavery, Federalism, and Comity.* Chapel Hill: University of North Carolina Press, 1981.

Foley, William. *A History of Missouri.* Vol. 1. Columbia: University of Missouri Press, 1971.

Fremont, John C. "In Command in Missouri." In *Battles and Leaders of the Civil War.* Vol. 1. New York: Century, 1887; reprint, Secaucus, N.J.: Castle, n.d., 278–88.

Gentry, North Todd. *The Bench and Bar of Boone County Missouri, Including the History of Judges, Lawyers and Courts, and an Account of Noted Cases, Slavery Litigation, Lawyers in War Times, Public Addresses, Political Notes, etc.* Columbia, Mo.: Author, 1916.

Grant, Blanche C., ed. *Kit Carson's Own Story of his Life as Dictated to Col. And Mrs. D. C. Peters About 1856–1857.* Santa Barbara, Calif.: Narrative, 2001.

Grant, Ulysses S. *Personal Memoirs of U. S. Grant.* New York: Library of America, 1990.

Grasty, Rev. John S. *Memoir of Rev. Samuel B. McPheeters, D.D.,* with an introduction by Rev. Stuart Robinson. St. Louis: Southwestern, 1871.

Harris, William C. *With Charity for All: Lincoln and the Restoration of the Union.* Lexington: University Press of Kentucky, 1997.

Henderson, John B. *Speech of Hon. J. B. Henderson of Missouri on the Abolition of Slavery delivered in the Senate of the United States, March 27, 1862.* Washington, D.C.: L. Towers, 1862.

Hesseltine, William B. *Lincoln and the War Governors.* New York: Alfred A. Knopf, 1948.

Heyrman, Christine Leigh. *Southern Cross: The Beginnings of the Bible Belt.* New York: Alfred A. Knopf, 1997.

Hobson, Charles F. *The Great Chief Justice: John Marshall and the Rule of Law.* Lawrence: University of Kansas Press, 1996.

Horwitz, Morton J. *The Transformation of American Law, 1780–1860.* Chapel Hill: University of North Carolina Press, 1977.

Howe, Daniel Walker. *The Political Culture of the American Whigs.* Chicago: University of Chicago Press, 1979.

Huebner, Timothy S. *The Southern Judicial Tradition: State Judges and Sectional Distinctiveness, 1790–1890.* Athens: University of Georgia Press, 1999.

In Memoriam: Hamilton Rowan Gamble, Governor of Missouri. St. Louis: George Knapp, 1864.

Jaffa, Harry V. *Crisis of the House Divided: An Interpretation of the Issues in the Lincoln-Douglas Debates,* with a new preface. Chicago: University of Chicago Press, 1959; reprint, 1982.

Johnson, Michael P., ed. *Abraham Lincoln, Slavery, and the Civil War: Selected Writings and Speeches.* The Bedford Series in History and Culture. Boston: Bedford/St. Martin's, 2001.

Journal of the House of Representatives of the State of Missouri at the First Session of the Seventh General Assembly, Begun and Held at the City of Jefferson, On the Nineteenth Day of November, in the Year of our Lord, one thousand eight hundred and thirty-two. St. Louis, Mo.: John Steele, Free Press Office, 1833.

Journal of the House of Representatives of the State of Missouri of the First Session of the Thirteenth General Assembly, Begun and Held at the City of Jefferson, On Monday, the Eighteenth Day of November, in the Year of our Lord One Thousand Eight Hundred and Forty-Four. Jefferson City: James Lusk, printer to the state, 1845.

Journal of the Missouri State Convention Held at the City of St. Louis, October 1861. St. Louis: George Knapp, 1861.

Journal of the Missouri State Convention, Held in Jefferson City, June 1862. St. Louis: George Knapp, 1862.

Journal of the Missouri State Convention, Held in Jefferson City, June 1863. St. Louis: George Knapp, 1863.

Journal of the Senate of the State of Missouri at the First Session of the Seventh General Assembly, Begun and the Held at the City of Jefferson, on the Monday the Nineteenth Day of November, in the Year of our Lord, One Thousand eight hundred and thirty-two. Jefferson City: Calvin Gunn, Jeffersonian Office, 1833.

Karsten, Peter. *Heart versus Head: Judge-Made Law in Nineteenth-Century America.* Chapel Hill: University of North Carolina Press, 1997.

Kaufman, Kenneth C. *Dred Scott's Advocate: A Biography of Roswell M. Field.* Columbia: University of Missouri Press, 1996.

Klement, Frank L. *Dark Lanterns: Secret Political Societies, Conspiracies, and Treason Trials in the Civil War.* Baton Rouge: Louisiana State University Press, 1984.

Laws of a Public and General Nature of the District of Louisiana of the Territory of Missouri and of the State of Missouri up to the Year 1824. Vol. 2. Jefferson City: W. Lusk and Son, 1842.

Laws of a Public and General Nature of the State of Missouri, Passed Between the Years 1824 and 1836, not published in the Digest of 1825 Nor in the Digest of 1835. Vol. 2. Jefferson City: W. Lusk and Son, 1842.

Leopard, Buel, and Floyd C. Shoemaker, eds. *The Messages and Proclamations of the Governors of the State of Missouri.* Columbia: The State Historical Society of Missouri, 1922.

Mathews, Donald G. *Religion in the Old South.* Chicago: University of Chicago Press, 1977.

McCandless, Perry. *A History of Missouri.* Vol. 2. Columbia: University of Missouri Press, 1972.

McCormick, Richard P. *The Second American Party System: Party Formation in the Jacksonian Era.* Chapel Hill: University of North Carolina Press, 1966.

McCoy, Drew R. *The Elusive Republic: Political Economy in Jeffersonian America.* Chapel Hill: University of North Carolina Press, 1980.

McDonough, James L. *Schofield: Union General in the Civil War and Reconstruction.* Tallahassee: Florida State University Press, 1972.

McPherson, James M. *Battle Cry of Freedom: The Civil War Era, The Oxford History of the United States.* Vol. 6, edited by C. Vann Woodward. New York: Oxford University Press, 1988.

Mering, John Vollmer. *The Whig Party in Missouri.* University of Missouri Studies, vol. 91. Columbia: University of Missouri Press, 1967.

Meyers, Marvin. *The Jacksonian Persuasion: Politics and Belief.* New York: Vintage, 1957.

Miller, John C. *The Federalist Era, 1789–1801.* New York: Harper and Brothers, 1960.

Miller, William Lee. *Arguing About Slavery: The Great Battle in the United States Congress.* New York: Alfred A. Knopf, 1996.

Missouri Reports. Vols. 1–11, 15–20, 22.

Monaghan, Jay. *Civil War on the Western Border, 1854–1865.* Lincoln: University of Nebraska Press, 1955.

Monroe, Dan. *The Republican Vision of John Tyler.* College Station: Texas A & M University Press, 2003.

Neely, Mark E., Jr., *The Fate of Liberty: Abraham Lincoln and Civil Liberties.* New York: Oxford University Press, 1991.

Norton, E. H. *Speech of Hon. E. H. Norton of Missouri on Confiscation and Emancipation delivered in the House of Representatives, April 24, 1862.* Washington, D.C.: n.p., 1862.

O'Brien, Gail Williams. *The Legal Fraternity and the Making of a New South Community, 1848–1882.* Athens: University of Georgia Press, 1986.

Parrish, William E. *Turbulent Partnership: Missouri and the Union, 1861–1865.* Columbia: University of Missouri Press, 1963.

Peters, Richard. *Reports of Cases Argued and Adjudged in the Supreme Court of the United States.* Vol. 5. Philadelphia: Thomas, Cowperthwait, n.d.

Penick, James Lal, Jr. *The New Madrid Earthquakes.* Rev. ed. Columbia: University of Missouri Press, 1981.

Peterson, Merrill D., ed., *The Political Writings of Thomas Jefferson.* Monticello: Thomas Jefferson Memorial Foundation, 1993.

———. *Thomas Jefferson and the New Nation, A Biography.* New York: Oxford University Press, 1970.

Phelps, John S. *Confiscation of property and Emancipation of Slaves: Speech of Hon. John S. Phelps of Missouri in the House of Representatives, May 22, 1862.* Washington: n.p., 1862.

Phillips, Christopher. *Missouri's Confederate: Claiborne Fox Jackson and the Creation of Southern Identity in the Border West.* Columbia: University of Missouri Press, 2000.

Potter, David M. *The Impending Crisis: 1848–1861.* Completed and edited by Don E. Fehrenbacher, the New American Nation Series. New York: Harper and Row, 1976.

Primm, James Neal. *Lion of the Valley: St. Louis, Missouri.* Boulder, Colo.: Pruett, 1981.

Proceedings of the Missouri State Convention Held at the City of Jefferson, July 1861. St. Louis: George Knapp, 1861.

Proceedings of the Missouri State Convention Held at the City of St. Louis, October 1861. St. Louis: George Knapp, 1861.

Proceedings of the Missouri State Convention Held in Jefferson City, June 1862. St. Louis: George Knapp, 1862.

Proceedings of the Missouri State Convention Held in Jefferson City, June 1863. St. Louis: George Knapp, 1863.

Randall, James G. *Constitutional Problems Under Lincoln.* Urbana: University of Illinois Press, 1951.

Rehnquist, William H. *All the Laws but One: Civil Liberties in Wartime.* New York: Alfred A. Knopf, 1998.

Report of the Committee of the House of Representatives of the Twenty-second General Assembly of the State of Missouri Appointed to Investigate the Conduct and Management of the Militia: Majority and Minority Reports with the Evidence. Jefferson City, Mo.: W. A. Curry, Public Printers, 1864.

Rosin, Wilbert Henry. "Hamilton Rowan Gamble: Missouri's Civil War Governor." Ph.D. diss., University of Missouri, 1960.

Ryle, Walter H. *Missouri: Union or Secession.* Nashville, Tenn.: George Peabody College for Teachers, 1931.

Schlesinger, Arthur M., Jr. *The Age of Jackson.* New York: Book Find Club, 1945.

Schofield, John M. *Forty-Six Years in the Army,* with a foreword by William M. Ferraro. New York: Century, 1897; reprint, Norman: University of Oklahoma Press, 1998.

Sears, Stephen W., ed. *The Civil War Papers of George B. McClellan: Selected Correspondence, 1860–1865.* New York: Ticknor & Fields, 1989; reprint, New York: Da Capo, 1992.

Shalhope, Robert E. *Sterling Price: Portrait of a Southerner.* Columbia: University of Missouri Press, 1971.

Sherman, William Tecumseh. *Memoirs.* New York: Library of America, 1990.

Snead, Thomas L. "The First Year of the War in Missouri." In *Battles and Leaders of the Civil War.* Vol. 1. Secaucus, N.J.: Castle, n.d.

Sprague, Dean. *Freedom Under Lincoln.* Boston: Riverside Press Cambridge, 1965.

Stampp, Kenneth M. *The Peculiar Institution: Slavery in the Ante-Bellum South.* New York: Vintage, 1956.

Steward, Dick. *Duels and the Roots of Violence in Missouri.* Columbia: University of Missouri Press, 2000.

Tap, Bruce. *Over Lincoln's Shoulder: The Committee on the Conduct of the War.* Lawrence: University of Kansas Press, 1998.

Trexler, Harrison Anthony. *Slavery in Missouri, 1804–1865.* Johns Hopkins University Studies in Historical and Political Science, series 32, no. 2. Baltimore: Johns Hopkins Press, 1914.

United States Reports. Vols. 30, 49, 51, 56–57, 59, 62–63.

Wade, Richard C. *Slavery in the Cities: The South, 1820–1860.* London: Oxford University Press, 1964.

The War of the Rebellion: A Compilation of the Official Records of the Union and Confed-

erate Armies. 128 vols. Washington, D.C.: U.S. Government Printing Office, 1880–1902.

Warren, Charles. *The Supreme Court in United States History,* vol. 1, *1789–1835.* Rev. ed. Boston: Little, Brown, 1926.

Watson, Harry L. *Liberty and Power: The Politics of Jacksonian America.* New York: Hill and Wang, 1990.

Wells, Robert W. *Letter from Judge Wells, Jefferson City, June 6th 1862.* St. Louis: George Knapp, 1862.

Wilentz, Sean, ed. *Major Problems in the Early Republic, 1787–1848.* Lexington, Mass.: D. C. Heath, 1992.

Wyatt-Brown, Bertram. *Southern Honor: Ethics and Behavior in the Old South.* Oxford: Oxford University Press, 1982.

Young, William. *History of Lafayette County, Missouri.* Vol. 1. Indianapolis: B. F. Bowen, 1910.

Zarefsky, David. *Lincoln, Douglas, and Slavery: In the Crucible of Public Debate.* Chicago: University of Chicago Press, 1990.

Articles

Blum, Virgil C. "The Political and Military Activities of the German Element in St. Louis, 1859–1861." *Missouri Historical Review* 42 (January 1948): 103–29.

Boman, Dennis K. "Impeachment Proceedings as a Partisan Tool: The Trial of Judge David Todd." *Missouri Historical Review* 94 (January 2000): 146–59.

———. "Conduct and Revolt in the Twenty-fifth Ohio Battery: An Insider's Account." *Ohio History* (Summer–Autumn 1995): 163–83.

———. "The Dred Scott Case Reconsidered: The Legal and Political Context in Missouri." *American Journal of Legal History* 44, no. 4 (October 2000): 405–28.

Bushnell, Eleanore. "The Impeachment and Trial of James H. Peck." *Missouri Historical Review* 74 (January 1980): 137–65.

Cain, Marvin R. "Edward Bates and Hamilton R. Gamble: A Wartime Partnership." *Missouri Historical Review* 56 (January 1962): 146–55.

Castel, Albert. "Order No. 11 and the Civil War on the Border." *Missouri Historical Review* 57 (July 1963): 357–68.

Chroust, Anton-Herman. "The Legal Profession in Early Missouri." *Missouri Law Review* 29 (1964): 129–37.

Clark, Thomas C. "The Impact of Nineteenth Century Missouri Courts upon

Emerging Industry: Chambers of Commerce or Chambers of Justice?" *Missouri Law Review* 63 (1998): 51–114.

Covington, James W. "The Camp Jackson Affair." *Missouri Historical Review* 55 (April 1961): 197–212.

Curtis, Michael Kent. "The 1837 Killing of Elijah Lovejoy by an Anti-Abolition Mob: Free Speech, Mobs, Republican Government, and the Privileges of American Citizens." *UCLA Law Review* 44 (1997): 1109–84.

Foley, William E. "The Political Philosophy of David Barton." *Missouri Historical Review* 58 (April 1964): 278–89.

———. "Slave Freedom Suits Before Dred Scott: The Case of Marie Scypion's Descendants." *Missouri Historical Review* 79 (October 1984): 1–23.

Gates, Paul Wallace. "Private Land Claims in the South." *Journal of Southern History* 22 (May 1956): 183–204.

Kirkpatrick, Arthur Roy. "Missouri on the Eve of the Civil War." *Missouri Historical Review* 55 (January 1961): 98–108.

———. "Missouri in the Early Months of the Civil War." *Missouri Historical Review* 55 (April 1961): 235–66.

McCandless, Perry. "Benton v. Barton: The Formation of the Second-Party System in Missouri." *Missouri Historical Review* 79 (July 1985): 425–38.

———. "The Political Philosophy and Political Personality of Thomas H. Benton." *Missouri Historical Review* 50 (January 1956): 145–58.

Mink, Charles R. "General Orders, No. 11: The Forced Evacuation of Civilians During the Civil War." *Military Affairs* 34 (December 1970): 132–36.

Nelson, Earl J. "Missouri Slavery, 1861–1865," *Missouri Historical Review* 28 (July 1934): 260–74.

Philips, John F. "Hamilton Rowan Gamble and the Provisional Government of Missouri." *Missouri Historical Review* 5 (October 1910): 1–6.

Schroeder, Walter A. "Spread of Settlement in Howard County, Missouri, 1810–1859." *Missouri Historical Review* 64 (October 1968): 1–37.

Stychin, Carl F. "The Commentaries of Chancellor James Kent and the Development of an American Common Law." *American Journal of Legal History* 37 (October 1993): 440–63.

Thomas, Arthur Dicken, Jr. "Moses Hoge: Reformed Pietism and Spiritual Guidance." *Journal of Presbyterian History* 7, no. 2 (Summer 1993): 95–98.

Thomas, Raymond D. "A Study in Missouri Politics, 1840–1870." *Missouri Historical Review* 21 (January 1927): 166–84.

Turkoly-Joczik, Robert L. "Fremont and the Western Department." *Missouri Historical Review* 82, no. 4 (July 1988): 363–85.

Viles, Jonas. "Old Franklin: A Frontier Town of the Twenties." *Mississippi Valley Historical Review* 9 (March 1923): 269–82.

Violette, Eugene Morrow. "Spanish Land Claims in Missouri." *Washington University Studies* 8 (1921): 167–200.

Williams, T. Harry. "Fremont and the Politicians." *Journal of the American Military History Foundation* 2 (Winter 1938): 178–91.

Wyatt-Brown, Bertram. "Honor's History Across the Academy." *Historically Speaking* 3, no. 5 (June 2002): 13–15.

Index

Miller, John, 12, 25
Mills, Adam, 40–42
Mills v. Stoddard et al., 40–41
Mine la Motte, 62
Missouri at the relation of Douglas v. Scott,
    53–54
Missouri at the relation of Richardson v.
    Ewing, 49–50
Missouri Compromise, 78, 85–86, 90
Missouri constitution, 168–70, 210, 212,
    214
Missouri General Assembly, 22–36,
    47–50, 54, 58, 76–78, 100, 102,
    109–10, 112, 114, 184–86, 196–98,
    218–19, 235–37
Missouri Pacific Railroad, 237
Missouri state convention: Commit-
    tee on Federal Relations, viii, 105,
    106; election of delegates to, viii,
    99, 102–3; legislation and purpose
    of, 102; military bill repealed by,
    112; November 1861 elections set
    by, 112, 136; reconvened in July
    1861, 112; replacement of exile state
    government by, 112, 188; debate over
    committee proposals in, 113–14; re-
    convened in October 1861, 133–38;
    militia bill passed by, 135; and delay
    of statewide election, 136, 164–65;
    abolition of state offices by, 136–37;
    and loyalty oath, 137, 143, 150, 185;
    defense warrant bonds issued by,
    137–38; June 1862 slavery debate
    in, 163, 165, 169–71; reconvened
    in June 1863 to reconsider eman-
    cipation, 209–14; Committee on
    Emancipation, 212; state constitution
    amended by, to allow emancipation,
    212; resolution for HRG to recon-
    sider resignation, 215
Missouri State Militia: recruitment for,

117, 121, 138, 156, 159, 175; early
    condition of, 117–18, 156–57; acqui-
    sition of arms by, 133, 140, 156–57;
    and military law, 133–35, 156; pay
    in, 135; funding of, 137–39, 143;
    coordination with federal troops by,
    143, 146–47, 157–58, 181, 183, 211;
    command of, 146–47; organization
    of, 146–47, 158, 175, 233; appoint-
    ments in, 147, 158, 179, 236; security
    provided by, during 1862 election,
    186; operations of, 201, 219–20,
    235; investigated by state legislature,
    218–19
Missouri Supreme Court: HRG elected
    to, viii, 42–43; HRG's practice be-
    fore, viii, 7, 31; *Scott v. Emerson,* viii,
    65–66, 69, 78, 81, 83–92, 239;
    judicial offices made elective, 42–43;
    freedom suits of, 65, 67–92; state
    convention proposal to increase num-
    ber of judges, 112
Monaghan, Jay, 222*n*21
Moore, John R., 148–49
Morton, Quinn, 226
Mount Sterling, Missouri, 7–8
Mulligan, James A., 131

Napton, William B.: appointed to
    Missouri Supreme Court, 79;
    proslavery jurisprudence of, 79–
    81, 82*n*42, 85–86, 90; failed elec-
    tion to Missouri Supreme Court,
    93; ousted from Missouri Supreme
    Court, 137
Natural rights ideology, 91, 169
New Light preaching, 4
New York *Herald,* 94–95
New York *Times,* 230
Newtonia, Missouri, 131
Nicolay, John G., 147